CLIMATE CHANGE AND THE MORAL AGENT

Climate Change and the Moral Agent

Individual Duties in an Interdependent World

ELIZABETH CRIPPS

OXFORD

UNIVERSITY PRESS

OXFORD
UNIVERSITY PRESS

Great Clarendon Street, Oxford, OX2 6DP,
United Kingdom

Oxford University Press is a department of the University of Oxford.
It furthers the University's objective of excellence in research, scholarship,
and education by publishing worldwide. Oxford is a registered trade mark of
Oxford University Press in the UK and in certain other countries

© Elizabeth Cripps 2013

The moral rights of the author have been asserted

First Edition published in 2013

Impression: 1

British Library Cataloguing in Publication Data
Data available

ISBN: 978-0-19-966565-5

Printed in Great Britain by the
MPG Printgroup, UK

For my parents, Harry and Vivien

Preface

Global climate change raises profound challenges for theories of moral accountability. Traditionally, we are considered responsible for harms we do or could easily have prevented, either as individuals or as members of some collective body capable of acting intentionally. Climate change is undoubtedly harmful, but no one person causes or could prevent it on her own. Nor is it the result of intentionally collective action at the global level. So why should we assume—as a great many of us do—that we ought to be doing something about it? And what does that mean for us as individual moral agents?

These are under-considered questions. Much of the debate in political philosophy has focused on what would be a fair distribution of the burdens of tackling climate change, sometimes only in terms of emissions cuts, but increasingly in terms of the wider costs of mitigation, adaptation, and compensation. There is also a highly developed literature on how theories of distributive justice might be expanded to include members of other states, of future generations, or even of other species. However, important as these debates are, there is an even more urgent question from the point of view of the individual as things currently stand. That is: 'Exactly *whose* problem is this, morally speaking, and—crucially—where does that leave me?'

To answer the question, this book goes back to the moral foundations. It asks whether we can acquire moral duties as neither individuals acting in isolation nor formalized collective entities: as sets of individuals who could organize themselves to bring about some morally salient end. In a globalized world, the limits of our interdependence go far beyond those situations in which we think of ourselves as co-members of a group. Should not our duties to one another expand in the same way? If we have duties to aid the needy at the individual level, do we not also (as some eminent theorists have suggested) have positive duties to organize to prevent serious suffering? And do we not have duties even harder to deny in this case, because the harms brought about by climate change are harms that we, between us, are causing? Such duties would be collective in a weak sense, but there would be nothing weak about their moral salience.

Against such a background, the question for the individual can be reframed. If this is what *we* should be doing, but aren't, what should *I* do? Should I cut my own emissions because that is what a fair collective scheme to mitigate climate change would require of me? Should I attempt to bring such collective action about? Or should I try directly to mitigate the harm or aid the victims of climate change?

These are the core questions for this book. However, it also goes beyond them in two key ways. Although there is an extensive body of work on ecological justice, and on the moral status of non-human animals, there is hardly any on the moral implications of the damage that climate change does to non-humans. Redressing this, at least in the context of my own project, I ask what it would mean for our weakly collective moral duties if we took seriously the moral status of those with whom we share this planet. I also go beyond the question of our individual *duties*—of what we can be blamed or criticized for not doing—to consider more generally the plight of the moral agent in the face of failure to act collectively on climate change. Is there anything we can do, as individuals, that will leave us able to live fully at peace with ourselves in the face of increasingly probable catastrophe? If there is not—if, as I argue, we are marred by the choices with which such collective failure presents us—then does not this, too, give us a duty to act collectively: a duty that we, between us, owe to each of us?

My aim is to contribute to the lively scholarly debate on climate change ethics, as well as the overlapping fields of environmental justice, and environmental and ecological ethics. The arguments should also be of interest to global justice theorists, to moral and political philosophers more generally, and philosophers of social science. However, this is a problem of practical urgency as well as philosophical interest. As such, I hope my readership will stretch beyond academic institutions.

With this in mind, I end this preface with a brief reading guide for non-specialists, to whom some sections will be more relevant than others. Chapter One, section (v), Chapter Two, sections (i) and (ii), Chapter Four, sections (i) and (iv), Chapter Five, section (vi), and Chapter Seven, section (iii) could be omitted by readers who are less interested in engaging with philosophical puzzles for their own sake. A reminder of key definitions has been included at the close of the book, as well as a glossary of some of the general philosophical terms to which I refer throughout. I hope that this will help to make my arguments accessible not only to other researchers but also to those whose predicament was what first inspired me to write this: those many motivated but bewildered moral agents who are struggling, in their everyday lives, with the very real dilemma of how appropriately to respond to climate change.

Elizabeth Cripps
Edinburgh

Acknowledgements

This book is the product of a British Academy Postdoctoral Fellowship at the University of Edinburgh (2009–12). It also draws on my doctoral research at University College London (2005–8), funded by the Arts and Humanities Research Council and a Jacobson Fellowship from the Institute of Philosophy. I gratefully acknowledge the support of all these institutions.

Sections (i) and (ii) of Chapter Two draw extensively on my earlier paper, 'Collectivities without Intention', *Journal of Social Philosophy*, 42 (1) (2011b), 1–20. (Copyright: Wiley-Blackwell.) Material is reproduced with permission of John Wiley & Sons. An earlier version of Chapter Three, section (iii) can be found in: 'Climate Change, Collective Harm and Legitimate Coercion', *Critical Review of International Social and Political Philosophy*, 14 (2) (2011a), 171–93. Material is reproduced with permission of Taylor & Francis Group (http://www.tandfonline.com). Parallel points to some in Chapter Four are made in 'Saving the Polar Bear, Saving the World: Can the Capabilities Approach do Justice to Humans, Animals *and* Ecosystems?' *Res Publica*, 16 (1) (2010), 1–22. Material is reproduced with permission of Springer.

The quote from 'An Inspector Calls' at the start of Chapter Three is reproduced by kind permission of United Agents on behalf of the J. B. Priestley estate. (Original publisher: William Heinemann.) The quote from Tim de Christopher at the start of Chapter Six is reproduced by kind permission of Scott Rosenberg, executive editor, Grist.org.

Chapters Two and Three build on my PhD thesis. They have benefited accordingly from the generosity and expertise of my supervisors, Jonathan Wolff and Michael Otsuka, and examiners, Leif Wenar and Susan James. I also received insightful comments on sections of Chapter Two from the Stirling Political Philosophy Group. Chapter Four has been greatly enhanced by constructive feedback from the Edinburgh Political Theory Research Group and at the Climate Ethics Workshop, Oxford, April 2012. I am grateful for perceptive criticism of Chapters Five and Six from my fellow participants in the workshop on Climate Change, Distributing Burdens and Motivating Action, Edinburgh, June 2012; the Climate Justice and Non-Ideal Theory Panel, ECPR Conference, Reykjavik, August 2011; and the British Academy Workshop on Climate Change and Responsibility, Edinburgh, June 2012. Chapter Seven was much improved by discussion at the Governance and Sustainability Research Programme, University of Westminster; the Philosophy Senior Seminar, University of Glasgow; the Stapledon Colloquium, University of Liverpool; and the Centre for Political Theory and Global Justice, University of Sheffield. Particular thanks go to those with whom I had productive discussions at more than one of these events, including Simon Caney, Clare Heyward, Aaron Maltais, and Henry Shue.

I am also very grateful for thoughtful written comments on draft chapters from Christina Boswell, Lynn Dobson, Stephen Gardiner, Clare Heyward, Robert Jubb, Chris Macleod, Aaron Maltais, Catriona McKinnon, David Schlosberg, Kerri Woods, and three anonymous reviewers for Oxford University Press. A number of others were kind enough to comment on individual arguments at earlier stages, including Cecile Fabre, Dominic Roser, David-Hillel Ruben, Anders Schinkel, and Jonathan Wolff.

Finally, this project would not have been possible without the enthusiastic support of the team at Oxford University Press or the kindness and encouragement of my friends, family, and colleagues. Special thanks are due to my editor, Dominic Byatt, and my postdoctoral mentor, Tim Hayward, to Harry Cripps for being my test-case non-specialist reader, to Vivien Cripps for fine-tuning my prose, and to Tom Baird and Sarah Jones for endless patience during the writing process.

Contents

1

Introduction

The scientific evidence is now overwhelming: climate change presents very serious global risks, and it demands an urgent global response.[1]

The Stern Review

[O]ver the past few decades, something has changed . . . [O]ur most humdrum activities may harm people in myriad ways we have never thought about before.[2]

Judith Lichtenberg

There are some situations in which it is easy, on most moral theories, to say what should be done. A student could gain thousands of roubles if he attacks and kills two old women. He shouldn't. A businessman could save a drowning child by getting his suit wet. He should.[3] The board of a corporation could save billions of dollars by suppressing evidence that its products are killing its customers. It shouldn't. Of course, the agents concerned might not do this, but that is a different problem.

Unfortunately, our current situation is not one of these. Climate change does very bad things to very many people. It brings with it death, serious illness, starvation, the loss of livelihood, of home, even of homeland. It also threatens mass extinction of plant and animal species. Given this, many of us take it as read that we have a duty, between us, to do something about it. Indeed, there is a highly developed empirical and normative literature on what exactly this *thing* should be—mitigation, adaptation, compensation, or all three—and how the costs of doing it could be fairly allocated between states.

However, on traditional theories of moral accountability, it is hard to explain where this duty comes from.[4] Not, it seems, from our standard thinking about individual responsibility, which focuses primarily on the direct results of individual actions or failures to act. After all, it's not as though any one of us causes climate change on her own. Nor could any individual prevent (or even perceptibly mitigate) it on her own. We are a very long way from those 'paradigm moral problems' where, as Dale Jamieson puts it, 'an individual acting intentionally harms another individual; both the individuals and the harm are identifiable; and the individuals and the harm are closely related in time and space'.[5] We are just as far from the core case of a positive duty, or duty to aid: where an individual knows she (and only she) could easily rescue some other individual from a significant, identifiable, and immediate threat.

Nor are standard models of collective, corporate, or even political responsibility much better equipped to help, revolving as they do around decisions made intentionally at the collective level, and in particular on the degree to which individual citizens can be held responsible for the policies of their states. There is no single collective body which can be blamed for causing climate change. It isn't even caused by individuals acting together intentionally, each knowingly contributing to some collective act of which this is a foreseeable side-effect. Rather, a great many persons (present and future) face a global-level threat from which we could protect them by organizing ourselves effectively to act together in certain ways, but which instead we are making much worse, through the combination of billions of individual actions.

With this comes a further question, one both theoretically intriguing and, for us as individuals, practically imperative. In the absence of any effective collective action, what should *I* be doing? As a moral agent, my connection with harmful climate change is very different from that I have with the harms I do, or fail to prevent, as an individual. It introduces questions beyond those— widely debated already by moral and political philosophers—of whether temporal, social, or physical distance can affect what one human being owes another.

Climate change is what Judith Lichtenberg calls a 'new harm'. I can't avoid being part of it simply by a few clear-cut omissions: 'Don't kill people, don't rape them, don't attack them, don't rob them.' Rather, I am part of it as part of almost everything I do: 'Every bite we take!' says Lichtenberg, with understandable emphasis. 'Every purchase we make!'[6] What's worse, if I don't take those bites—or limit them to local, vegan products—I can expect to make no difference. Harmful climate change will be unalleviated by my isolated sacrifice. So what should I do? Refrain anyway? Cut my own emissions? Or should I do something else instead? Devote myself to campaigning for collective action? Try to help the victims of climate change? And, in either case, why?

This book is my response to these twin challenges: of specifying what kind of moral duty we have to act on climate change, and of fathoming out what that means, as things currently stand, for the individual moral agent.[7]

My approach is as follows. I focus neither on the duties we acquire as individuals acting in isolation, nor on those acquired as members of established, often formalized, collective bodies. Rather, I argue that sets of individuals—as not-yet-organized collectivities or potential collectivities—can acquire weakly collective duties. These duties require them to organize as necessary to respond collectively to collective problems. (It is worth stressing that the 'weakly' qualifies the sense in which the harm is collective, not its force as a moral duty.) Individual duties, in such cases, are derivative of these weakly collective demands.

I make a fourfold case for a weakly collective duty to take action on global climate change, with the arguments complementary but largely independent. In each case, this is a duty to the victims of climate change, including many who are currently alive as well as future generations. Although the primary focus is on climate duties to our fellow humans, the weakly collective duties can also be defended as duties to non-humans.

The Young (younger generations, globally) have a weakly collective duty to mitigate climate change. This is grounded in moralized collective self-interest. As The Able (the global affluent) we have a weakly collective duty to secure mitigation and adaptation to harmful climate change, no matter who caused it. This is defended by an argument from collective ability to aid. As Polluters, we have a weakly collective duty to mitigate climate change caused by current generations, to enable adaptation to such change as cannot now be prevented, and to compensate (where possible) if neither is achieved in time to prevent serious harm to individuals. This is grounded in an expanded notion of collective responsibility for foreseeable harm. The last, most controversial, argument appeals to self-interest of a different kind: our interest in finding ways to live and act together which enable us to live at peace with ourselves, as simultaneously moral agents and human beings.

At the individual level, it is often thought that being 'green' means doing what we would have to if everyone were cooperating to mitigate climate change. In driving less, turning down the heating, eating less meat, and so on, we aim to reduce our own contribution to greenhouse gas emissions. However, I argue that individual moral agents should give priority to promoting collective action, supplemented by duties to aid victims or mitigate some part of the harm directly (probably as part of a like-minded subset). While we may be required to do many of the things we standardly think of as green, they cannot straightforwardly be defended as what I will call mimicking duties: as required because they are what a fair collective scheme would ask of us. Rather, where a convincing case can be made for such actions, it is generally because they are a means to fulfilling promotional or direct duties, and they do not take priority in cases of conflict with these duties.

In making these arguments, I have, of course, to start somewhere. Accordingly, I clear the ground by laying out five relatively uncontroversial starting assumptions: assumptions about climate science, about human flourishing, and about moral philosophy. On the latter, I take as read two widely accepted individual moral principles. I also assume away one peculiarly problematic philosophical niggle, the non-identity problem, which apparently undercuts any attempt to ground moral duties in avoiding harm to future individuals. I make no claim fully to defend these starting points. However, in introducing them, the following sections will also outline my reasons for accepting them as relatively uncontroversial and, in the case of the moral principles, fill out precise definitions to be adopted here. I then comment on methodology and respond to a potential objection regarding the scope of this project, before closing this introductory chapter with a more detailed summary of what is to follow.

(I) ASSUMPTION 1: CLIMATE CHANGE AND SCIENTIFIC CONSENSUS

The first two ground-clearing assumptions are that climate change is being caused by humans, and that it is bad for them.

I make no claim to engage in detail with climate science: with the ever-increasing understanding of the processes through which we are raising the average temperature of our planet, and through which this climate change has its detrimental impact on human lives. A number of climate ethicists and political theorists have already surveyed this literature, some in considerably more depth than I need to here.[8] My moral arguments begin with only two general—and increasingly undeniable—points. One is that we are causing global climate change through our combined actions: our actions, ultimately, as individuals, whether we are acting *as* individuals or through corporations, states, and other collective structures. The other is that this climate change will do many of us (present and future) very serious harm. Accordingly, this section will spell out my reasons for accepting the first, and section (ii) those for accepting the second of these.

Climate change is happening. The Intergovernmental Panel on Climate Change (IPCC) makes this extremely clear:

> Warming of the climate system is unequivocal, as is now evident from observations of increases in global average air and ocean temperatures, widespread melting of snow and ice and rising global average sea level...Eleven of the last twelve years (1995–2006) rank among the twelve warmest years in the instrumental record of global surface temperature (since 1850). The 100-year linear trend (1906–2005) of 0.74 [0.56 to 0.92]°C is larger than the corresponding trend

of 0.6 [0.4 to 0.8]°C (1901–2000)...The linear warming trend over the 50 years from 1956 to 2005 (0.13 [0.10 to 0.16]°C per decade) is nearly twice that for the 100 years from 1906 to 2005.[9]

The IPCC is equally clear on the anthropogenic nature of this change. It states 'with *very high confidence* that the global average net effect of human activities since 1750 has been one of warming'. This warming is driven by 'changes in the atmospheric concentrations of [greenhouse gases] and aerosols, land cover and solar radiation... [which] affect the absorption, scattering and emission of radiation within the atmosphere and at the Earth's surface'. According to the 2007 report, human activities have increased global atmospheric concentrations of carbon dioxide, methane, and nitrogen dioxide to the extent that they 'now far exceed pre-industrial values determined from ice cores spanning many thousands of years... Most of the observed increase in global average temperatures since the mid-20th century is *very likely* due to [this] observed increase in anthropogenic concentrations.'[10]

Warming already takes a toll on natural systems. The IPCC reports with '*high confidence* that natural systems related to snow, ice and frozen ground (including permafrost) are affected'. Glacial lakes are bigger and there are more of them; there are more rock avalanches; and ecosystems have changed in the Arctic and Antarctic. There is high confidence that hydrological systems are also already affected, with increased run-offs from many glacier or spring-fed rivers, rising temperatures in lakes and rivers, and implications for water quality. The report has very high confidence that changes in terrestrial biological systems, and high confidence that changes in marine and freshwater biological systems, can be attributed to climate change.[11] Recent research by the UK Met Office and the American Meteorological Society explicitly links some of the extreme weather events of 2011 to anthropogenic climate change.[12]

The IPCC conclusions have been robustly supported by a plethora of reputed scientific bodies.[13] In the United States—the heartland of so-called climate sceptics—these include the American Meteorological Society, the American Geophysical Union, and the American Association for the Advancement of Science (AAAS).[14] In 2006 the AAAS stated unambiguously: 'The scientific evidence is clear: global climate change caused by human activities is occurring now.'[15] In 2009 the US Global Change Research Programme produced its own synthesis report, stating:

Observations show that warming of the climate is unequivocal. The global warming observed over the past 50 years is due primarily to human-induced emissions of heat-trapping gases. These emissions come mainly from the burning of fossil fuels (coal, oil, and gas), with important contributions from the clearing of forests, agricultural practices, and other activities.[16]

In 2001 the national science academies of sixteen countries issued a statement acknowledging the IPCC as 'the world's most reliable source of information on climate change and its causes'.[17] This was reinforced in 2005 by a joint statement from the national science academies of the G8 nations and Brazil, China, and India, citing 'strong evidence that significant global warming is occurring' and calling for a prompt response by all nations.[18] Other bodies supporting the scientific consensus include the International Council of Academies of Engineering and Technological Sciences, the European Academy of Sciences and Arts, the European Geosciences Union, and the Network of African Science Academies.[19]

This reflects overwhelming agreement within the underlying scientific research. In 2004 Naomi Oreskes surveyed peer-reviewed articles on climate change published in scientific journals between 1993 and 2003. None disagreed with the view that most of the observed global warming of the previous fifty years is likely to have resulted from increased greenhouse gas emissions.[20] In 2009 Peter Doran and Maggie Zimmerman surveyed individual earth scientists directly. Of the 3,146 respondents, 90 per cent thought mean global temperatures had generally risen from pre-1800 levels, and 82 per cent that human activity was 'a significant contributing factor in changing mean global temperatures'. Among climate science specialists, these rose to 96.2 and 97.4 per cent, respectively.[21]

As Denis Arnold points out, insofar as there is a dispute about this consensus, it emerges neither in the well-vetted research that makes it into leading scientific journals nor in the summary statements presented by respected bodies of scientists. So where does it come from?[22] From 'opinion pieces in newspapers, blogs, industry-sponsored position papers, and even vanity journals published with the intention of advancing an ideological perspective rather than advancing science'.[23] Even without the widespread concerns about the influence of vested interest groups, such organs are not exactly known for matching the loudness of their assertions with comparable rigour of research.[24]

I am, accordingly, going to take scientific consensus on anthropogenic climate change as a starting point, and the IPCC reports as acknowledgedly authoritative. This consensus extends to some very stark projections.

On current trends (that is, with no more than current climate policies), global temperatures are projected to grow by around 0.2°C a decade until nearly 2030. Depending on the specific emissions scenario (that is, depending on the development pathway taken but assuming no additional climate policies), the IPCC puts global average temperatures in 2090–9 at between 1.1 and 6.4°C higher than 1980–99.[25] The Stern Review, commissioned by the British government to assess the evidence and report on the economics of climate change, reports a 50 per cent risk that a 'business as usual' approach will yield an increase of more than 5°C over the following decades. This, the review warns, 'would take humans into unknown territory': territory whose extreme dangers are highlighted by the fact 'that we are now only around 5°C warmer than in the last ice age'.[26]

(II) ASSUMPTION 2: CLIMATE CHANGE AND FUNDAMENTAL INTERESTS

Climate change is bad—very bad—for individual human beings. To fill out this assumption, this section outlines a relatively uncontroversial account of fundamental human interests, then returns to the IPCC evidence to show that climate change will deprive very many persons of just such interests. I also briefly explain a subsidiary assumption: that both mitigation and adaptation are required in order to prevent these deprivations.

I am taking it as read that there are certain prerequisites to living a fully flourishing human life: that in order to do so an individual must have the capability, or meaningful opportunity, to enjoy continued life (at least to a normal human length), bodily health, bodily integrity, affiliation (relationships with others), and practical reason. This last includes being able to develop and pursue a plan for her own life, with such education as this requires.[27] These human functionings are so centrally important that it is a serious harm to an individual to be deprived of her opportunity to exercise any one of them. Moreover, they cannot fully be traded off against one another: if one is lost, gains in the others cannot fully make it up to the individual.

To some extent, I am borrowing from the capabilities approach. I draw on the notion, central to that school of thought, of certain necessities for the kind of life that can properly be called human. (A life, as Amartya Sen puts it, that 'we have reason to value'.[28]) The idea is to move away from assessments of well-being that rely on either the satisfaction of potentially adaptive preferences, on the one hand, or a narrower notion of resources, on the other. Individual preferences are not formed in isolation, and so can adapt either to extremely poor circumstances (leading to individuals ranking as acceptable lives where they suffer from severe objective deprivation) or to extremely luxurious ones (the problem, in the distributive justice literature, of expensive tastes).[29] Autonomy, a hard-to-dispute prerequisite for human flourishing, involves more than not being forcibly prevented from pursuing one's immediate goals. (I will return to this point shortly.) However, differences between humans or their social situations are such that two individuals with the same income or wealth, or even the same formal rights and opportunities, can have radically different qualities of life.[30]

However, capabilities theorists tend to adopt a broader range of central human functionings than those listed above. Martha Nussbaum, listing central capabilities, includes: life; bodily health; bodily integrity; senses, imagination, and thought; emotions; practical reason; affiliation; other species; play; and control over one's environment.[31] Some of these, especially other species, have proved controversial.[32] Accordingly, it is important to stress that I do not, and do not need to, commit myself to her list as a whole. Rather, I am taking as read only those elements which it is hardest to deny are central to human life.

In fact, life, health, bodily integrity, affiliation, and practical reason could all be defended as central human functionings by appeal only to a combination of basic needs—or, as Frances Stewart puts it, means to achieve 'a minimally decent condition of life'—with the conditions for human autonomy, or being what Joseph Raz describes as '(part) author of one's own life'.[33] On even relatively austere accounts, basic needs include nutrition, health, and at least some opportunity for education.[34] Scope to exercise practical reason, some kind of affiliation, and bodily integrity can be defended as basic requirements for an autonomous life. This, Raz has argued, 'consists in the successful pursuit of self-chosen goals *and relationships*' and requires being free from coercion and manipulation, appropriate mental faculties, and an adequate range of long- and short-term options.[35]

However, one thing is explicitly incorporated from the capabilities approach. (I make no apology for this, because it makes the assumption less controversial rather than more so.) This is the distinction between actually exercising some central functioning and having the capability or meaningful opportunity to do so. The claim is not the strongly paternalistic one that an individual cannot fully flourish if she does not choose to enjoy one of these central elements; rather, it is that she is seriously harmed by being permanently deprived of the capability—or meaningful opportunity—to do so. There is a world of difference between the unemployed, poverty-stricken woman, barely able to feed herself, and the rich girl, immortalized by the Britpop band Pulp, slumming it because she wants 'to live like common people'.[36]

Jonathan Wolff and Avner de-Shalit have filled out this distinction, identifying a capability as a genuine, secure opportunity to exercise a central functioning. An opportunity, they argue, is genuine if an individual could exercise it without jeopardizing another central functioning. It is secure if the individual can rely on being able to exercise it going forward: that is, if it is not subject to risk she cannot control.[37] Chapter Two will return to this point, because the argument from moralized collective self-interest relies on this incorporation of some avoidance of risk in the model of human flourishing. However, the arguments from collective ability to aid and weakly collective harm require us only to accept in general terms that we have certain fundamental interests, corresponding to our ability to enjoy continued life, health, bodily integrity, affiliation, and practical reason.

Against this background, let us return to the science. Again, this is very clear. As the Stern Review puts it: '*Climate change threatens the basic elements of life for people around the world—access to water, food production, health, and use of land and the environment.*'[38] The IPCC report spells out serious implications of climate change for the fundamental interests of a great many individual human beings, present and future.[39]

Expected temperature changes most obviously threaten those least controversial of fundamental human interests: health, and continued life itself. The IPCC puts it starkly:

> The health status of millions of people is projected to be affected through, for example, increases in malnutrition; increased deaths, diseases and injury due to extreme weather events; increased burden of diarrhoeal diseases; increased frequency of cardio-respiratory diseases due to higher concentrations of ground-level ozone in urban areas related to climate change; and the altered spatial distribution of some infectious diseases.[40]

Other fundamental interests are also threatened, especially for those in low-lying and small island communities. The IPCC predicts with very high confidence that floods will affect 'many millions more people than today' by 2080. Those hit hardest will be on small islands and highly populated, low-lying areas of Asia and Africa. Sea-level rise is also 'expected to exacerbate inundation, storm surge, erosion and other coastal hazards, thus threatening vital infrastructure, settlements and facilities that support the livelihood of island communities'.[41]

By undermining whole communities, these changes can deprive individuals of ties essential to affiliation, as well as the ability—central to practical reason—to live in any meaningful sense according to their own plan of life. If environmental refugees are treated as badly as many political and economic refugees, even bodily integrity could be threatened, by depriving individuals of freedom of movement. However, this last is not so much a direct consequence of climate change as—like the increased potential for resource conflict—a likely consequence of human reaction to its effects.[42] Finally, as Breena Holland has pointed out, for many people religious or spiritual practices hinge on interaction with threatened environments.[43] These, too, would be undermined.

Having outlined the rather bleak situation in which we find ourselves, it remains to lay out the basic moral principles which I am also taking for granted. Before doing so, however, I must make a subsidiary but significant point. The arguments of Chapter Three will rely implicitly on the assumption not only that climate change threatens fundamental human interests, but that both mitigation and adaptation are needed to protect them. Again, I do not defend this in detail. However, I should briefly give my reasons for taking it as read.

Let us begin with the IPCC definitions. Mitigating climate change involves reducing total greenhouse gas emissions and enhancing carbon sinks. Adaptation involves '[i]nitiatives and measures to reduce the vulnerability of natural and human systems against actual or expected climate change effects'.[44] In other words, mitigation involves attempting to prevent the changes to the global environment; adaptation is about changing the way we live in order to stop those changes from affecting human lives too badly.[45] For the purposes of this book, the adaptation required can be taken to be such as will protect fundamental human interests from any climate change which is not prevented by mitigation.

Again, the IPCC is clear. It states with high confidence that 'neither adaptation nor mitigation alone can avoid all climate change impacts'. Adaptation is 'necessary both in the short term and longer term to address impacts resulting from the warming that would occur even for the lowest stabilisation scenarios assessed', while '[u]nmitigated climate change would, in the long term, be *likely* to exceed the capacity of natural, managed and human systems to adapt'.[46] The 2005 joint statement by national science academies calls for action 'to reduce the causes of climate change, adapt to its impacts and ensure that the issue is included in all relevant national and international strategies'.[47] The AAAS is also adamant: 'In addition to rapidly reducing greenhouse gas emissions, it is essential that we develop strategies to adapt to ongoing changes and make communities more resilient to future changes.'[48]

Insofar as there is disagreement on this point, it has its roots not in science but in economics.[49] The counter-argument is that it is better to concentrate on adaptation because it can be secured more cheaply than mitigation. Again, I need not go into this debate, which is well covered elsewhere. I note only that such claims have been robustly criticized on moral grounds: for (implicitly or explicitly) unacceptably discounting the value of future human lives.[50] I am taking these rebuttals, in combination with the above IPCC conclusions, as conclusive.

(III) ASSUMPTION 3: THE NO-HARM PRINCIPLE

Let us turn, then, to the moral principles to be taken as the next two starting assumptions.

Whatever else matters morally, it matters that individual human lives go well, or at least that they don't go very badly indeed. This much, I think, can be taken as read. In beginning with this, I am not denying that other things might also have moral significance. In this context, the most obvious contenders are the flourishing of non-human animals and the preservation of species, ecosystems, or even the 'natural world' as a whole. Indeed, as Chapter Four will discuss, it is highly plausible that the sphere of moral concern should be extended beyond the human being. However, for the purposes of the rest of the book, I need start only with the claim that moral value attaches to individual human flourishing, or—to put it even less controversially—moral disvalue attaches to the reverse. It is a bad thing if individual humans are seriously harmed.

In terms of what this means for us as individual moral agents (that is, as actors to whom the rules of morality apply), I am taking two widely held moral principles for granted. The first is this:

No-harm principle
An individual (moral agent) has a moral duty to avoid inflicting serious harm (deprivation of a fundamental interest) on another human being or human beings (moral subject(s)) *at least* if she can avoid so doing without suffering comparable harm herself.

This prohibition is implicit in John Stuart Mill's harm (or liberty) principle: 'That the only purpose for which power can rightfully be exercised over any member of a civilized community, against his will, is to prevent harm to others.'[51] It is explicit in W. D. Ross' duty of non-maleficence, or 'not injuring others', and in Henry Shue's re-statement of 'the liberal no-harm principle': '*It is wrong to inflict avoidable harm upon other people*, and it ought often to be prohibited by law.'[52] In adopting it here, I begin with about as generally acknowledged a moral principle as I could hope to find. Even the most stalwart libertarian would accept at least some version of the no-harm principle. Whatever our positive duties to one another, we have, by virtue of our common humanity, at least this negative one.

Moreover, I have made it even less controversial, in two key ways, than many would accept. Firstly, in limiting 'serious harm' to the deprivation of fundamental interests—to the permanent loss of the capability to exercise some central human functioning—I am being relatively cautious. Clearly, there has to be some limit to the harms prohibited, given the almost infinite range of ways in which even our individual actions can impinge on others. If I buy the only dress on the sale rack, or take the last seat on the bus, there is a trivial sense in which I am harming the next comer, by depriving them of it. However, to prohibit all such actions would be a very unreasonable restraint on my scope to live my own life.

However, many would put the bar lower than I have done. For example, even temporary disruptions of the exercise of central functionings—those which I identify below as 'significant costs'—might be prohibited by the no-harm principle. I am certainly not denying this. However, for the purposes of the argument from weakly collective harm, which takes the individual no-harm principle as its starting point, it is necessary only to rely on this relatively permissive version. Accordingly, I limit myself in this way here simply to make the premises as uncontroversial as possible.

Similarly, the cost condition might be disputed. As Lichtenberg points out, we generally acknowledge *some* limits to what can be demanded of individuals even in restraint from harm: '[d]uress and necessity are defences that mitigate a person's guilt even in violent harm'.[53] However, we also tend to limit what counts as necessity. For example, on most intuitions, I shouldn't murder a bystander even if this were the only way in which I could save my own life or that of a loved one.[54] Again, I am very far from denying this. However, the arguments of Part One need only this weaker—and accordingly still less controversial—version of the no-harm principle.

Having laid out this first moral principle, I have one further remark to make before moving on to the principle of beneficence. Section (ii) closed with a brief discussion of the need for both mitigation and adaptation. We can now add to this. On most plausible readings, the no-harm principle requires not only that we avoid causing serious suffering, but also that we attempt to make up for it where we have inflicted it: that is, that we compensate for harms for which we are responsible. To make a parallel point to Simon Caney, this is directly relevant to the climate change case.[55]

Adaptation and mitigation are both necessary to protect the fundamental interests threatened by climate change, but would not be jointly sufficient, even if collective action were taken rapidly now, to prevent all harm. It is this danger—or the too plausible possibility of continued failure to act collectively on either mitigation or adaptation—that gives rise to the third category of duty. This is a duty to compensate: to attempt to make it up to the deprived individuals in some other way (or at least, as Caney points out with grim realism, to those among them who aren't already dead).[56] I will come back to this in Chapter Three.

However, as Caney also stresses, it is crucial to retain the distinction between adaptation and compensation. Adaptation enables the fundamental interests to be protected; compensation reacts to their loss. We can make this point at the individual level. Assuming I am aware of the situation, I have a moral duty to refrain from pushing a large boulder so that it rolls down a hill towards you. If I have pushed it, I have a duty to attempt to prevent you from being crushed (perhaps by yelling at you to move). If I do neither, and you are seriously injured, I have compensatory duties to attempt to make it up to you. However, it goes almost without saying that this 'making it up' is always second-best. If you have to spend your life in a wheelchair because of what I did, I can never fully make it up to you, even if I buy you the most expensive wheelchair going.[57]

(IV) ASSUMPTION 4:
THE PRINCIPLE OF BENEFICENCE

The second widely held moral principle is the principle of beneficence. Two versions will be used in Part One, one of which is weaker (and so less controversial) than the other.

Weak principle of beneficence

An individual (moral agent) has a moral duty to prevent the serious suffering (deprivation of a fundamental interest) of some other human being or human beings (moral subject(s)) if she can do so at minimal cost to herself.

Moderate principle of beneficence

An individual (moral agent) has a moral duty to prevent the serious suffering (deprivation of a fundamental interest) of some other human being or human beings (moral subject(s)) if she can do so at less than significant cost to herself.

The moderate principle corresponds to that defended by Peter Singer: 'if it is in our power to prevent something very bad from happening, without thereby sacrificing anything morally significant, we ought, morally, to do it'.[58] However, one can accept it without being an act-utilitarian: without thinking there is no more to the rightness or wrongness of our actions than their impact on aggregate (or average) well-being.[59] Thus, for example, Ross defends a duty of beneficence, alongside a duty of non-maleficence, within his pluralist account of moral duties.[60] Moreover, neither of the two versions above goes as far as Singer's strong principle, on which we are required to prevent the 'something very bad' up to the point at which we would have to sacrifice something of comparable moral importance.

The weak principle is very weak: the agent is required to incur only minimal costs. These might be immediately trivial. For example, if I could preserve your life by flicking a switch, then I would have a duty to do so. Alternatively, they might be only minor changes to what I would have to do anyway in pursuit of some end of my own. Suppose I have two choices of route for my run tomorrow morning. By taking one of these—which is only marginally less pretty and almost as good exercise—I could also collect the drugs you need to treat your very serious asthma. Even if the moderate principle of beneficence were denied, so that it would be too demanding to require me to run four miles just to save your health, the weak principle could still require me to do so in this case. I would be running the same distance anyway, so the extra effort is minimal. (I will return to this in Chapter Two, for although the principle in itself is not at all controversial, I will take a slant on it there that some would consider more so.)

The moderate principle is more demanding, but does still impose limits. As phrased above, it immediately raises the question of what counts as a morally significant cost, so I must say something briefly about this. There is a spectrum from comparable cost to the agent, at one end, to trivial costs which even the weak principle would exclude, at the other. There is also considerable shared understanding. For example, it can safely be deemed overdemanding to require me to save someone's life by devoting the rest of mine to reading him the collected works of Charles Dickens, but not to claim that I should spend ten minutes reading to a stranger if there arises some unlikely situation in which my doing so would save him.[61] However, it could be impossible to draw an exact line.

Fortunately, the interests- or capabilities-based model of flourishing lends itself to a plausible working suggestion, which sets the bar between these two extremes. It might reasonably be deemed a significant cost to the agent to do something which seriously interferes, even on a temporary basis, with the exercise of a central human functioning. This is so even if she is not permanently deprived of the relevant capability.[62]

Examples of such costs include a broken limb or a short-lived but excruciating pain. Neither deprives the individual of her ability to live a healthy life overall. However, they do significantly interfere with it in the short term. Similarly, being required to delay her education by a year interferes seriously with an agent's exercise of practical reason, even though it does not deprive her overall of the capacity to plan her own life. Comparable examples arise in other core areas: being separated from one's young child for a week, incarcerated for a fortnight, or exiled for months from one's community.[63] Of course, the period required for such interruption to count as serious will depend on the particular functioning: the kind of good at stake. Not being able to write another chapter of my *magnum opus* today (or even this month) would not outweigh a duty to save the life of a stranger; being deprived thereby of all future opportunity to pursue my plan of life would do so. Even a few moments of agonising, torturing pain might do so.

In retaining the focus on the central elements of a flourishing human life, this avoids appeal to trivial costs. However, it remains considerably less demanding than a requirement to fulfil the principle up to the point of giving up all future capability of functioning in the relevant way. To return to the example above, even if it would save the suffering stranger, I would have no moral duty to abandon my own projects for six months and spend my working days reading Dickens to him instead.

Accordingly, I start with this version of the moderate principle of beneficence. However, it is important to acknowledge one influential rival view. Liam Murphy argues that the cost condition for the principle of beneficence should be set by reference to the number of other duty-bearers. On his compliance condition, no more can be demanded of me in saving others from severe suffering than would be required if everyone else were doing their bit towards the same end.[64] If there are a thousand famine victims and a thousand potential helpers, each of whom could send a little of her own plentiful food to a victim and save his life, then as one of the duty-bearers I am required to do just that: send that bit of food (or more realistically send the money to some charity to supply it). The effort demanded of me should not increase because those around me are failing to do anything.

As I will argue in Chapter Six, there are reasons to question this condition: it seems arbitrarily to put all the cost of a moral default on the victim, rather than also on other potential duty-bearers. Moreover, even if we were to accept it, questions would remain concerning the limits of beneficence where there are no other (absconding) duty-bearers, or when all are prepared to help. If I am the only person in a position to save your life, how much am I required to give to do it? My own life? One of my kidneys? A thousand pounds? A vial of my blood? A first class postage stamp?[65] However, most of the rest of the book does not stand or fall on rejecting the compliance condition. Even if we accepted it as determining the limits of the demands of beneficence in cases where there are many potential duty-bearers, the general defence—both of the weakly collective duty and of the derivative individual duties—would still follow. (Chapters Five and Six will return to this point.)

Having outlined the moral principles to be taken as starting assumptions, it is worth briefly considering their relation to one another. The principles of beneficence, on the one hand, and the no-harm principle, on the other, are presented as independent but not as mutually exclusive. I leave open the widely held possibility that, if both are accepted, then the individual no-harm principle takes priority: avoiding inflicting serious harm trumps simply preventing it. However, I am not committing myself to the view that, if all three of the arguments for the weakly collective duty convince, there is the same absolute priority at the weakly collective level: in terms either of collective fulfilment of the duty or of derivative individual duties. As Lichtenberg argues, the reasons we tend to think of negative duties as being more stringent—efficacy, integrity, demandingness—become blurred when taken to the weakly collective level.[66]

(V) ASSUMPTION 5:
EVADING THE NON-IDENTITY PROBLEM

This brings us to the fifth and final objection. As a philosopher, I am bound to acknowledge one persistent difficulty facing any attempt to ground moral duties in harm to future individuals: Derek Parfit's non-identity problem.[67] The puzzle is this: those same combined actions that cause such suffering to members of future generations also determine who those future individuals *are*. Different behaviour patterns mean children being conceived at different times, perhaps even by different pairs of parents. Since we can safely assume (at a minimum) that changing a conception date by a month or more will result in having a different child, future generations will be composed of different individuals from those who would have made them up had we acted otherwise on climate change. But then, assuming that the lives of those individuals are still worth living, how can we say that we have harmed them? Consider someone born in Bangladesh in 2100. Deprived though she is of fundamental interests as a result of the combined actions which worsened climate change, how can we say that she has been made worse off by them? Had we acted otherwise, she wouldn't have existed at all.

My fifth starting assumption is that there is a way around this problem. I do not attempt to resolve it here. Instead, I appeal on the one hand to a number of promising attempts by others to do so, and on the other to the hugely repugnant consequences of taking it seriously in practice. These implications extend from small- to very large-scale cases. The non-identity problem could give us a mandate to do anything, no matter how awful in terms of undermining the fundamental interests of future persons, so long as in the process we did two things: changed who those future persons were, and did not make them so badly off that their lives were not worth living at all.

Consider the following example, which I have borrowed from Barbara Vine's novel of the same name.[68]

Blood doctor
A Victorian doctor, determined to research haemophilia, deliberately marries a woman whose family has the gene, in the hope of having a haemophiliac son to observe at close quarters. They do indeed have such a son, who later dies of the disease.

While some of our repugnance results from the man's treatment of others (notably the boy's mother), much of it results from the infliction of such a terrible disease on his son, even though—or even assuming—the boy's short life was still worth living. The non-identity problem seems to deprive us of this line of criticism: if the man had acted otherwise, that particular child would never have been born at all, so how can he be said to have been harmed by it?

At the collective level, consider the following.

Community cost saving
A community is deciding whether to introduce a new chemical into its water system. If the chemical is used, money will be saved. However, as a result of drinking the water, all women who would otherwise have conceived healthy children this month will conceive severely disabled children next month instead. The lives of these children, though they involve much suffering, will still be worth living.

Again, such a policy is abhorrent. However, according to the non-identity problem, it cannot be criticized by appeal to the harm done to the future children.

Given such implications—quite apart from those in the climate change case—it is unsurprising that many philosophers have made ingenious attempts either to dissolve or to resolve the non-identity problem. I will briefly survey three relevant possibilities here.[69]

The first option is to step back from the impact on specific individuals and appeal to comparisons across individuals, across actual and possible worlds. Parfit himself appeals to his principle Q, a variant on a principle of beneficence.

If in either of two outcomes the same number of people would live, it will be worse if those who live are worse off, or have a lower quality of life, than those who have lived.[70]

For cases where the number of people is changed, he posits—but does not ultimately identify—a Theory X. Straightforward appeal to the number of flourishing individuals in such cases gives rise to its own problematic implications, including a duty to go on and on creating more new persons simply because they would live worthwhile lives.

Caspar Hare appeals to *de dicto* goodness or badness: goodness or badness in terms of the interests of those (whoever they are) who occupy certain positions. This is in contrast to *de re* concern for the interests of specific, actual individuals.[71] In *Blood doctor*, the man acts wrongly because he causes the person occupying the role of his own child to be worse off than whoever (else) had been occupying that role would have been otherwise. The same is true of Parfit's own examples of mothers deciding whether to conceive disadvantaged children now or wait to conceive children with every opportunity to flourish.[72]

Other proposed solutions retain the focus on the impact on—the harm to—specific future individuals. One possibility is to dissolve the non-identity problem by showing that future persons don't have an interest in existence, in itself, at all. On Rivka Weinberg's argument, existence is not a benefit conferred (or harm averted), which can be used to 'cancel out' the infliction of suffering: it is a prerequisite for having any interests at all.[73] Accordingly, in assessing the goodness or badness of an action there is no need to consider either the fact that it conferred existence on an individual, or the interests that those not brought into existence would have had fulfilled if they had been born.

The alternative is to accept existence as a benefit, but insist that there is still a sense in which future individuals are wronged or harmed by those actions which significantly curtail their quality of life. James Woodward cites specific rights, grounded in specific interests, which can be wrongfully violated even without their holder being made worse off overall. He uses the example of Smith, who is wronged when a racist airline official denies him a ticket, even though that decision saves his life because the plane crashes with no survivors.[74] Caney defends a climate justice model based on goal-rights (or rights to have certain interests secured).[75]

Elizabeth Harman and Seana Shiffrin argue that the future individuals in these difficult cases are harmed because certain serious impacts constitute harms even if they come bound up with benefits. (Examples are serious disfigurement, or early death.) Harman argues that, in cases of people who would not otherwise exist, the fact that a harm also benefits them is 'ineligible to justify the harm' if, in failing to harm, it would have been possible to give the benefit to someone else instead.[76] Shiffrin argues that harms involve central, alienating costs. These, she reasons, can be justified if they prevent some other greater harm but not simply because they also confer a benefit. Benefits, while they take a person up from an already perfectly acceptable level to some higher threshold of well-being, are not central in the same way.[77]

Given the interests- or capabilities-based model of valuable human flourishing, the second two ways around the non-identity problem look particularly promising. Nothing in section (ii) required that coming into existence be ranked as a fundamental interest. Of course, there is such an interest in being able to continue one's life to a normal length. However, in general there is no problem with the idea that we can have interests that we would not have acquired without acquiring something that is not itself in our interest, nor with the view that we can have an interest in keeping something we didn't have an interest in getting in the first place. In the case of life itself, this seems peculiarly so, since existence is not only a prerequisite for other interests but for being the kind of being who has interests.

Moreover, the focus on specific, fundamental interests—each a prerequisite for full flourishing and irreplaceable by one another—suggests a solution close to Shiffrin's. The idea would be that being deprived of a fundamental interest (the capability for continued life, health, bodily integrity, affiliation, or practical reason) is a morally significant harm (involves serious suffering), unless the only way of avoiding this is by the sacrifice of another such.

This is, of course, only a brief survey. The debate still continues, with further objections to many of the solutions still outstanding.[78] However, I take the range of promising solutions, combined with the extremely repugnant implications, above, as legitimate reason simply to assume that the two principles can be reformulated to avoid the non-identity problem. That is: that the no-harm principle can require avoiding foreseeably depriving other human beings of fundamental interests, if the agent can do so without sacrificing such an interest herself, *whether or not those other individuals would have existed at all had she acted otherwise*; and that the principles of beneficence require action to secure the fundamental interests of other human beings, subject to the cost condition, *whether or not they would have existed had the agent acted otherwise*. However, I am also assuming that the latter do not demand the creation of additional future persons simply because they would have their fundamental interests secured. The idea is that there can be a duty to create flourishing people in order to avoid creating deprived future persons, but not to create them simply for the sake of it.

(VI) METHODOLOGY AND SCOPE

Having laid out the five starting assumptions of this book, I will now offer a brief comment on methodology, and then respond to one potential objection on the scope of this project.

My approach is that of the analytic philosopher. The idea is to start from some fixed points about which we can be relatively confident (some accepted principles, on the one hand; some clear-cut intuitions on the other) and reason clearly and consistently from there. Although I do not offer anything like an adequate defence of this method here, it is a widely used one in moral and political theory, and I am very sympathetic to the defence offered by Daniel McDermott. Like him, I consider it the aim of this kind of normative theory 'to provide better understanding of the requirements of morality'.[79]

This method does appeal to intuitions. However, as McDermott stresses, intuitions are not themselves taken as the last word on what we ought to do. Rather, intuition is one means of testing possible conclusions as to what the rules of morality are. Of course, our intuitions are more or less strong, and more or less reliable, in different cases. Equally, in accepting some core moral principles (even those two relatively uncontroversial suggestions, above), I risk losing some of my audience before I start. However, as McDermott maintains, such problems are not specific to analytic methods in moral philosophy: scientists, too, must rely on assumptions which could later turn out to be false and, ultimately, can convince others only on the basis of judgements those others make about the combination of theory and fact with which they are presented. As he puts it: 'No matter how sensible a normative theory may appear, we can be sure that people will disagree about it, and we can also be sure that they will continue to disagree regardless of the outcome of any tests.'[80]

Moreover, in offering three largely independent arguments for the weakly collective duty, building on two different principles (and two different versions of one of them), I hope to strengthen the case that there is such a duty. My reasoning here is akin to that employed in the highly practical task of leading a rock climb. There, the aim is to provide a belay as secure as possible by fixing the rope to the rock face in two or three different places, before trusting it to hold the weight either of oneself or one's climbing partner. In this case, my conclusions in Part One are derived from three different starting points—one of which is wholly independent of the others, and the other two of which are at least partially so—with a view to embarking with greater confidence on the arguments of Parts Two, Three, and Four.

As part of this analytic process, I will make extensive use of one device very common to such reasoning: the thought experiment, or hypothetical example. (Indeed, I have done so already, even in this introductory chapter.) Thought experiments play an important role. They enable us to focus intuitions with greater clarity, and trigger greater awareness of the implications of potential moral principles.[81] (The analogy, continuing McDermott's defence, would be with a controlled experiment in natural science.) As a result of such 'tests', we may, as practical philosophers, have either to abandon some of our in-practice intuitions, or to reframe some potential principles, but this again is part of a familiar, well-established process—that of reflective equilibrium—and it is a process through which scientists have also to go.

Turning from methodology to scope, the potential objection is this: what's so special about climate change? After all, there are many situations in which we might have a weakly collective duty to protect the fundamental interests of human beings.[82] Indeed, Shue and Robert Goodin, on whose arguments I draw in Chapters Two and Three, defend duties to establish institutions to protect the vulnerable (or secure basic rights) in the broader context of a cosmopolitan approach to global justice.[83]

I hope and expect that the arguments defended here, if they prove convincing, will transfer to other cases. However, I focus on climate change for the following reasons. Firstly, because it is so peculiarly global: we are all on the same planet, even if we aren't all in the same institutional structures, committed to the same way of life, or even buying from the same corporations. Secondly, because it is also so peculiarly urgent: as far as mitigation is concerned, these are duties which, if not fulfilled soon—if we commit ourselves through collective failure to a future of five or even six degrees of temperature increase—become even collectively unfulfillable.[84] As section (ii) stressed, there is a limit to what adaptation can do. Thirdly, relatedly, because while there are many other situations in which one or even two of the three arguments to be made in Part One can be defended, climate change combines all three. Our weakly collective duty, in this case, can be established on the basis of moralized collective self-interest, collective ability to aid, and weakly collective responsibility for harm.

I am also deliberately focusing on climate change rather than on other environmental problems: more localized pollution, for example, or biodiversity loss in general (rather than the threats posed by climate change to biodiversity, which will be considered in Chapter Four). Again, the model will almost certainly also have implications for these. However, it is the truly global nature of the challenge, and its negative impact at an equally global level, that makes climate change special, and makes it my focus here.

(VII) STRUCTURE

Part One provides a threefold defence of our weakly collective duty to organize ourselves to act on climate change. It does this by expanding dominant models of when a set of individuals constitutes a collectivity, and of collective responsibility for (by causing, or for failing to prevent) serious harms.

However, it is worth stressing from the start that I do not commit to any particular form of collective action. I leave it open whether fulfilling the weakly collective duty would involve an effective agreement between states (that is, one unlike anything we have seen hitherto), an extended remit for an existing international organization, the establishment of some stronger global-level institution, or even—at the other extreme—a global-level agreement between individuals or sub-state collectivities. This might be the kind of 'global citizens' movement' advocated by Jamieson, which would stigmatize high-emitting lifestyles and bring about a widespread change in ways of life.[85] My focus in Part One is on providing a moral grounding for the weakly collective duty to identify and pursue some effective, fair, and legitimate means of acting collectively on climate change. Later, it is on exploring the implications of this duty for individual moral agents, as things currently stand.

Chapter Two presents the argument from moralized collective self-interest. This has three steps. Firstly, I defend a non-intentionalist account on which a collectivity is constituted by individuals mutually dependent for the achievement or satisfaction of some common or shared goal, purpose, or fundamental interest, whether or not they are aware of this themselves. This is contrary to the influential intentionalist model, on which a set of individuals can only constitute a collectivity (or social group) if its members think of themselves as doing so. Secondly, I ask whether we constitute a global-level 'collectivity of humanity' because of the threats posed by climate change to continued life, health, bodily integrity, affiliation, and practical reason. Drawing on the idea of fundamental interests in retaining secure opportunities to function, I argue that younger generations are relevantly mutually dependent. This gives The Young a prudential incentive to cooperate to mitigate global climate change.

I then moralize this appeal to collective rationality. Drawing on work by Larry May, Virginia Held, Robert Goodin, and Shue, I defend a collectivized version of the weak principle of beneficence.[86] I argue that a special case application of this principle gives The Young a weakly collective moral duty (a duty of all to each) to mitigate climate change. The argument, briefly, is as follows. The harm is severe enough to bring the principle into force. Moreover, because the set whose interests are at stake includes that of potential helpers, the minimal cost clause must be satisfied. It is not only a minimal cost: it is to each member's advantage that the collective action takes place.

Chapter Three argues from collective ability to aid and weakly collective responsibility for harm. I introduce the notion of a potential collectivity: a set of individuals who are not yet organized to act collectively but could become so. Within this, the possibility arises of a *should-be* collectivity: a potential collectivity with a moral duty to organize to act collectively in pursuit of a particular goal. Two such are identified at the global level: The Able (or affluent) and Polluters.

Applying a collectivized moderate principle of beneficence, I defend a weakly collective duty of The Able to mitigate and enable adaptation to climate change, regardless of who or what caused it. I then defend an expanded notion of negative moral responsibility, on which a set of individuals are weakly collectively responsible for harm resulting predictably and avoidably from the aggregation of their individual acts. 'Predictable' is used in a twofold sense: it is reasonably foreseeable to each both that the aggregation of actions would do harm, and that sufficient others are similarly motivated to act for the harm to result. Drawing on this, I argue that Polluters have a weakly collective duty to organize to mitigate and enable adaptation to climate change for which current generations are responsible, and to compensate where such efforts come too late to prevent serious harm. (By Polluters, I mean those whose greenhouse gas emissions are higher than those at which, were everyone to emit at that level, climate change would be made no worse, and could avoid so emitting without sacrificing fundamental interests themselves.) Finally, I indicate how, in practice, fulfilment of these three weakly collective duties might be approximated by one fair collective scheme at the level of The Able.

Part Two pushes the boundaries. I expand the non-intentionalist model to include at least sentient non-human animals as members of collectivities. I then explore the implications of extending the collectivized no-harm principle and principles of beneficence to non-humans as moral subjects. I begin relatively cautiously with individual, sentient non-humans. On the interests- or capabilities-based model of flourishing, this expansion of the moral sphere is a philosophically compelling next step. However, taken in isolation, it turns out to have highly problematic implications, both in general and in terms of climate duties. Thus, I am pushed into going further again: to allowing for similarly derived duties to (or at least in respect of) species and systems.

This rather complicates the moral landscape. Rather than three weakly collective duties which are at least broadly collectively mutually fulfillable, we face conflicting cases for collective action on climate change, each morally salient. Because we should (more than ever) undoubtedly do *something* but we cannot now do *everything*, there is yet another step involved in fulfilling our collective moral duties: that of deciding how to trade these incompatible ends off against one another.

Part Three turns from the weakly collective to the individual level. As a member of The Young, The Able, or Polluters (or, in many cases, of all of them), what should the individual moral agent be doing now? There is no existing collective scheme to fulfil the duty—never mind a fair, legitimate scheme—in which she can simply do her part.

I consider three possible kinds of duty: mimicking duties (to do what would be one's duty in some fairly organized collective response), promotional duties (to promote collective action), and direct duties (to alleviate the harm or aid victims directly, oneself or in combination with a like-minded subset). Because actions standardly thought of as 'green' generally involve individual emissions cuts, we might naturally take mimicking duties to be primary (that is, to take priority). We might even think they are exclusive, or all that can be asked of us. However, Chapter Five rejects this view. Without promotional duties, many weakly collective duties would be doomed to non-fulfilment. Moreover, even where mimicking actions in aggregate would secure a weakly collective end, an individual mimicking duty cannot be convincingly defended as primary or exclusive.

Five possible philosophical defences for mimicking duties are considered: a 'fair shares' argument drawing on the compliance condition; an appeal to the chances of individual emissions triggering some increase in overall harm; a rule-consequentialist defence; Aaron Maltais' appeal to the fairness of anticipating a collective scheme; and virtue-ethics and Kantian defences.[87] I argue that none succeeds in defending mimicking duties as exclusive, or even primary. Rather, where the arguments convince, they make a better case for promotional or direct duties. However, I acknowledge that where it is impossible to fulfil either promotional or direct duties there may be a 'clean hands' case for mimicking among Polluters, and that Maltais' argument from fairness to future cooperators could uphold mimicking duties so long as they don't conflict with promotional or direct duties.

Chapter Six then defends promotional rather than direct duties as primary, on the grounds of efficiency, effectiveness, and fairness. It also distinguishes the argument from a parallel (but less extensive) one offered by Walter Sinnott-Armstrong.[88] Promotional duties are duties to try to bring about effective collective action, not simply by getting one's government to do 'its job', but if necessary via the establishment of international institutions or agreements, or by collective action which bypasses such institutions altogether. Climate change may not be 'my' fault, but it is—at least on the weakly collective harm argument—'ours'. And it is certainly our problem.

Direct duties are defended as supplementary: when it is impossible or unfeasibly costly successfully to promote collective action, or if they are one way of fulfilling promotional duties. Returning, against this background, to the question of emissions cuts, a derivative case is made for some such mimicking actions as a necessary or efficient means of fulfilling promotional or direct duties. Finally, Chapter Six considers the demandingness of these moral duties. Drawing on the individual principles outlined as starting assumptions above, it briefly suggests some reasonable limits. Two objections are then rejected, in the process of which I argue against the compliance condition. I then briefly consider how what can be demanded or expected of individuals might vary within the collectivity or potential collectivity, depending on natural abilities, resources, or institutional or social position.

Finally, Part Four goes beyond the question of correlative duties to consider more generally the plight of the individual moral agent in the face of current collective failure to act on climate change. In so doing, it provides the fourth argument for the weakly collective duty to act on climate change: the argument from marring choices.

Building on Thomas Nagel and Stephen Gardiner, I make four claims.[89] The first is the familiar point that collective action on climate change could make it significantly less burdensome for us to fulfil our moral duties. The second, going further, is that we need collective action on climate change in order fully to reconcile the three standpoints from which each of us faces the world: the personal, the interpersonal, and the impersonally moral. The third is that many individuals are marred by finding these standpoints irreconcilable. This is not a point about being forced to violate moral duties. Rather, it concerns the gap between what can reasonably morally be demanded of an agent and what she can nonetheless, also reasonably, feel deep moral regret for not doing. Accordingly, collective action on climate change is needed to avoid wronging such individuals in a special kind of way. The fourth claim is that we are *all* so marred, as moral agents. The idea, then, is that we (between us) owe it to each of us to act collectively on climate change.

Because this is my most controversial argument, it is worth emphasizing that nothing in the rest of the book stands or falls with it. The reader left unmoved by my appeal to a distinction between grounds for blameworthiness (or guilt) and for fundamental regret, can still accept my reasoning up to the close of Chapter Six, and consider herself to have been offered a three- rather than a fourfold case for our weakly collective duty to take action on climate change.

Part 1

Climate Change and Us

*Collective self-interest, collective inaction,
and collective harm*

2

In the Same Boat

In a little community like ours, my dear...we have a general number one...[W]e are so mixed up together, and identified in our interests, that it must be so...The more you value your number one, the more careful you must be of mine; so we come at last to what I told you at first—that a regard for number one holds us all together, and must do so, unless we would all go to pieces in company.[1]

Charles Dickens, *Oliver Twist*

No country can hide from the dangers of carbon pollution.[2]

Barack Obama, Speech to the UK Parliament

This chapter offers the first of three arguments for the weakly collective duty to act on climate change. By this, I mean a duty to organize ourselves to achieve some end collectively. It does so building on starting assumptions spelled out in Chapter One: the fact of anthropogenic climate change; the identification of some prerequisites for individual human flourishing so universal as to count uncontroversially as fundamental interests; and the weak principle of beneficence. For now, the relevant 'us' is The Young: younger generations of humans across the globe. The action required is limited to mitigation.

Sections (i) to (iv) make a prudential case, identifying mitigation as collectively rational in a particularly salient sense. I begin by defending a non-intentionalist model, according to which we can form collectivities through mutual dependence for the satisfaction of our fundamental interests. This binds us to one another in many more situations than those in which we standardly think of ourselves as members of groups. I then argue that members of The Young have a fundamental interest in climate change mitigation, because climate change will expose their central human functionings to significant risk and so render their capabilities insecure. Drawing these threads together, I defend The Young as a collectivity. I note the possibility of further expansion to include members of future generations.

Sections (v) and (vi) move from the prudential to the moral: collectivizing the weak principle of beneficence, building on this to establish a principle of moralized collective self-interest, and so defending a weakly collective duty of The Young (a duty of all to each) to mitigate climate change.

(I) RE-THINKING COLLECTIVITIES[3]

For many years, the dominant view was that sets of individuals constitute collectivities because they think of themselves as doing so: either because each individual considers herself to be a member of some group with the others, or because they all jointly intend to do something. This, broadly put, is the intentionalist view. It can be filled out in more precise terms as follows.

Gilbert's intentionalist model
A collectivity is a set or aggregate of individuals with at least one shared purpose or goal, all of whom are aware of that goal or purpose, aware that it is shared, aware of the awareness of other members of this, aware of each member's joint readiness to commit to achieving the joint goal or purpose as a body, aware of each member's awareness of *this* (and so on).

This account is in line with that of probably the most influential proponent of intentionalism, Margaret Gilbert.[4]

I have two reasons for questioning this view, both in general terms and as it has been more narrowly expressed. Firstly, in practice as well as in normative philosophy, we face a globalized world. This was stressed in Chapter One. However, it sits oddly with a restricted notion of collectivityhood. We can influence one another's lives at previously unthought-of levels, across both distance and time. As a result we find ourselves frequently in situations calling for collective action, even if we are neither 'set up' for such action nor consider ourselves in any way bound together.

Secondly, the intentionalist cannot fully account even for those collectivities which are standardly taken as central. These include the family, the tribe, or even the state. It cannot adequately account for the membership of special case individuals: infants, those with severe intellectual disabilities, or certain kinds of rebels. Although often intuitively regarded as members, these individuals are not or cannot be aware of a shared purpose or goal, do not or cannot consider themselves as being part of a group, and do not or cannot jointly intend to do anything.

Instead, I defend the following:

Non-intentionalist model
A set of individuals constitutes a collectivity if and only if those individuals are mutually dependent for the achievement or satisfaction of some common or

shared purpose, goal or fundamental interest, whether or not they acknowledge it themselves.

This includes not only genuinely shared goals, but also mutual dependence through individual (selfish) goals, purposes, or fundamental interests which can only be achieved through cooperation.[5]

As I will argue, this can straightforwardly accommodate the three special case members. Moreover, although it does allow for more controversial, entirely non-intentional cases, these can meet three generally plausible conditions for collectivityhood: the collectivity does something distinct from what its individual members do, it survives changes in who those members are, and it plays a necessary part in adequately capturing the significance of some of their individual acts.

This section addresses the first of these points. The intentionalist model revolves around individual awareness: awareness of being part of a group or intentionally pursuing shared ends.[6] However, without appealing to actual interdependence through fundamental interests, we cannot explain how non-intentional individuals can truly become members of a collectivity. The discussion is in terms of the family, but could be formulated in terms of tribes or even states.

Let us begin with the first special case: the infant. Families are central collectivities. Babies, intuitively, are members of families. The rest of the family treats them as such, and all the family are tied to one another through the ongoing routine of family life, on which they all depend. However, babies are not aware of being part of a collectivity. They cannot participate in any joint intention. They are not consciously aware of all the various things a family does together.

The intentionalist model might be adapted to accommodate infants. It might specify that those who do not currently think of themselves as members of the group will do so in time: that those members not currently aware of the shared goals or purposes can be expected to become so. However, this remains problematic. On the one hand, some account is needed of what it means to say the infant can be expected to espouse the goals. On the other, even this expanded model could not accommodate the next problematic case: the family member with severe intellectual disabilities. Although she is a part of the family in the same way as the infant, she can, sadly, never be expected to become aware of this.

The model might be adapted again, this time to require that all individuals within the group who can think of themselves as such, do so—that all those capable of being aware of the goals or purposes (aware that they are shared, etc.) will be so aware—but to allow also for some who cannot. However, this takes us further still from the core intentionalist idea. Moreover, difficulties arise parallel to those above. Firstly, it leaves open the question of who can or cannot be included in this 'some'. What determines their membership status?

Secondly, even this change would leave untouched the third problematic case: the teenage rebel.[7]

The rebel is not a baby, nor does he have severe intellectual disabilities. His parents think he is part of the family and theirs seems a reasonable conviction given the many ways in which their lives are intertwined. However, he would deny being part of the family and resent any demands made on him by other members. It might be that he espouses the goal of living a comfortable and secure life and continues to reap the advantages of being in the family home, but refuses to acknowledge this reliance or consider himself in any way committed to the goal of furthering their comfort and security. Alternatively, he might deny needing the kind of security provided in his parents' house (food on the table, a welcoming home, educational opportunities, reassurance and conversation, and so on), which he dismisses as bourgeois.

To include the rebel, on either of these versions, we would need to stretch the intentionalist model still further, relaxing the requirement that all individuals within the set capable of being so are committed to shared goals or purposes. Here, however, the same difficulty arises: how to explain which other (non-aware) individuals are part of the collectivity.

Gilbert suggests that babies can be members of collectivities because those 'core' members who are intentionally committed to the joint goal or purpose determine that they should be. She does this in two ways. The first is via entry rules.

> [T]he existing members may establish rules that determine who may become a member... The rules can in principle be so capacious as to allow those lacking the ability to be members of the initial plural subject to be considered members none the less. Thus infants can be thought of as 'members of the tribe', though they have no conception of the tribe as a whole.[8]

Her later suggestion, focusing on political societies, is that infants can be assigned imputed membership as a kind of stopgap until full membership can be achieved.

> [Core members] may stipulate that others, for instance, their children, are to be regarded as members for some or all practical purposes. These others then have imputed membership. They will not be core members or members proper unless they come to participate in the joint commitment that constitutes the political society in question.[9]

However, neither of these fully resolves the difficulty because it is unclear what limits there are on rule-setting or stipulation.[10] To make clear the absurd implications of this, suppose two of my young cousins are besotted with *Twilight* star Robert Pattinson. They decide to set up a fan club, devoted to maintaining a website about him, collecting pictures, seeing all his films repeatedly, sending him fan mail, and so on. As it stands, the first quote from Gilbert suggests that they could simply write an entry rule which makes all their first cousins, including my sister and me, members of the collectivity. On Gilbert's second suggestion, while they couldn't make us full members without our signing up to the common ends, they could still count us as members 'for all practical purposes'.

This implication—which is clearly contrary to the spirit of Gilbert's own argument—might be avoided by stipulating that entry rules or imputed membership can only apply to those individuals who are incapable of committing to the shared goals themselves. However, this is problematic on two fronts. In one way, it doesn't go far enough: if even imputed membership cannot be assigned to those who could commit to the common goals or purposes of a collectivity and who might reasonably be expected to do so (by virtue of lives actually interconnected) but do not, then the teenage rebel can never even be an imputed member of his own family.

In another, it goes too far: the powers of core members are still dangerously open-ended with regard to infants or persons with severe intellectual disabilities. While my cousins could not include my sister or me in their fan club, they could still stipulate that my baby nephew count as a member. A couple could stipulate not only that their own baby or adopted baby count as a member of their family, but that any baby at all does so: their neighbour's newborn son, for example, or Harper Beckham, or the African orphan who melted their hearts on a news programme.

What is needed is not unqualified rule-setting authority for core members but a way of identifying those others who, in each case, they are entitled to consider as belonging to the same collectivity. That is, of specifying which entry rules can reasonably be set. Presumably, for Gilbert, the relevant difference between the ludicrous stipulation of membership of the fan club and parents assigning their baby imputed membership of the family is that the child can be expected later to commit to the family but not the fan club. To make this a condition, however, simply pushes back the question. Under what circumstances can the core members reasonably expect this? (Their actually expecting it is not enough: they might be delusional.) Some objective criteria are needed. Biological ties are too restrictive: they would exclude adoptive children.

The alternative is actual interdependence. However, to specify interdependence criteria which include individuals who do not or cannot espouse shared goals or purposes, it is necessary to appeal to something else. This is what explains the inclusion, in the non-intentionalist model, of fundamental interests. It is just such mutual dependence which characterizes all three of the special cases highlighted above.

The baby is mutually dependent with his parents and siblings for the achievement of the goals of family life (broadly, living peacefully and happily together). Of course, the baby does not have goals: he cannot formulate them. Moreover, the conscious, practical pursuit of common ends will be done by the others. However, the dependence is mutual because not only is it part of their shared aims that the baby be included, and be healthy and contented, but this positive family atmosphere is in *his* interest. The same argument can be offered for the family member with severe intellectual disabilities. The rebel is also tied to his family in various ways. He inhabits the same house. They all, including him, benefit from a supportive family atmosphere. There are common interests in play: fundamental interests in a stable family life, which can only be secured together. In the first variant, he acknowledges some of these as selfish interests while mistakenly denying the mutual dependence for their achievement; in the second, he mistakenly denies them even as interests.

At this point, there are two options.[11] One is to adopt the following:

Modified intentionalist model
A collectivity must have a 'core' set or aggregate of individual members with at least one shared purpose or goal, all of whom are aware of that goal or purpose, aware that it is shared, aware of the awareness of other members of this, aware of each member's joint readiness to commit to achieving the joint goal or purpose as a body, aware of each member's awareness of *this* (and so on). These core members can set entry rules to assign membership or imputed membership to additional individuals, so long as they are mutually dependent with core members in the sense that securing the common goal is either necessary to some selfish end of their own, or in their fundamental interest.

The alternative is the non-intentionalist model. Having demonstrated the central role played by interdependence through fundamental interests, I would suggest we could reasonably put the burden on the other side: to show why we should not go all the way and allow for collectivities constituted entirely by such dependence through interests. Moreover, although the modified model could accommodate the three special case individuals, it retains the idea that membership is assigned to these special case individuals according to the inclination of core members, rather than being something to which they are entitled. I at least find this extremely unappealing. Is the individual with severe intellectual disabilities only a member of his family insofar as the other members choose to recognize him as such? However, this intuitive repugnance is not necessarily universally shared, so I do not rely on it here. Instead, the following section will offer a more positive defence of the non-intentionalist model.

(II) NON-INTENTIONALIST COLLECTIVITIES

Having motivated this move via a critique of intentionalism, I begin this section with some clarificatory points concerning the non-intentionalist alternative. The central claim, recall, is that a set of individuals constitutes a collectivity if and only if those individuals are mutually dependent for the achievement or satisfaction of some common or shared purpose, goal, or fundamental interest, *whether or not they acknowledge it themselves.*

Firstly, this is a broad understanding of 'common'. The mutual dependence clause requires that the individuals have goals, purposes, or fundamental interests that it only makes sense to consider as being pursued together: whether because they are genuinely shared goals, or individual goals, purposes, or fundamental interests which can only be secured together. This accommodates either a group of friends setting off to climb a mountain together (a model intentionalist example) or a group of strangers washed up on a remote island, none of whom care about each other's welfare but who need to cooperate to survive. (Think of something akin to the start of the television series *Lost*.) In these latter cases, the goal is a common one because the individuals are mutually dependent for its achievement, rather than the other way round.

Secondly, there are two ways in which an individual can become a member without acknowledging herself as such. One is if she acknowledges some individual goal or purpose but denies what is in fact the case: that she is mutually dependent with others for its satisfaction. The other is if she is mutually dependent with them for the securing of her own fundamental interests. This second restriction is crucial and I will return to it throughout the chapter. These are not trivial ends. An individual can become a member of a collectivity through some interest she does not acknowledge even as a selfish goal, but only if what is at stake is so central as to count relatively uncontroversially as a prerequisite for a flourishing human life. As laid out in Chapter One, such fundamental interests include retaining the capability for continued life, bodily health, bodily integrity, practical reason, and affiliation.

Finally, this is not a one-size-fits-all model: there are several distinctions within the account. Collectivities can be pre-existing or new: compare a village school with a few parents setting up a fundraising committee. They can be lasting or *ad hoc*, by which I mean constituted by individuals mutually dependent through a very short-term goal, purpose, or interest. (Paul Sheehy suggests four prisoners escaping in a rowing boat.[12]) Collectivities can be small or large, voluntary or involuntary, passive or active, or can overlap categories. Thus, for example, the campaign group Fathers for Justice is a small, voluntary, active subset of the large, partially involuntary collectivity of divorced fathers unhappy with their legal access entitlement. This wider set is mutually dependent in the sense that the goal (legal change) is one that, if achieved for any, must be achieved for all. Finally, collectivities can be entirely intentional (the fundraising parents) or only partially so (the family or state). Most controversially, they might be entirely non-intentional. It is to this possibility that I now turn.

In these last collectivities, no members consider themselves part of a group, jointly intend to do anything, or acknowledge common goals or purposes.

This section will defend the model with the following small-scale examples, before I turn to the possibility of a global-level collectivity.

Second homes
A number of commuters own second homes set round a green. Because of other commitments, each owner uses his second home on different days each fort-night. Each wants the green to be pleasant but only for his own sake. They are so far from considering themselves a group that none even knows whether any of the others uses the green. However, because they all do use it, they can only keep it pleasant by *de facto* cooperation. Each one could undermine the common end for all.

Rival gangs
Nine young men, members of three deeply opposed gangs in their home city, are cast ashore on an island. In order for each to survive for more than a few days, they would all need to cooperate to find food, build shelter, and so on. However, such is the mutual loathing between the gangs that they deny any such idea and would prefer to spend their time trying to kill each other.

In each of these cases, the relevant individuals are mutually dependent. In the first case, it is only between them that they can secure an individually espoused goal for each; in the second, cooperation is required to secure a fundamental interest. Both are involuntary, unintentional collectivities.

Even such controversial non-intentionalist collectivities meet the three plausible conditions for collectivityhood listed at the start of section (i). These are borrowed from the philosophy of social science, but are in line with common-sense ideas about groups or collectivities.[13] I will fill them out in general terms, in relation to the non-intentionalist model, then reinforce the point by considering them in relation to the two examples.

The first condition is that the significance of certain actions by individual members cannot be captured without reference to the collectivity as a whole. (To put it another way, reference to the collectivity is ineliminable.) This may not be significance in the familiar social sense of some extra meaning assigned to certain actions by some group. (For example, the significance that both the border control guard and I associate with a small booklet containing my picture and various bits of text.) However, it is a significance derived from exactly those relations that render the set of individuals a collectivity. They are mutually dependent for the securing of ends that can only be achieved, *for each individual*, by the set as a whole. Thus, actions which contribute (unwittingly or otherwise) to either the achievement or failure to achieve that overall end rebound back in a particular way onto each of those individuals.

Reference to the collectivity is ineliminable in capturing this significance, in the sense that it enables us to state truths we would otherwise be unable to express.[14] For certain statements, such as 'the collectivity has lost three members' or 'the castaways destroyed themselves', there is no way of avoiding reference to the collectivity. To borrow an argument made by Graham MacDonald and Philip Pettit (the so-called multiple realizations argument), because of the relations those individuals are in, there are indefinitely many combinations of individual acts that could bring about any given outcome at the collective level. Thus, it is necessary to refer to that collective level—to the set of individuals *in those relations*—to capture all of these possibilities in one statement.[15]

The second condition is that what the collectivity does is distinct from what the individuals do. Here, two situations can be identified: those where it is impossible by definition for individuals to do what the collectivity does and those where individuals are merely physically unable to do so. Only the US electorate could elect Barack Obama president; individuals could only vote for him. A crowd destroys a park: something one individual could not physically achieve. However, in all cases—intentional or otherwise—collectivities 'do' or achieve something distinct from what their individual members do.

The third condition is that lasting (as opposed to *ad hoc*) collectivities persist even as individual members leave and are replaced. At first glance, this faces difficulties when it comes to small collectivities. However, some very small groups can sustain some changeover: for example, a family is still a family when an extra child is born or one parent dies. Moreover, these concerns apply equally to intentionalist collectivities. They cannot be presented as a particular difficulty for the non-intentionalist account.

Now recall the two examples. In *Second homes*, indefinitely many combinations of individual action could secure the common end. Some individuals might pick up litter while others only refrain from spreading it, or vice versa; one person might put out food to encourage bird-life, another refrain from wearing his spiked boots to play football, a third clean up after his dog, and so on. Although each individual acts thus because he wants to keep the green pleasant for himself, their actual if unacknowledged relations mean these acts can only lead to the satisfaction of the individual goals in combination. The significance of each individual's behaviour—including its significance for her—can only fully be captured once it is seen in this context. The green is kept tidy (which is the end she pursues) only because, unbeknownst to her, there is a *de facto* common goal of keeping it so. To put it another way (and satisfy the second condition), it is this identifiable collectivity, rather than individuals in isolation, which keeps the green pleasant and tidy. The third condition is satisfied because individual houses could be sold and, assuming the new owners also want a pleasant green, the collectivity would persist.

In *Rival gangs* (a kind of *Lost/The Wire* hybrid), each individual's action also has a significance, for him and precisely those others, which can only be brought out by reference to the relations which render them a collectivity. In fighting, each is contributing to a situation in which his own interests are undermined. The outcome (disaster or cooperation) could come about in innumerable ways. Whether Marlo strikes Jack and Chino retaliates, or Jack attacks Tony and Marlo runs off with the food, or another combination, the collective-level outcome is the same: tragedy. This is not a coincidental aggregation of individual acts. It is the result of the combined acts of individuals—who are, but needn't have been, those particular individuals—connected in a certain way. Thus, it is not each individual or the individuals in aggregate, but the collectivity constituted by individuals in those particular relations, that brings about this catastrophe. Finally, Marlo and Chino could build a raft and leave, and other gang members be washed ashore, without threatening the persistence of the collectivity.

Non-intentionalist collectivities can, then, meet the three plausible criteria for the establishment of a collectivity. To complete this quick defence of the model, it remains to respond to two obvious, if conflicting, objections.

These are: that the model's conditions for collectivityhood are too weak, and that they are too strong. I will begin with the latter, according to which it is unnecessary to require mutual dependence of all members on all other members. Consider, for example, the state. I have argued elsewhere, although I have not reproduced this here, that the state is a collectivity through actual mutual dependence for the securing of certain fundamental interests for all.[16] The objector points out that the state can get along very well without everyone paying taxes, so long as enough people do so to support the health, security, and education institutions which secure our fundamental interests.

The response to this is twofold, corresponding to two distinct scenarios. On the first, I have already noted the possibility of passive collectivities, or collectivities of which only a subset is active. One example was Fathers for Justice, a subset of those divorced or separated fathers who would like to see changes to the law. Another is the suffragettes as an active subset of the largely passive collectivity of women. In such cases, the goal, by its nature, would be achieved for all if achieved for any. This could be because it is a genuinely shared goal (for example, if all women genuinely espoused the goal that *all* women should have the vote) or simply because of the nature of the end sought (votes for all women means votes for you if you are a woman, and it is in each woman's fundamental interest to have a vote). The mutual dependence clause is met because each individual's achieving her goal or interest depends on the others achieving theirs. This is true even if the positive effort is put in by only the active subset. The climate change mitigation case, as we shall see in later sections, falls into this category.

The second scenario concerns goals or interests which do not by their nature need to be achieved for all, but do under the circumstances. In this case, membership of the collectivity is contingent both on individuals having the fundamental interest, goal, or purpose and on cooperation being required for its achievement. The state falls into this category. However, the objection can be rejected as narrowing down unnecessarily the ways in which an individual could cooperate. Omissions, as well as actions, can count. Thus, not everyone has to pay taxes for a peaceful, secure environment to be provided for all.

However, satisfaction of common interests does require everyone to refrain from bombing government buildings or public places, poisoning the drinking water, and so on. Given modern technology, even one individual could cause general devastation.

This leaves the converse objection: that it renders the model implausibly weak to include as a collectivity any set of individuals who would benefit from cooperating with one another. For example, my neighbour and I would each be better off being fitter. Running together would help us to become so. However, it would be counterintuitive to consider us a collectivity with the common end of running together if we had no wish actually to do so.

This objection misrepresents the model by glossing over a distinction between mutual dependence and the weaker condition of potential mutual advantage. As was stressed at the start of this section, a set of individuals does not constitute a collectivity unless they are in one of the following three situations. The first is that the individuals have an acknowledged shared goal in the simplest sense of wanting to achieve some particular end together. Recall the friends climbing a mountain together. Call this *Shared goal climbers*.

Secondly, a set of individuals can constitute a collectivity without an acknowledged shared goal if cooperation is required for the achievement of each individual's goals or purposes. Consider the following.

Wet weather climbers
By scrambling independently, several individuals have got halfway up a mountain. It has started to rain and each wants to get down by the quickest route, but this would require them to rope together and use all the equipment they have between them.

Because of the situation, the climbers constitute a collectivity even if none cares about getting down quickly *together*. They are mutually dependent in the sense that each has the relevant goal (getting down as fast as possible) and this could only be secured between them.

Thirdly, a set of individuals can constitute a collectivity with neither a genuinely common goal nor mutual dependence for the achievement of acknowledged individual goals, but only if they are mutually dependent through a fundamental interest each individual has. Consider for example:

Stranded climbers
By scrambling individually, several individuals have got halfway up a mountain. The weather has deteriorated to the point that to attempt to go on or stay put would almost certainly kill them. None has the equipment or expertise to get down alone, but all could do so if they cooperated. However, some of the climbers wish to push on for the summit despite the changed conditions.

It is important to distinguish cases like this from two others. The first is where cooperation is necessary only to secure some trivial interest. To use his own example, Robert Nozick might have an interest in a neighbourhood public address system, the achievement of which would require cooperation with others in his street, but this is not enough to render him and them a col-lectivity.[17] In *Wet weather climbers*, it was left open that the individuals could get down independently by some other (albeit slower) route. Accordingly, the establishment of the collectivity there depended on each espousing the (com-paratively trivial) goal of avoiding being unpleasantly cold and wet. However, in *Stranded climbers*, as in the family, state, or tribe including any of the com-plex case individuals discussed in section (i), the interests in question are exactly the kinds of central element of a human life taken as prerequisites for individual flourishing in Chapter One.

The second case from which to distinguish this is where there is a funda-mental interest at stake but no mutual dependence, either because some or all could secure the interest in some other way or because even by cooperating they cannot secure it. On the first possibility, my neighbour and I both have a fundamental interest in retaining the capability of enjoying bodily health. However, running, let alone running together, is by no means the only way to secure this. On the second, two men stranded in the path of an exploding volcano have the same fundamental interest at stake, but even by cooperating they cannot make a difference to their fate.

This concludes my introduction of the non-intentionalist model. I have indi-cated the range of situations—many more than we acknowledge—in which we are bound together into collectivities by our goals, purposes, or fundamental interests and in which, like it or not, there is an ineliminable collective sig-nificance to what we do. Now, I will turn to the possibility that the threat of anthropogenic climate change renders at least some of us just such a collectiv-ity. The first step is further to explore the sense in which climate change is bad for humans, so we can see how many of us it is bad *for*.

(III) CLIMATE CHANGE, RISK, AND FUNDAMENTAL INTERESTS

In highlighting some key human functionings, Chapter One left open just how many others there might be. Importantly, I did not take for granted the more controversial inclusions on Nussbaum's list of capabilities.[18] However, as will become important later in this section, I did insist on the distinction between the functionings themselves and the capability—or genuine, secure opportunity—to exercise them. It is the latter which we have a fundamental interest in retaining.

As Chapter One spelled out, climate change will permanently under-mine central human functionings for many current and future persons. To reiterate, the Intergovernmental Panel on Climate Change (IPCC) predicts climate-change-related deaths through heat and increased precipitation, as well as through various diseases.[19] Disruptive economic and agricultural consequences are also anticipated, and rising sea levels threaten whole small-island states, as well as many other low-lying communities. Both will undermine affiliation and the capacity of many persons to plan their own lives. As I also outlined, there is an indirect threat to freedom of movement, if environmental refugees are not treated better than many political and economic refugees currently are.

This takes us a long way. For the arguments of Chapter Three, it takes us far enough: many persons have been and many more will be seriously harmed by climate change. However, this chapter appeals to collective self-interest in climate change mitigation. Accordingly, it is important to bring out the widest sense in which we can reasonably say climate change is seriously bad for us. These predictable, permanent losses of central functionings, though terrible, are not in themselves sufficient to show that we all have a fundamental interest in mitigating climate change. Not everyone will actually suffer in this way although very many can be expected to do so, even in the developed world.

At the other extreme, it might be argued that the degradation of the natural world in general, and that brought about through climate change in particular, is in itself a central loss to each human being. For example, Nussbaum defends other species as a central capability: 'Being able to live with concern for and in relation to animals/plants/world of nature.'[20] According to the IPCC, between 20 and 30 per cent of plant and animal species are at increased risk of extinction if global average temperature increases by more than 1.5–2.5°C.[21]

However, this is insufficient to show that climate change would impose a fundamental interest loss on each of us. Quite apart from the difficulty of the move from needing some interaction with nature to the claim that losing these particular species would undermine that fundamental interest, this conflicts with the deliberate limitation of the model to the least controversial elements of human flourishing. (That is, to those which could also be defended as basic needs combined with something like Joseph Raz's conditions for autonomy.[22])

By including other species, Nussbaum captures the fact that the non-human world is hugely important to some human beings, in a way arguably irreducible to its contribution to other fundamental interests, such as health and life. The extinction of a species of mockingbird may be a loss to a birdwatcher which cannot fully be compensated. For me, experience of mountain areas such as the Scottish Highlands, the Lake District, and Snowdonia is incommensurate with and irreplaceable by other valuable experiences. However, it might be argued that this is simply because of our particular conceptions of the good. After all, many people do not share that sense of importance. Jonathan Wolff and Avner de-Shalit, testing the capabilities list against the views of the disadvantaged and those working with them, found other species to be widely contested.[23]

Attempts to specify a broader environmental capability are ultimately problematic in the same way. For example, Edward Page considers replacing or supplementing other species with 'the capability to experience life in an environment devoid of dangerous environmental impacts such as climate change'.[24] Breena Holland defends an ecological 'meta-capability'. However, it is unclear why 'an environment devoid of dangerous environmental impacts' should be considered necessary to individual flourishing—or, as Holland puts it, 'make human life *meaningful*'—over and above the sense already captured via more central capabilities, except in precisely the controversial sense that other species appeals to.[25] Why should environmental damage matter to me, except insofar as it threatens my life, health, or affiliation, or insofar as engagement with the natural world is central to my plan or life or conception of the good?

So it is a step too far beyond any of Chapter One's relatively uncontroversial starting assumptions to take the impact of climate change on the natural world as being itself a fundamental loss to all human beings. However, there are more people in the set of those mutually dependent through a fundamental interest in mitigation than those who would, as it happens, actually lose central functionings through climate change. This is because many more of us will have our central functionings put at risk, and it is impossible to know, evaluating the situation as it is now, who will be the unlucky ones. The avoidance of such risk is already built into the interests-based model of flourishing adopted in Chapter One.

The distinction between functioning and capabilities is an appealing aspect of the capabilities approach. As stressed in Chapter One, it avoids the paternalism of claiming that an individual cannot be fully flourishing if she chooses not to exercise certain functionings. However, it also brings out the more positive point that living a flourishing human life is not simply a matter of happening to enjoy central functionings at any time, but of being able to rely on the continued genuine opportunity to do so: in other words, of the individual's central functionings not being exposed to serious risks that she cannot control.[26]

This is intuitively plausible. It seems obvious, for example, that an Indian honey-gatherer is disadvantaged by the constant threat posed by the Bengal Tiger even though, as it happens, he may never be attacked. It is bad for Bedouin children to be exposed to toxic chemical waste even though they may not actually contract the diseases associated with such exposure.[27] However, borrowing from Wolff and de-Shalit, the claim can be more systematically defended.

Firstly, someone whose functioning is insecure might actually lose the functioning.[28] In many ways, this is the most obvious point. However, it is also the most controversial because it is a matter for debate whether being at risk is in itself bad for someone: bad for them over and above the badness of the actual loss of functioning (if this happens) or the ill effects of living knowingly with risk.[29]

Wolff and de-Shalit think it is. '[I]t seems natural', they argue, 'to say that [the Bedouins] were disadvantaged in one or more ways, regardless of whether or not they were aware of the risks they were facing.'[30] I am inclined to agree: it seems clearly worse for me if, to use Henry Shue's example, someone is playing Russian roulette with my head, or if I carry the gene for a high risk of a serious medical condition, even if I don't know it.[31] However, the counter-claim is that the risk of bad consequences, in itself, constitutes no harm to an individual. Until the threat becomes a reality, the individual continues to function in the relevant way, and it might never become a reality. If I am ignorant of the danger and I am never shot, or never get the medical condition, my life will have been in all relevant respects the same as it would have been if I had not run the risk. How, then, was it bad for me?

I find this unconvincing. To rely on such reasoning is to presuppose either that the only appropriate moment for evaluation of a human life is after it finishes, or that such evaluations must be both individual and entirely subjective. Not only is the first possibility morally questionable, but it is also the least helpful standpoint from the point of view of determining appropriate collective action. Whether or not it can be said afterwards that there is no difference between a life run with an ongoing, unknown, and unfulfilled risk and one without it, it must be significant *as long as the risk is live* that Person A is liable at any moment to have her life snatched away from her by a bullet, and Person B is not. Other things being equal, the reasonable third person would want to be B rather than A.

The second assumption is equally problematic. Not only does it defer entirely to the individual's own preferences (adaptive or otherwise), but it defers also to her own perception of the facts, however wrong about them she might be. Any claim that quality of life is unimpaired because the individual does not know the real situation is liable to 'Experience Machine' objections.[32] Person A is in an important sense analogous to Jim Carey's character in *The Truman Show*.[33] Unbeknownst to him, Truman is the protagonist of a TV drama, with actors playing the parts of his friends and family. It is no more convincing to say that a person is fully flourishing who is making plans and forging ties, all the time unaware of the bullet or disease that could at any moment sever those ties and render those plans meaningless, than it is to say so of him. One would not choose to be Truman any more than one would choose to be the individual in Robert Nozick's machine, who believes herself to be having desirable experiences but is in fact floating in a tank. The same can be said of threatened A, even a happily ignorant A.

However, we need not rely on this argument. As Wolff and de-Shalit argue, once a risk to a functioning is known to an individual (and information on the risks associated with climate change is widely available, especially in developed countries), there are a number of further ways in which it is bad for her. It will cause the individual stress and anxiety, adversely affecting her chances

of enjoying this or other functionings, especially health.[34] She might therefore take steps to reduce either the probability, the scale of the event, or its
impact on her (for example through purchasing insurance). These in turn can
have costs in terms of other capabilities. Moreover, individuals whose central
functionings are insecure can have problems developing other central elements of their lives. Often, this is a rational reaction: someone living under
the genetic threat of contracting a serious disease, or liable to lose their home
at any moment, might be reluctant to start a family.[35] However, living with risk
can also lead to a more general paralysis of the will, so that even in those other
areas in which it would remain perfectly rational to form plans, individuals
feel unable to do so.

There is an obvious objection to this line of reasoning: taken to its limits,
it would have absurd implications. If any exposure to risk is contrary to my
fundamental interests, then I can never fully flourish: the slight risk that I
will get knocked off my bike tomorrow by an impatient van driver would
mean—implausibly—that I do not genuinely enjoy the opportunity for
health. Moreover, given the very many occasions on which I choose to take
even greater risks myself, it would look unacceptably paternalistic to claim
that I am always thereby harming myself.

This concern can be mitigated by clarifying what is meant by a functioning's being 'secure'. The idea is not that any risk constitutes such harm. Rather,
I limit my claim to the following:

> *Secure functionings claim*
> Significant, ongoing risks to *central functionings*, from which an individual *can-
> not opt out*, render those functionings insecure and so deprive the individual of
> the associated capability. Accordingly, she has a fundamental interest in avoid-
> ing such risks.

The italicized words make three points clear. Firstly, the relevant risks are
those which the individual has no option not to take, or at least cannot opt
out of, once taken. A woman at constant risk of eviction by a temperamental
landlord, with nowhere else to go, is in a very different position from one who
moves without booking from hotel to hotel at peak season but who could easily get a mortgage.[36] Secondly, it concerns only risks to central human functionings. An ongoing risk of breaking a fingernail is hardly on a par with one
of becoming seriously ill.

Finally, even such ongoing risks to central functionings only undermine
capabilities if they are significant. Of course, 'significant' is a placeholder.
However, it is one I appeal to because I think there is sufficient shared understanding of when a risk counts as significant for the discussion to move forward. If I inhabit an island where a violent storm washes away all habitation
on average every 10,000 years, the risk is not high enough to render my central
functionings insecure.[37] If, however, the chance of such a storm in my lifetime

is 25 per cent, most of my future functionings are too insecure for me fully to enjoy the corresponding capabilities.

On this model, younger generations can be said to have a fundamental interest in mitigating climate change. Section (iv) will fill this out. Firstly, however, there is a further objection to acknowledge. With climate change, the situation is one not simply of risk but of uncertainty: it is not known how high the risk is. This need not undermine the argument. As Shue points out, a risk can be known to be significant even if the probability of the outcome is not precisely calculable: '[t]he fact that something is uncertain in the technical sense, that is, has no calculable probability, in no way suggests that its objective probability, if known, would be small'. This is so in cases where '(a) the mechanism by which the losses would occur is well understood, and (b) the conditions for the functioning of the mechanism are accumulating'.[38] Although I do not reproduce his reasoning here, Shue has argued persuasively that the risks posed by anthropogenic climate change meet these conditions.

(IV) (NOT QUITE) A COLLECTIVITY OF HUMANITY

Suppose I lose a kidney. Suppose also that my family has a high rate of kidney failure. I must now live with a significant risk of permanent loss of my bodily health. No matter how the risk was incurred—whether I lost the kidney in an accident, through disease, or even by selling it or giving it away—I cannot decide, at any point in the future, to opt out of taking that risk. Even if I continue, by good fortune, to be healthy, I no longer enjoy the capability for bodily health because I cannot rely on enjoying it on a sustained basis.[39]

This, I suggest, is analogous to the situation in which younger generations will find themselves as a result of climate change. Significant risks to central functionings will be incurred even in developed countries. For example, the US Global Change Research Programme predicts an increase in some diseases transmitted by food, water, and insects, difficulty meeting 'air quality standards necessary to protect public health', and increasing risks of illness or death through extreme heat (although some reduction in cold-related deaths), all in the United States. It also warns of exacerbated conflicts over water.[40] The Stern Review warns that 'heat waves like that experienced in 2003 in Europe, when 35,000 people died and agricultural losses reached $15 billion, will be commonplace by the middle of the century'.[41] The IPCC predicts intensifying water security problems in areas of Australia and New Zealand by as early as 2030.[42] These are risks which we will not, as individuals, be able to choose not to take.

However, this is not sufficient to identify a collectivity including all of humanity, for two reasons. Firstly, not everyone has a fundamental interest at stake. Consider a rich, middle-aged Westerner. Call him George. Suppose, further, that it is no part of his plan of life that the natural world be preserved. There is some chance that climate change will deprive George of a central functioning: for example, via an extreme weather event or water war. However, this is too low a risk to count as significant in the relevant sense.[43]

It could be argued that George is likely to have some kind of a stake in at least the next couple of generations, giving him strong reason to care about harm to them. Probably he has children, maybe even grandchildren. If he doesn't, he may well have nieces or nephews or care about the children of friends. This argument could go in several directions. It might be argued that significant risk of severe harm to one's own children is an irreplaceable cost to oneself, incommensurate with those other fundamental interest losses noted above, and sufficient to ground membership of a collectivity. Alternatively, we might say that George and all other parents/grandparents who do care strongly about what happens to their own descendants have a common goal in the second sense identified in sections (i) and (ii): an individually held goal which can only be secured by cooperation.

Either of these lines might profitably be explored. However, I do not rely on them here. This is in part because the moral argument, of the next two sections, does not extend to those who are mutually dependent only through their goals, rather than their fundamental interests. Moreover, however intuitively plausible it is to those of us who do care deeply about at least some members of future generations, it goes beyond anything espoused in Chapter One to claim that it is necessarily a fundamental loss to any parent (never mind grandparent, uncle, aunt, or parent's friend) that their child should be at significant risk of suffering. (Chapter Seven will return to such questions.) Affiliation might get us some way, but retaining the capability for affiliation doesn't necessarily depend on having a certain tie to some member of the next generation, or even on having it with your own child, if you happen to have one.

The other point against the collectivity of all humanity is that there are two sides to being mutually dependent in the required way. One is that it is necessary to secure some fundamental interest for each individual. The other is that cooperation could actually secure it for them. To recall an earlier example, if two men are stranded in the path of an exploding volcano, they have a common interest in the weak sense that they will almost certainly live or die together. However, that does not render them mutually dependent if even between them they can neither stop the volcano nor get away in time.

In the climate change case, this requirement has two apparent implications: one correct, one a mistaken objection. It excludes from the collectivity current older generations even in the developing world. Although many will be (or are) deprived of fundamental interests by climate change, mitigation, which will not show its effects for some forty years or more, would not benefit them.[44] Let us, accordingly, call the relevant collectivity The Young, leaving open exactly how young they need to be. (Note, however, that I am not thereby ruling out the possibility of some other, all-inclusive, collectivity. This might be bound, for example, by a common end of avoiding nuclear war. However, it is not the topic under consideration here.)

Moreover, recalling *Stranded climbers*, it might be claimed that there is no collectivity here because even if mitigation would preserve a fundamental interest for The Young, it is impossible to achieve. Like the volcano, climate change cannot now be curtailed. (Of course it cannot now be prevented altogether: as Chapter One made clear, there is no scientific doubt that we are committed to *some* anthropogenic climate change; indeed it is already happening.) This claim might be made at various levels. The first is that already dismissed in Chapter One: that climate change is nothing to do with human action. It is not a part of this book to attempt to engage with such views, which have been widely scientifically discredited.

The next level acknowledges this, but maintains that mitigation is now scientifically impossible. This, too, can be rejected. According to the Stern Review, '[t]here is still time to avoid the worst impacts of climate change if strong collective action starts now'.[45] Even Bjørn Lomborg, in his vigorous defence of a focus on economic growth and adaptation rather than mitigation, does not deny the possibility of mitigating climate change. Indeed, he concedes that this could be done at very much less than significant cost to its members.[46] The window in which this is so may be closing, but it remains—for now—open.

This leaves the third possible objection: that, whatever is possible scientifically, politically we cannot achieve timely collective action on climate change. Such a claim would gain rhetorical force by appeal to the recent catalogue of failures to achieve adequate and meaningful international action.[47] Certainly, there is every reason to doubt, with Dale Jamieson, 'that our political institutions are up to it'.[48] However, to move from this to the claim that collective action is impossible is to misunderstand the distinction between physical impossibility and obstacles created by those who could themselves, between them, overcome them.

Recall the *Rival gangs*. There is a clear distinction between the situation in which it is practically impossible for them to cooperate (because, say, they cannot speak the same language) and either of the following two situations. In one—the situation as described—the members of the different gangs hate each other and are unwilling to cooperate. Moreover, the knowledge that this dislike is mutual will add distrust, making it harder to break the deadlock even if all wanted to do so. On the other variant, as well as their history of rabid mutual conflict, each gang has an established, complicated decision-making process. Thus, even if members were willing to cooperate with the members of other gangs, a protracted, multi-level process of discussions and voting would be demanded before committing to anything.

In neither case is it impossible to secure the common end. In the first, it is a matter of the unwillingness to change of precisely those whose actions are required to secure that change. The mutual distrust does, of course, give rise to a collective action problem. Questions arise as to what sort of mutually guaranteed system of potential punishment for default will be needed to secure sufficient mutual trust for the cooperation to work. In this extreme example, they echo questions of how it would be possible to leave the every-man-for-himself state of nature posited by Thomas Hobbes.[49] However, we can still say of the men that, were they all to decide to cooperate to save their own lives, they could do so.

In the second scenario, existing organizational structures slow the process of establishing collective action. To each individual, these structures seem immutably fixed. However, the members of each of the gangs could, between them, decide to change or overlook the rules in this emergency situation. Claiming otherwise would be equivalent to claiming that a few members of the board of a company, stuck together in the same fast-sinking lifeboat, couldn't start bailing out the water until they had gone through a three-stage voting process to determine whether they should.

Moreover, although there are some points of resemblance, the climate change case is by no means this extreme. There is an existing international communication and cooperation structure which both gives the lie to a universal aversion to any international cooperation, and suggests some means through which change could begin. Insofar as existing decision-making structures have impeded progress, it is not because there are no means of making decisions promptly. For example, the UN is perfectly capable of imposing sanctions on countries for other reasons.

Thus, there is a four-level distinction between: scepticism that any progress will be made by leaving things to existing institutions; scepticism that those institutions could make such progress; the claim that it is impossible to change those institutions or develop new ones capable of acting effectively; and the claim that it is impossible to bypass them to achieve effective action. We can accept the first, and even the second, while strongly denying the third and fourth. (As Jamieson himself effectively does, by calling for mass activism.[50])

Thus, we can reject the claim that the scientific or political impossibility of mitigating climate change undermines The Young as a collectivity, even while acknowledging that the impracticability of its making a difference to them excludes older generations.

However, another interesting possibility arises: that of extending member-ship of the collectivity in the opposite direction: to include future generations. Recall the possibility, highlighted in section (ii), of active subsets of wider, largely passive, collectivities. Whoever they turn out to be, whether anyone born into a future generation will have their fundamental interests secured will depend on current decisions on whether or not to act to mitigate climate change.[51] As also noted earlier, climate change mitigation is an example of an end which, by its nature, is achieved for all if achieved for any. Thus, future generations could be included as members of a largely passive collectivity of which some members of current generations are—or could be—an active subset.[52]

I do not defend this in detail, as the argument from collective self-interest can be made without it (although it does serve to reinforce the moral argu-ment in later sections). However, it is worth briefly considering this expanded version of The Young, in the context of the three conditions for collectivity-hood discussed in section (ii).

As with Fathers for Justice or the suffragettes, it is the active subset that does something over and above what the individual members do: that miti-gates or—on current form—worsens climate change. However, the contrib-utory individual actions (driving—or not driving—a gas guzzler, waving a placard outside international talks, standing for election on a green mani-festo, signing an international treaty on emissions reductions, and so on) have their significance for the wider set of individuals. The combination undermines—and other actions in combination could secure—the funda-mental interests of precisely these individuals. This significance cannot be expressed without reference to the relations that make them into a col-lectivity. Including future generations also captures the sense of chang-ing membership over time. Indeed, it makes sense in the context of those familiar examples discussed earlier: the state, the family, and the tribe. There are some actions whose significance can only adequately be captured by reference to the collectivity as existing across generations; for example, a family farmer planting trees which will not come to maturity until after his own death.[53]

One final point before turning to the question of moral duties. The Young are defended as a collectivity at the global level only through their funda-mental interest in mitigation. This is not to say that they do not each also need adaptation. However, adaptation, unlike mitigation, neither requires the cooperation of all to secure it for any, nor is something that, if secured for some, is secured for all. By acting together through existing, already formal-ized, smaller-scale collectivities (for example, as members of wealthy states), some could secure the interest for themselves alone. They are not mutually dependent in the right way, any more than *Stranded climbers* would be if two of the climbers could get down safely by cooperating only with one another.

It is because of this that the weakly collective duty, in this case, is only to mitigate climate change.

(V) COLLECTIVE BENEFICENCE

This chapter has made a prudential case for The Young to act collectively on climate change mitigation. It has done so by identifying them as a collectivity bound by a fundamental interest each has in such mitigation. However, it has not yet made a moral argument. This will be the work of the next two sections.

We acquire special duties through membership of collectivities in various familiar ways. In some small-scale cases, such as the family, we are often thought to acquire duties directly, regardless of whether we had any choice about entering the relationship. In forming other close personal ties, such as friendships, we can be said implicitly to accept duties.[54] At the political (especially state) level, special duties are defended by appeal to an implicit contract or to some allegedly unique feature of the relationship, such as the fact of mutual coercion.[55] The non-intentionalist model, in allowing for collectivities forged by mutual dependence through fundamental interests, raises a further possibility. I will defend the following.[56]

Principle of moralized collective self-interest
A set of human beings (moral agents) who are mutually dependent through a common fundamental interest have a weakly collective duty to cooperate to secure that interest, so long as this is possible without those individuals having to sacrifice some other fundamental human interest.

I will defend this principle, on which The Young have a weakly collective duty to organize to mitigate climate change, in two stages. The first (this section) is to collectivize the principles of beneficence, drawing on existing work by Larry May, Virginia Held, Robert Goodin, and Shue.[57] Although I am concerned for now only with the narrower set of cases where there is overlap between victims and duty-bearers, I will defend the collectivized principles more generally. This is because I will need the collectivized moderate principle in Chapter Three, for the argument from collective ability to aid. Section (vi) will then defend the principle of moralized collective self-interest via a special case application of the weak principle of beneficence.

Let us begin with the individual principles of beneficence taken as starting assumptions in Chapter One.

Weak principle of beneficence
An individual (moral agent) has a moral duty to prevent the serious suffering (deprivation of a fundamental interest) of some other human being or human beings (moral subject(s)) if she can do so at minimal cost to herself.

Moderate principle of beneficence
An individual (moral agent) has a moral duty to prevent serious suffering (deprivation of a fundamental interest) by some other human being or human beings (moral subject(s)) if she can do so at less than significant cost to herself.

Given their acceptance at the individual level, it is a natural next step to weakly collective versions of the principles of beneficence. As Goodin argues, we can be vulnerable to one another individually, disjunctively, or conjunctively. As May brings out, our potential to prevent serious harms to others is not restricted to what we can do as individuals, on the one hand, or as existing groups, on the other.

Consider the following variants on Peter Singer's classic example.[58]

Easy rescue 1
On his way to work, Peter passes a pond in which a child is drowning. He could easily stop and save the child, although it would slightly damage his clothes to do so.

On either principle of beneficence, Peter has a moral duty to stop and rescue the child.

Easy rescue 2
Peter is a member of the Olympic rowing team. One morning, he and his teammates pass a lake in which a child is struggling. The weather is bad and it would be dangerous if not impossible for any to swim out to the child in time. However, there is a rowing boat at the water's edge and the team could easily row to the child and save her. They might be a few minutes late for training, but would not be so tired as to make any discernible difference to their performance.

It is consistent with the previous case to attribute a duty to the team to save the child. They are an established group, used to acting together. By doing so, they can save the child at very low cost to each of them and indeed to the shared ends of the group.

Easy rescue 3
Peter and Quentin are on their way to work when they simultaneously reach a lake in which a child is struggling. The weather is bad and it would be dangerous if not impossible for either to swim to the child in time. However, there is a two-person rowing boat at the water's edge. If they both got in and rowed to her, they would be in time to save the child, although each would be a few minutes late for work. The men are strangers but are obviously healthy and can speak the same language.

If Peter has a moral duty in *Easy rescue 1*, and the team a duty in *Easy rescue 2*, it is implausible to deny that Peter and Quentin have a moral duty to get themselves into the boat and act together to save the child. Although they lack an established way of making collective decisions, not only are the various required actions (getting into the boat, rowing, pulling out the child) possible in the time, but it is clear to both what it is that needs to be done.[59]

This is what I will refer to as a weakly collective duty: a duty to act together so as to achieve some end. In May's more backward-looking terminology, if they failed to organize to save the child, Peter and Quentin would share responsibility.[60]

Now consider the following.

Easy rescue 4
As in *Easy rescue 3*, except that three men, Peter, Quentin, and Rob, reach the lake simultaneously. Only two are needed to organize to rescue the child.

May would describe the three as a putative group; on the vocabulary I will adopt in Chapter Three, they are a potential collectivity.[61] Although the situation is over-determined, in the sense that no one individual is strictly speaking necessary for the collective result, it remains true of them that they could have saved the child at low cost to each: they could, between them, ensure the child is saved. To bring this out, suppose they fail to do so, and imagine how the mother might respond if she later finds this out. 'You', she might say, 'failed to save my child when you could easily have done so'. She would be understandably and (on most intuitions) justifiably angry. Her 'you' would be a 'you plural', picking out all three of them taken together.

Any one of them might object that the others could have done it without him: that his failure was neither necessary nor sufficient for the collective failure. However, this would not excuse them, taken together, any more than it excused the bystanders in the Kitty Genovese case, where a woman was murdered in the sight of nearly forty people, none of whom intervened.[62] The relevant point, for each of Peter, Quentin, and Rob, is that he-and-either-of-the-others could have saved the child, at low cost to each, and they didn't.

These cases implicitly appeal to the collectivized principle of beneficence:

Collectivized weak principle of beneficence
A set of human beings have a duty to cooperate to prevent the serious suffering (deprivation of a fundamental interest) of another human being or human beings if they can do so at minimal cost to each.

Collectivized moderate principle of beneficence
A set of human beings have a duty to cooperate to prevent the serious suffering (deprivation of a fundamental interest) of another human being or human beings if they can do so at less than significant cost to each.

As we move away from this stylized case, two points must be made. Firstly, especially in bigger-scale cases, preventing the deprivation of fundamental interests is likely to demand more complex coordination. Given this, the two elements involved come apart: organizing to act collectively, and actually performing the actions involved. The distinction becomes clearer between just any random collection of individuals and a set capable of organizing itself to act collectively. To ascribe moral responsibility, there must, as May puts it, 'be some sense in which a group was not formed that could have been formed'. It must be 'plausible to think that the [putative] group could have developed a sufficient structure in time to prevent the harm'.[63]

Moreover, consistently to apply the collectivized principle of beneficence, the cost condition must be met at both levels. It is required both that the collective action itself does not impose too high a cost on each individual (call this the *cost of action condition*) and that getting organized to act collectively does not do so (*cost of coordination condition*).

Secondly, applying this reasoning to ongoing cases undermines any attempt to categorize all positive duties into either individually held duties of rescue or duties of existing institutions. The fact of vulnerability to a collection of individuals taken conjunctively, on the one hand, and the possibility of organization to become capable of responding to it, on the other, suggests an intermediate case: duties to create institutions through which to protect fundamental interests.[64]

Consider the following.

Easy rescue 5
Peter, Quentin, Rob, and many others occupy smallholdings in a remote area. Nearby is a small but deep lake, a site of great beauty loved by all, but into which visiting children frequently fall. None of the smallholders can afford to mount a guard on the lake all the time, but by giving up an hour or so a month each they could prevent the drownings.

In the absence of any background institutions whose primary responsibility this would be and to whom effective appeal might be made, Peter and the others could best fulfil the demands of the principle of beneficence by organizing in this way.

This completes the defence of the collectivized principles of beneficence. I will return to the moderate principle in Chapter Three, but have now to appeal to a special case application of the weak principle.

(VI) COLLECTIVITIES, PRUDENTIAL INCENTIVES, AND MORAL DUTIES

Consider the members of a collectivity bound by a shared fundamental interest. A central element of a flourishing human life is at stake for each if they do not cooperate. This section argues that, *once the moral agents within the set can reasonably be expected to be aware of their mutual dependence*, the peculiarities of this situation, in combination with the collectivized weak principle of beneficence, yield the principle of moralized collective self-interest.

The italicized clause is important. Although this extends to cases where the relevant individuals do not consider themselves part of a group, or even do not accept pursuit of the fundamental interest as a personal goal, it would be implausible to assign moral duties in cases where the individuals cannot know there is any mutual dependence. Such duties would be unfulfillable. However, it would also be implausible to absolve the agents of the duty were they simply denying the situation in the face of evidence readily available to them. The requirement that they can reasonably be expected to be aware of the situation is analogous to the standard requirement of reasonable foreseeability in the no-harm principle.

The argument then has two stages. Firstly, note that the collectivized principle of beneficence applies even if the victim himself is one of those whose cooperation is required to secure his fundamental interests. In that case, the rest have a duty to cooperate *with each other and him* to save him from serious harm.

Consider the following:

Easy rescue 6
Peter, Rob, and Quentin are on their way to work when they simultaneously reach a lake in which Sami is struggling. It would be dangerous if not impossible for any to swim to the child in time. However, there is a two-person rowing boat at the water's edge. If any two of the three got in and rowed to Sami, then they would be able *with his help* to detach him from the reeds in which he is entangled. To do so would make each of the three a few minutes late for work. The men are strangers but are obviously healthy and can speak the same language.

The fact that Sami would also need to cooperate does not, as things stand, change the moral situation. (I am, of course, assuming that Sami would co-operate: that he wants his own life to be saved; this is a point to which I will return.) It would be inconsistent to claim that Peter, Rob, and Quentin would have a duty to save him between them, if they could do so without his coopera-tion, but that they have no duty between them to help him save himself.

The next stage of the argument has two interlocking parts. Consider any given individual in the mutually dependent set. Were she and the others to cooperate, they could preserve her fundamental interests. The possibility of such coordination in time is implicit in the non-intentionalist definition of a collectivity (and explicitly defended, in the climate change case, in section (iv)). Thus, according to the collectivized weak principle of beneficence, the rest have a duty to cooperate with her to preserve her fundamental interests if they can do so at minimal cost to each. However (the second interlocking part), those required to cooperate also each have the fundamental interest at stake. The cooperation is thus to their own advantage, so by definition the minimal cost condition must be met: it cannot be too costly for you to do something, in a morally relevant sense, if it actually benefits you to do it. The only proviso—and this is an important one—is that it must be possible to organize to secure that fundamental interest for each without sacrificing another such interest.

This same argument applies with each individual in turn considered as vic-tim, giving each set of all-minus-one a weakly collective duty to cooperate to secure the interests of that one, and so all a weakly collective duty to cooperate to secure the interests of each.

To illustrate this, recall *Stranded climbers* from section (ii). Call them Anne, Beth, Calah, and Delilah. Each got independently to the same point on the mountain but it would now be extremely dangerous for any either to continue or to stay put. To descend safely, they need to cooperate.

Begin by considering the position of each individual as potential sufferer. If Anne is to stay alive (a fundamental interest if ever there was one), she and the other three must cooperate to descend safely. Thus, according to the weak principle of beneficence, the other three have to cooperate to help her to descend, if this can be done at minimal cost to each. The same can be said of each of Beth, Calah, and Delilah, thereby assigning the weakly collective duty to each of the other three possible three-person subsets of the collectivity: Anne, Calah, and Delilah have a duty to Beth; Anne, Beth, and Delilah a duty to Calah; and Anne, Beth, and Calah a duty to Delilah. Turning to the position of each individual as potential cooperator, we can say of her that because the cooperation required would also save her own life, without in the process costing her some other fundamental interest, the minimal cost condition must be met. She cannot claim it imposes too great a cost on her to do something which is also so fundamentally to her own advantage.

This is so even if Beth wants to push on for the summit. Maybe she overestimates her own ability, or underestimates the (fairly obvious) danger facing them all, or has simply got it into her head to go on whatever the cost. It remains the case that retaining the opportunity for continued life is a fundamental human interest for her as it is for the others. Cooperation would secure this for them, without costing her another such interest. She knows this. Accordingly, she cannot claim that the cost of cooperation to her is such as to undermine the case for the weakly collective duty.

This makes the case for the principle of moralized collective self-interest. However, before applying this to the climate change case, a point of clarification must be made and two objections considered. To begin with the former, it is worth reiterating that the minimal cost condition applies to both the cost of action and the cost of coordination. This is so even though the two are blurred in this small-scale case. However, because of the peculiar nature of the situation—because of how much is at stake for each of precisely those who are required to cooperate—all that this requires here is that cooperation, like collective action, does not cost each any other fundamental interest.

The first objection is that it is unacceptably paternalistic to claim that Beth should do something she doesn't want to do because that thing is in her own interest. However, this misunderstands the argument. The claim is not that Beth—or any of the others—has to descend the mountain safely *because* it would save her own life. Rather, her duty to cooperate is derivative of the weakly collective duty she, Calah, and Delilah have to Anne, that she, Anne, and Delilah have to Calah, and that she, Anne, and Calah have to Delilah. (Anticipating Chapter Five, any duties she might have to promote cooperation are also derivative from the weakly collective duty.) The weakly collective duty is grounded primarily in the serious harm to be prevented: harm to Anne, Calah, or Delilah. The appeal to her own interests comes in only secondarily: as grounds for rejecting any appeal to the cost of cooperation to justify not acting to protect the others in this way.

To reinforce this, compare this situation with that in which all four climbers, while knowing the risk, would still rather face the almost certainty of death and push on for the summit. In this case, although they are still a collectivity and although they still have a prima facie weakly collective duty to each, this might be overridden. If all those who would be protected by a certain action freely and knowingly reject it, then to insist on it looks unacceptably paternalistic.[65] (Suppose, in *Easy rescue 6*, that Sami did not want to cooperate in saving his own life.)

The other objection accuses me of focusing on an inappropriate interpretation of cost. On this line of reasoning, the cost condition should take into account whether each individual is required to bear any immediate cost, not whether she is better or worse off in some fundamental, 'overall' sense. I find this implausible. If immediate (in)convenience were to determine the extent of our moral duties, the consequences would be absurd. Significant immediate disruption is compatible with low-level impact on one's quality of life, and vice versa. Compare, for example, selling your expensive house for one slightly less expensive with signing away a small inheritance the moment you hear of and before you receive it, and so ruling out ever purchasing a house in the future. The morally relevant impact in determining the limits of our duties must surely be the impact that fulfilling them would have on the duty-bearer's life overall.[66]

With all this in mind, let us return to The Young. From sections (i) to (iv), they constitute a collectivity (perhaps 'we', since my own generation is probably around the cut-off point). They are mutually dependent through the interest each has in climate change mitigation. Thus, according to the principle of moralized collective self-interest, they have a weakly collective duty—a duty of all to each—to organize to secure climate change mitigation. However, one potential obstacle remains, recalling the proviso acknowledged above. If it were impossible for collective action to secure this fundamental interest without sacrificing another for some members of the set, then it could no longer be said to be to each of their own advantage (and so a relevantly minimal cost) to cooperate to do so. This, I contend, is not the case here.

Begin with the cost of action condition. The Stern Review sets a mitigation cost of around 1 per cent of annual gross domestic product (GDP).[67] This, in itself, is hardly a threat to fundamental interests. Even assuming it were being divided only among The Young, rather than across all generations, it need not be so.

There are a number of objections to this claim. The first appeals to the fact that The Young includes some who are already extremely badly off. An equal division of mitigation costs would undoubtedly impose central interest deprivations on them. Accordingly, it is claimed, the cost of action condition is not met.

However, in requiring that the end could be collectively achieved at relatively low cost to each, the collectivized principle of beneficence does not demand that it could be so achieved at equal cost to each. To do so would be wrongly to assume that there is only one way (or only one fair way) of assigning duties within a group. Recall *Easy rescue 3*. Even if Peter were considerably stronger than Quentin, who could not physically bear half of the burden of rescuing the child, so long as there is *a* way of distributing that effort such that the cost to each is comparatively low, the duty holds.[68]

In the climate change case, the same reasoning applies. So long as there is some distribution of costs across the collectivity which would mitigate climate change without sacrificing any other fundamental interests, the cost of action condition is met. There is every reason to suppose that there is. Suppose The Young bore all the costs of mitigating climate change and suppose this were to amount to 3 or 4 per cent of their resources. Even if those who are also in The Able were required to bear all the costs—protecting poorer members of The Young from fundamental interest losses—there is no reason to believe it would impinge on their fundamental interests. How much, after all, could most of us give up by way of economic income and wealth, or of emissions, without actually sacrificing anything fundamental: anything that really counts as a precondition for an individual flourishing life?[69] A good deal more than 3 or 4 per cent. There is no reason why the actual distribution of costs should not increase in proportion to individual income and wealth.

The second objection focuses not on economic burdens but on the impact of action to mitigate climate change on one's pursuit of a particular plan or life, or conception of the good. It might even be claimed that play, another of Nussbaum's more controversial capabilities, is undermined.[70] The idea is that inability to engage in fuel-intensive activities will render certain ways of life impossible, thereby undermining scope for practical reason (or play) and so counting as a fundamental interest loss. Four obvious points can be made against this argument.

Firstly, there are frequently less environmentally expensive ways of achieving more or less the same satisfaction, or exercising the same skill. For example, those drivers obsessed with maximizing their speed between London and Glasgow could, if they drive at all, focus instead on the challenge of doing so in the most fuel-efficient manner (or, still better, attempt to hone their speed skills on a bicycle instead, and improve on another central functioning at the same time).

Secondly, ruling out some particular elements of a way of life does not equate to destroying a life plan, let alone to undermining an individual's entire potential for such planning. Consider the difference, for example, between preventing all travel and radically curtailing opportunities to fly. Equally, it is one thing to be unable to ski five times a season; another to be deprived of all opportunity 'to laugh, to play, [or] to enjoy recreational activities'.[71]

Thirdly, there is a distinction between the cost to the individual of pursuing some end in isolation, and the cost to each of doing so—as this duty requires—as part of some collective endeavour. Chapters Five, Six, and Seven will return to this theme. Even if it would impose a serious cost on an individual, acting alone, to minimize her emissions to what they would be in a fair collective scheme, it need not be so through the collective scheme. Suppose my childhood-imbued love of spending time in the mountains means that, as things are currently structured, I find it extremely difficult to pursue my plan of life without access to a car. This is a problem only insofar as I attempt to mitigate climate change by acting in isolation; effective collective action could minimize the costs to me by, for example, investing in effective, reliable public transport.

Fourthly, in line with the discussion above, if anyone could show that certain actions would genuinely require sacrificing a fundamental interest, or central capability (not just an expensive taste), then there is a case for adjusting whatever distribution of individual duties is determined as part of the collective scheme. It is only if there is no scheme which could mitigate climate change without imposing fundamental interest losses that the argument against the weakly collective duty could be made.

Let us turn, then, to the cost of cooperation. Here, to meet the minimal cost condition in these peculiar circumstances, all that is required is that it not undermine a fundamental interest.

Again, two points can be made. Firstly, as with the cost of action condition, there is a distinction between the requirement (which would be harder to meet) that it would be possible for all individuals to put exactly the same effort into developing a collective scheme without any losing a fundamental interest, and the requirement that there are combinations of individual efforts on which this would be possible. Recall *Easy rescue 5*. Perhaps, while all of the smallholders would be able easily to do their hour a month, there are great disparities in what they could do by way of setting up the scheme. Some might not be able to leave their small children to go out to canvass support. Others might be cripplingly shy and unable to bring themselves to ask anyone else to sign up. Still others might have plenty of spare time, and abundant leadership skills.[72]

Similarly, in the climate change case, some persons are in a position—or have particular skills—to make more difference at rather less cost to themselves. Others are sufficiently deprived, or in sufficiently oppressive political systems, that there is very little they can do by way of promoting collective-level change without sacrificing fundamental interests. Anticipating Chapter Six, this may mean that different actions are required of them by way of fulfilment of derivative duties in the absence of effective collective action; it doesn't mean that there is no weakly collective duty.

One final point: this special case application of the weak principle of beneficence is reinforced by the inclusion in the collectivity of young children and future generations. The existence of this passive subset undermines any attempt (already unconvincing) to override the duty by appeal to a general willingness to forgo the threatened interest. Even if it could plausibly be claimed (which it can't) that all adult members of The Young would rather ignore their fundamental interest in climate change mitigation than organize to secure it, this cannot be said of future generations and young children, who are not yet capable of such decisions. (Recall *Stranded climbers*, and suppose a child is also stranded there, independent of any of them, but also dependent on the cooperation to save her life.)[73]

CONCLUSIONS

This chapter has argued from moralized collective self-interest for a weakly collective duty of The Young to organize themselves to mitigate climate change. Drawing on the non-intentionalist model and on collectivizing the weak principle of beneficence, it argued that The Young are bound together into a collectivity by fundamental interests, in a way giving rise to a prudential incentive and a weakly collective moral duty to act to secure them.

While I have appealed only to the weak version of the principle of beneficence, and so to some extent relied on less than I will in Chapter Three, it is worth acknowledging that in other ways some of the starting assumptions of this chapter are more controversial than those I will use next. I have appealed to a particular understanding of cost—in terms of overall impact on the agent's life—in applying the cost of cooperation and of action conditions. I have relied more extensively on details of the capabilities approach, in defending a widespread appeal to collective self-interest, than it is necessary to do in defending the claim that climate change seriously harms many individuals. As I will reiterate at the close of Part One, however, the idea is that these three arguments are complementary but largely independent. Thus, I hope that those unconvinced by these more controversial elements of this chapter can still approach the next with an open mind.

3

Doing and Preventing Harm

One Eva Smith has gone—but there are millions and millions and millions of Eva Smiths and John Smiths still left with us, with their lives, their hopes and fears, their suffering, and chance of happiness, all intertwined with our lives, and what we think and say and do.[1]

J. B. Priestley, *An Inspector Calls*

Today we face the possibility that the global environment may be destroyed, yet no-one will be responsible.[2]

Dale Jamieson

On the non-intentionalist model, there is at least one global-level collectivity or 'collectivity of humanity': younger generations are mutually dependent through the fundamental interest each has in climate change mitigation. This mutual dependence gives rise to a weakly collective duty: a duty of all to each and of each to each other to cooperate to mitigate global climate change. Or so I have argued.

However, mutual dependence—collective self-interest—will only take our moral accounting so far. Many of those alive today can legitimately deny having any such fundamental interest in climate change mitigation. Many of these, moreover, have no intention of signing up to the goal of tackling climate change. These are those middle-aged or elderly persons, living in the developed West or in affluent bubbles in other parts of the world, who are unlikely to suffer serious harm through climate change, have little or no concern for the fate of future generations, and are doing very nicely on the kind of high-polluting, high-consuming lifestyle on which environmental devastation feeds. This chapter argues that they, too, have collectively incurred climate duties: duties acquired, on the one hand, because the global affluent could between them prevent the serious harm to others done by climate change, and on the other because of weakly collective responsibility for at least a part of that harm.

To defend this claim, I will expand the model outlined in Chapter Two. Section (i) will introduce the idea of a *should-be collectivity*: a set of individuals who would constitute a collectivity were they to espouse some goal and who ought (morally) to espouse it. Two such are identified at the global level: The Able, who have a duty grounded in a collectivized principle of beneficence to cooperate to mitigate and enable adaptation to climate change, no matter who brought it about (section (ii)); and Polluters, who have a negatively grounded duty (a duty based in their weakly collective responsibility for harm) to stop worsening climate change, and to mitigate and enable adaptation to that climate change for which current generations are responsible (sections (iii) and (iv)).

By 'The Able' I mean the global affluent, or those who could contribute to action on climate change mitigation and adaptation at less than significant cost to themselves. This includes many (but not all) of those in the developed world, as well as the rich minority in developing countries. By 'Polluters' I mean those emitting greenhouse gases above the level at which, were all emitting at that level, climate change would not be worsened, and whose individual emissions over that level are avoidable without the loss to them of some fundamental interest. In both cases, this is a duty to the victims of climate change. (Accordingly, 'current generations' in the previous paragraph is shorthand for those in current generations who meet these two conditions: i.e. it picks out that climate change for which such moral responsibility can be assigned.)

Section (v) will conclude Part One with a comment on how all three weakly collective duties might, in practice, be fairly fulfilled by collective action at the level of The Able.

(I) SHOULD-BE COLLECTIVITIES

Chapter Two argued that a number of individuals make up a collectivity if they are mutually dependent for the achievement or satisfaction of some common or shared goal, purpose, or fundamental interest, regardless of whether they are aware of this. Building on this, I identify as a *potential collectivity* any set of individuals who would, were they to espouse some goal, be mutually dependent for its achievement and would, accordingly, constitute a collectivity. Suppose you and I were to find ourselves at the foot of a remote cliff which we need not ascend but, should we choose to, could only do so safely by climbing as a pair. We would constitute a potential collectivity because a goal each of us might espouse (that of getting to the top) would require cooperation.

Clearly, the set of potential collectivities is indefinitely and unhelpfully large. At its weakest, any two or more individuals could count as a potential collectivity, because they could espouse the goal of doing something together. However, those potential collectivities with which moral and political philosophers need concern themselves constitute a much smaller subset: those whose members ought (morally) to cooperate to pursue those ends through which they would be mutually dependent. To put this more formally:

Should-be collectivity
A set of individuals who:
    (i) would, were they to espouse some goal or goals, constitute a collectivity; and
    (ii) have a moral duty to espouse that goal.

In parallel with the two understandings of 'common end' outlined in Chapter Two, this could come about in either of two ways. There might be an individual goal the achievement of which, for each individual, would require the cooperation of all and which each individual has an individual duty to pursue, or there might be some goal which all could espouse together and which the potential collectivity has a weakly collective duty to pursue. (Recall that by a 'weakly collective duty' I mean a duty requiring a set of individuals which is not yet a collective agent in any strong sense to bring about some result between them, by organizing themselves, as necessary, to be capable of collective action. This can be distinguished from the strongly collective duty of a collective entity already capable of intentional action.)

The second possibility is the more relevant to this project. However, for completeness, it is worth briefly illustrating the first. Accordingly, consider the following.

Playground
A number of parents live in a housing estate. Each has promised his or her child that a playground will be built in the estate, but none has the time, money, or skill to build one without the cooperation of the others.

The parents constitute a potential collectivity because they are mutually dependent for the achievement of the end (to build a playground) and a should-be collectivity because each has a moral duty (an individual duty grounded in the promise to his or her own child) to pursue it.[3]

Turning to cases of the second type, I will offer two intuitively plausible examples, then use the following three sections to fill out the twofold philosophical model on which they rest, and apply them to the climate change case.

Beach rescue[4]
A number of unconnected holidaymakers are on a beach when a child starts to drown in the water. Her rescue would require most of them to organize themselves to act together, to drag a lifeboat into the water, row it to her, and to pull her out.

Swimming teenagers
A number of teenagers, all independently, decide to swim in a small lake. Each jumps in and swims around very flashily. Between them, they cause so much turbulence that a child also (independently) swimming in the lake is put in serious danger of drowning. To rescue her would require cooperation by the teenagers; to avoid putting more children in the same position, turbulence would have to be kept to a lower overall level.

In each case, there is some end which no individual could secure without the cooperation of others: in the first, the rescue of the child; in the latter, the cessation of harm to her and prevention of harm to other children. In both, I will argue, there is a weakly collective duty to coordinate to achieve that end: a duty positively grounded in the first instance, negatively in the second. The holidaymakers and the teenagers are alike should-be collectivities. So, by parallel reasoning, are The Able and Polluters. I will begin with the holidaymakers.

(II) HARM WE CAN PREVENT TOGETHER

This project takes two widely shared moral principles for granted, as I spelled out in Chapter One. One was the no-harm principle, to which I will return in section (iii). The other was the principle of beneficence, on which I have a moral duty to prevent serious harm to another person or persons if I can do so at comparatively low cost to myself. Chapter Two argued that a collectivized version follows naturally from the individual version of this principle.[5] If I should pull a drowning child out of a pond if I can do so at the cost only of my clothes, and if you should do so in parallel circumstances, it is hard to resist the conclusion that, if we could save the child between us, at similarly low cost, we should do so. Accordingly, I defended the following:

Collectivized weak principle of beneficence
A set of human beings have a duty to cooperate to prevent the serious suffering (deprivation of a fundamental interest) of another human being or human beings if they can do so at minimal cost to each.

Collectivized moderate principle of beneficence
A set of human beings have a duty to cooperate to prevent the serious suffering (deprivation of a fundamental interest) of another human being or human beings if they can do so at less than significant cost to each.

Chapter Two drew on the collectivized weak principle of beneficence to defend a principle of moralized collective self-interest, and so to uphold the weakly collective duty of The Young to mitigate climate change. Here, I appeal to the moderate version. This is more demanding, but remains weaker than the very demanding strong principle defended by Peter Singer at the individual level, on which I have a moral duty to act to prevent serious harm to another if I can do so at anything less than morally comparable cost to myself.[6]

Before I do this, however, I want briefly to acknowledge a potential objection: that the principle of beneficence, individual or collective, loses its moral force when we increase the distance between victims and potential rescuers. The idea is that I only have a moral duty to rescue those close (physically, socially, even temporally) to me; and accordingly that we only have a duty to organize to rescue those who are close to us. Compare, for example, the different reactions most people have to the following two cases:

Moderately easy rescue
On her way to work, Jane passes a pond in which a child is drowning. She can stop and save the child, although if she does she will miss an important business appointment, costing her £1,000.

Email
Oxfam sends Jane an email which gives her the opportunity to save several Third World flood victims, simply by making an online transfer of £100.[7]

While most people would think Jane had done something very wrong in leaving the child to drown, most people also don't consider themselves to have done anything wrong when they immediately delete emails such as that from Oxfam. That is despite the fact that the request is for less money, and to save more children.

Accordingly, it might be objected, however plausible it is to collectivize the principle of beneficence at the small scale, we don't have any such duties when the victims are far away from those who could rescue them.

I will return in Chapter Six to a parallel objection, according to which the individual duties we acquire in the climate change case must—because they are so generally treated as such—be much less demanding than those in immediate cases of harm or rescue. I will also address a related objection in section (iv). For now, I do not need to engage in detail with the problem of distance in morality, which is extensively discussed elsewhere.[8] The individual principle of beneficence, taken as a starting assumption in Chapter One, was accepted there in general terms—without any proximity requirement—and the fact that some might reject it as such was part of the reason for providing three different arguments, drawing on different principles, for my weakly collective duty.[9]

However, I will make a few brief comments. Firstly, it is not clear that individuals' moral reactions do consistently track physical or social distance in this way. Peter Unger's (admittedly unsystematic) gleaning of intuitions on hypothetical examples suggests this, while Judith Lichtenberg makes the point that most Americans, far from responding to all cases of serious close-to-home need, are also 'quite unmoved by the plight of people who live down the street or across town'.[10]

Secondly, as I will discuss in more detail in Chapter Six, there is reason to doubt that behavioural differences accurately reflect differences even in what the relevant individual thinks of as her moral duties, never mind in what those moral duties actually are.[11] Our different reactions can equally well be explained as the result of psychological or socio-psychological mechanisms: ways we have developed of denying what it would be too inconvenient, in terms of our own day-to-day lives, to face up to. As Lichtenberg also points out, it is easier to ignore even very great human suffering when:

> those suffering are strangers—not just people who we do not know, but people whom we have never seen, who lack names and faces and with whom we have little in common. In these cases it is not painful to do nothing, as it would be to watch a child drown or an accident victim bleed to death. Just don't think about it, and—for your own practical purposes—it does not exist.[12]

Recent sociological research has identified widespread denial mechanisms at work in the globalized, capitalist world, as the rich minority find ways of concealing from themselves the plight of the marginalized poor, rather than face up to the conflict between moral principles they claim to uphold and ever-growing evidence of avoidable human suffering.[13] Given evidence of such widespread severe suffering, it is easier to find excuses for failure to respond than to face up to our moral duties. (It is easier, that is, to exaggerate the good we already do, or to convince ourselves that those suffering are undeserving of aid.)

That is not to suggest that *Email* and *Moderately easy rescue* are not importantly different. However, the difference lies not in the demandingness of Jane's moral duty, in each case, but in what she could do to assist. In *Moderately easy rescue*, there is one victim and one duty-bearer (Jane). She could save the victim, and the situation would be resolved. In *Email*, she could not save all the victims herself however great her sacrifice. However, it might well be that collective-level action could do so. Accordingly, there is another option available to her: that of attempting to bring about such action. This, I suggest, may be another (more reasonable) explanation of our intuition that the cases are distinct.

Having thus clarified the position, let us return to the application of the collectivized principle. It is worth reiterating three points. Firstly, in referring to fundamental interests, the definition draws on the interests- or capabilities-based model of flourishing outlined in Chapter One. There, it was stated as another starting assumption that there are certain morally valuable central elements of human flourishing, or prerequisites for a human life going well, which cannot be traded off against each other and which we have a fundamental interest in retaining. These could be identified as capabilities, or genuine, secure opportunities to enjoy the central human functionings of life, bodily health, bodily integrity, affiliation, and practical reason.[14] However, they could also be defended as basic needs, or at least such needs combined with some core conditions for autonomy. As I have already stressed, I am not committed to the contents of Martha Nussbaum's rather longer list of central capabilities.

Being permanently deprived of such a central element of a flourishing human life would, uncontroversially, count as a severe loss: the kind of harm that morality must condemn if it condemns anything at all. Climate change—as was also made clear in both the previous chapters—imposes just such losses.

However—which is the second point—turning from duty-bearer to victim, an individual could incur morally significant cost to herself without such permanent deprivation of a central capability. I suggested in Chapter One that this would be so if she were required to do something which interfered, seriously but temporarily, with her exercise of a central human functioning.[15] For example, the loss of bodily health through a debilitating or painful disease would be a significant cost to me even if I were able to regain my health in time. On the moderate principle of beneficence (individual or collective) action is required only if the costs incurred in preventing the severe harm (costs to the individual or, in the collective case, to each individual) are less than significant in this sense.

Thirdly, in the weakly collective case, there are two ways in which the significant cost might arise. It could be associated with joint achievement of the end—with the actions contributing to some collective or combined endeavour to secure the common end—or with the process of bringing the necessary collective action about in the first place. Accordingly, Chapter Two identified two components to the cost condition: the *cost of action condition* and the *cost of coordination condition*. For the collectivized moderate principle to come into force, both must be possible without imposing morally significant costs on the individuals.

Applying the collectivized moderate principle of beneficence, The Able have a weakly collective duty to organize to prevent the serious harms that result from climate change. Most plausibly, this will involve a combination of mitigation and facilitating adaptation.

To fill this out, let us begin with the cost of action condition.[16] The Stern Review sets a mitigation cost of around 1 per cent of annual gross domestic product (GDP).[17] The costs of such adaptation as would then also be necessary are harder still to quantify, but, in the context of the global élite, can also be expected to be affordable. According to the same source:

> The additional costs of making new infrastructure and buildings resilient to climate change in OECD countries could be $15–150 billion each year (0.05–0.5% of GDP).
>
> The challenge of adaptation will be particularly acute in developing countries, where greater vulnerability and poverty will limit the capacity to act. As in developed countries, the costs are hard to estimate, but are likely to run into tens of billions of dollars.[18]

The sacrifice required by the global affluent would be of luxury goods: a point long familiar in political philosophical debate concerning the fairest distribution of the burdens of tackling climate change.[19] Moreover, collective solutions should require less individual sacrifice than would the isolated individual lifestyle changes that might, in combination, achieve mitigation. (This is an efficiency point to which I will return in Chapter Six.[20])

Now consider the cost of coordination. Again recalling Chapter Two, two distinctions must be drawn. One is that between the requirement (which would be harder to meet) that it would be possible for all individuals to put exactly the *same* effort into developing a collective scheme without incurring significant costs, and the requirement that there are combinations of individual efforts on which this would be possible. In the climate change case, as in the small-scale cases discussed previously, there are some individuals who (by virtue of their position or their particular skills) can do rather more by way of facilitating coordination, at rather less cost to themselves. I will return to such differences in Chapter Six. For now, it is sufficient to reiterate that they do not undermine the weakly collective duty.

The second distinction is between costs fixed outside the potential collectivity and hurdles which are collectively determined and could be overcome collectively at less than significant cost to each individual. Recall *Beach rescue*. In parallel with Chapter Two's rejection of the claim that cooperation in time is impossible, consider the following three situations in which the holidaymakers might claim that cooperation is too costly.

In the first, factors which cannot now be altered (collectively or individually) render it too costly for the holidaymakers to interact at all. Communication or cooperation might be possible, but very difficult or painful. This might be cooperation with anyone (suppose the holidaymakers can speak to one another but, because of a rare disease each has, only with extreme agony) or with some persons in particular. Imagine, instead of the holidaymakers, a number of hermits, each on his or her bit of headland, each of whom has devoted his entire life to religious isolation, and must according to sacred vows never interact in any way with a member of the opposite sex. Although they could coordinate, the cost to each—undermining his or her entire plan of life—is high. To assign them a moral duty to do so would require a more demanding principle of beneficence than that defended here.

Of course, there are limits to how far this can go. If you and your ex-spouse could save a stranger from drowning by spending half a day in each other's company, but claim you would rather pull out your own teeth than do so, I doubt very much that even a relatively undemanding principle of beneficence would let you off. However, for the purposes of this project, we need only the acknowledgement that some kinds of cooperation might in themselves impose significant costs.

In the climate change case, two points can be made against appeal to such costs. Firstly, anticipating the discussion below, there already is sufficient global-level cooperation to count against any claim that it is too demanding, in itself, to have to interact with persons of (say) different national allegiance, a different gender, or with different conceptions of the good. Secondly, even though some individuals might reject any scheme which required close interaction with some other individuals (say on religious grounds), we need not engage with the difficulties entailed by cooperation at this individual-to-individual level. It is likely that any cooperation required in the climate change case will be sufficiently formalized to require negligible day-to-day interaction beyond already established communities.

In the second and third scenarios, the costs or hurdles apparently faced could be collectively reduced or overcome. In the second, all holidaymakers are sleeping, sunbathing, building sandcastles, and generally reluctant to move. Each, being self-interested, is disinclined to take the initiative, especially if positive coordinated action by a subset less than the whole potential collectivity would be sufficient to save the child. From the individual point of view, this is doubly problematic.[21] Not only might individuals be inclined to hold back effort in the hope that enough others would volunteer, but even those otherwise willing to be part of the active subset might expect it to be extremely difficult to get sufficient others to overcome their indolence in time, and so not even try to do so.

However, so long as it is possible without significant cost to each for the members of the potential collectivity to communicate with each other in time to perform the physical actions required, such combined disinclination is no more sufficient to override the weakly collective duty than my disinclination to get salt in my hair would be to override my individual duty to save a drowning child if I were alone on the beach and she were within my reach. In cases of collective ability to aid, what is relevant in determining whether we have a duty is what we could do between us at less than significant cost to each, not what I could do alone without such cost, or even what I could bring about (that is, what I, as the only motivator, could persuade others to do).[22]

In the final scenario, the potential collectivity of holidaymakers is made up of several smaller, actual collectivities—families, friendship groups, a school party—each of which has agreed internally on a process of decision-making: a unanimous or majority vote, say, or a long process of deliberation followed by a compromise; in others, one person (the mother or teacher, say) decides. Previous negotiations have taken place between some of these little groups, for example over the best sunbathing spots. Various systems have evolved for this. Even if all were willing to cooperate, if all these processes had to be gone through before deciding on collective action, the child would drown.

Even in this final case, the collectivized principle is not necessarily overridden. The mere fact of impedimentary existing decision-making structures cannot automatically be taken to override a potential duty the fulfilment of which requires those structures to be changed by the very people who uphold them. To claim otherwise would be, to parallel an example from Chapter Two, to hold excused the board of a company who watched a man drown outside their office window because the constitution they had themselves agreed on did not allow them to break up a board meeting until after a unanimous vote, recorded at length in the minutes, on whether to do so. Morally, at least, saving lives is more important than abiding by rules you have created (and could un-create) for yourselves. To the extent, then, that collective action is hindered by existing structures which it would be impossible or extremely costly for any one individual (or even a small subset) to change, this need not count against the weakly collective duty. If the potential collectivity as a whole could change the structure at less than significant cost to each, it still holds.

In the climate change case, as in Chapter Two, we are somewhere between these two latter situations. While existing institutional structures have proved far from effective in tackling climate change, lack of progress can hardly be put down entirely to a lack of means through which to act. (Global action has been taken fast enough on other things.) Rather, it has been hindered by the fact that the supposedly cooperating entities (states) prioritize their own short-term, and sometimes even less-than-significant, interests over fulfilment of the weakly collective duty. At least so far as democracies are concerned, this is because so many in the electorate are similarly inclined to prioritize their own immediate ends (or, at least, would be avoided if that electorate were clearly to demand a different course of action).

However, in parallel to the points above, the weakly collective duty can be defended while remaining ambivalent on exactly how much of an impediment current structures are. This is because this project does not commit to any particular form of collective action. Rather, I leave open various ways in which the weakly collective duty might be fulfilled. Global institutional change is one possibility: a new global institution, or a more effective global-level deal than the summits of the United Nations Framework Convention on Climate Change have so far managed to produce. As already stressed in Chapter Two, the fact that there has been pitifully little progress, and that many see little grounds for optimism about any such future progress, does not mean either that we (between us) could not or that we do not morally have a duty to make the changes required for such progress.

Another possibility is that mitigation, at least, could be secured without a formal global-level deal, but by sufficient sub-collective groups (primarily states) acting independently, or making deals only between themselves, to secure the overall end.[23]

Finally, even if it were impossible (or too costly to each individual) to bring about the institutional change needed, this would not necessarily rule out global-level cooperation. Individuals could agree to bypass states and their unsuccessful negotiations, and commit to cut emissions themselves. For example, according to Dale Jamieson, the way to break through 'the world's largest and most complex collective action problem…is through the actions of a morally motivated global citizens' movement that acts as a highly committed political interest group. Such a movement would stigmatize coal, meat eating, trophy houses, overheating and overcooling, large living spaces, and private automobiles.'[24] With global means of communication and modern multimedia, this last possibility remains. Although it is harder to envisage meeting adaptation ends in this way, it is at least conceivable that, as part of this changed way of life, individuals could combine forces not only to invest adequately in low emissions technology, but also to promote technology to aid adaptation, which might then be distributed via NGOs.

Having defended the weakly collective duty of The Able to mitigate and enable adaptation to climate change, I now turn to the third argument: appeal to weakly collective responsibility for harm to defend a weakly collective duty of Polluters, including mitigation, adaptation, and compensation.

(III) HARM WE DO BETWEEN US[25]

These two sections will defend the claim that Polluters have a negatively derived weakly collective duty to act together to mitigate climate change.

On the second widely shared moral principle taken as read in Chapter One, an individual has a duty not to do serious harm to others (at least) unless in avoiding it she would incur comparable or greater harm. This has standardly been extended to assign collective moral responsibility to a group which has acted as a group to produce serious, foreseeable harm. However, collections of individuals who do not constitute formalized, acknowledged groups can and do also bring about serious, predictable harms.

Recall *Swimming teenagers*, who have all jumped into a lake and caused so much splashing and disruption, between them, as to put a child in danger of drowning. None, individually, harms the child: the minor turbulence caused by one alone would not have put her at risk. There is no collective intention to harm: there is no collective intention at all. Nor does each individual intend to contribute to some harmful activity or even some activity of which harm would be a foreseeable side effect. These considerations count against the attribution of individual or strong collective responsibility. Nonetheless, the child is harmed as a result of the combination of the teenagers' actions. This makes those teenagers at least a prima facie locus for moral condemnation.

What is peculiar about such cases is that, although the action is not collective in the strong sense of corporate action irreducible to the actions of individuals, the result (harm) could not have occurred were not those individuals situated, in relation to one another, in such a way that their pursuit of individual goals would have a certain predictable aggregative impact. It is only because of the way the individuals are grouped, in this weak sense, that harm is done.

Accordingly, I will defend the following.

Weakly collective responsibility claim
A number of individuals who do not yet constitute a collectivity (either formally, with an acknowledged decision-making structure, or informally, with some vaguely defined common interest or goal) can be held collectively morally responsible for serious harm (fundamental interest deprivation) which has been caused by the predictable aggregation of avoidable individual actions.[26]

'Predictable' has a double meaning here: individuals are acting predictably in that they are acting in pursuit of their goals or interests, and it is predictable (reasonably foreseeable) that those actions, in combination, will result in harm. More particularly, in line with May's treatment of collective inaction and with the conventional moral philosophical (and legal) treatment of individual responsibility, the following can be filled out.[27]

Three-part sufficient condition for weakly collective responsibility:

- the individuals acted in ways which, in aggregate, caused harm, and which they were aware (or could reasonably be expected to have foreseen) would, in aggregate, cause harm (although each only intentionally performed his own act);

- they were all aware (or could reasonably be expected to have foreseen) that there were enough others similarly placed (and so similarly motivated to act) for the combined actions to bring about the harm; and

- the contributory actions were avoidable at less than comparable cost to the individuals.

This model includes cases of overdetermination, where no individual's action need be necessary for the harm.

The first clause is to allow for the possibility that the individuals making up the potential collectivity are excusably ignorant of the situation. For example, in *Swimming teenagers*, it might be entirely unexpected—and not easy to spot—that there is a child in the water. Or it might not be foreseeable just how much turbulence lots of teenagers jumping about in the water would create. The second clause allows for excusable ignorance regarding the motivations of others. This would exclude responsibility if each teenager was unaware (and could not reasonably be expected to be aware) that others besides herself would want to dive into the lake. Suppose, for example, each had apparently good—if mistaken—reason to believe all the others to be terrified of water. In either of these cases, the child's death might be considered a tragic accident.

The third clause is intended to exclude situations in which it would not be possible to avoid the contributory action without unreasonable cost. For example, if each teenager had been chased into the water by a psychopath, or all were jumping out of the way of a forest fire, they would not be held weakly collectively responsible on the model above. Recall, however, that the threshold is standardly more demanding than in beneficence cases. For the weakly collective duty to be assigned, the alternatives available to each agent need only be 'non-terrible': in the terms of Chapter One, they would not cost her capability for continued life, health, bodily integrity, affiliation, or practical reason.[28]

I will defend this model by responding to three potential objections. The first is this. Although it does not require intention to harm, the ascription of moral responsibility does standardly require intention to do something—some individual or collective act—of which harm is a foreseeable side effect. To bring this out, compare the following.

Footbridge 1
A footbridge is unsafe and children are clearly visible playing in the water below it. There are no signs that the bridge is unsafe. I step on it, it breaks, and the children are harmed.

Footbridge 2
The situation is as in *Footbridge 1* except that there are clear signs that the bridge is in a state of poor repair and I can see the children in the water below it.

Footbridge 3
The situation is as in *Footbridge 2* except that the bridge can safely hold one person only and this is clearly signed. You and I are doing a three-legged race, in the course of which we knowingly step onto the bridge together.

In the first case, it is at least plausible that I am not morally responsible. I intended no harm and could not reasonably have been expected to foresee it.[29] In the second case, I could have foreseen that my actions would result in harm and it is plausible to hold me morally responsible.[30] In the third case, we are acting intentionally together and the harm is a foreseeable result of that action. In *Swimming teenagers*, however, not only is there no intention to harm, there is no intentional action at all at the level of the harm: there is neither collective intention to act nor individual intention to contribute to collective action.

My response to this objection is to point out that the weakly collective result picked out by the predictability conditions above is itself reasonably foreseeable. Each individual knows (or can reasonably be expected to know) that the combined actions of all those similarly placed, and so similarly motivated, would cause harm. Thus, for example, the following two cases can as clearly be contrasted as *Footbridge 1* and *2*, above.

Footbridge 4
As in *Footbridge 1* except the bridge can hold one person but not two, and you are approaching the bridge from exactly the same distance, at the same speed, as me. We step onto it at the same time; it breaks and the children are harmed.

Footbridge 5
As in *Footbridge 4* except that there are warning signs on each side of the bridge.
You and I see these, and each other, in plenty of time to stop. Each of us steps onto
the bridge and the children are harmed.

You and I can both reasonably be expected to know not only that harm would
result from certain actions in combination with those of any other person,
but also that another person is similarly placed and so similarly motivated
to act. To attribute weakly collective responsibility in *Swimming teenagers*,
the same must be true of them. In such cases, the collective result is not pure
coincidence but was reasonably foreseeable by each contributing to it. The
discussion, below, of the avoidability condition should reinforce this point.

The second objection centres on my inclusion of overdetermination cases.
Fulfilment of the weakly collective duty defended requires the should-be
collectivity to become an actual collectivity, acting formally or informally
together to bring about the overall result of preventing the harm. This will
in turn require something of each of its members. Correlative moral duties
are thus assigned to individuals at two levels: duties to play one's part in
collective action to prevent the harm, and duties in the absence of such collective action. (The primary latter such duty, I will argue in Part Three, is a
duty to promote the necessary collective action.) The objection at this stage
is: If what an individual did made no difference, why should she have any
moral duties in connection to it, at all?

The quick response is that she acquires such duties as a member of the relevant set: the potential collectivity. She may not be personally responsible,
but she is one of those collectively so. Thus, she acquires individual correlative duties in the same way as members of a harming corporation would do
so even if their individual actions had, as it happened, made no difference.
However, the objector could retaliate by asking why, if the individual's actions
have made no perceptible difference, she should count as a member of this
weakly defined group—this potential collectivity—at all.

One reply is that any one of the individuals was similarly unnecessary. Thus,
it would be arbitrary and unfair to identify the harming group as all acting in
that way less one specific individual. This draws on Liam Murphy's account of
morality as a collective project: the 'natural thought...that it is objectionable
to expect agents to take up the slack caused by the non-compliance of others'.[31] However, the individual might retort that she is not expecting any such
objectionable unfairness, because she does not think any of the others should
be held accountable either: she considers it impossible to identify a 'potential
collectivity' responsible for the harm.

In response, recall the third part of the three-part condition above: the
collective avoidability requirement. Another way of phrasing the objection
just made is that, in overdetermination cases, the harm could have been
avoided had only most of those held weakly collectively responsible acted

otherwise. Thus, any one individual can correctly claim that it could have been avoided without her changing her own behaviour, so long as enough others did so.

However, it can also correctly be observed that, given her membership of the potential collectivity, each individual *is* a member of some substantial subset(s) which could avoid the harm.[32] In parallel with *Beach rescue*, the members of the potential collectivity are potential members of the harm-avoiding subset. The potential collectivity is identified as the locus of responsibility, even though there are many different subsets which could in fact have prevented the harm. However, the combination of this clause with the other elements of the condition (specifying that the harm results predictably from the combined actions of the set of individuals) takes us out of the realm of positive and into that of negative responsibility.

Consider the following:

Footbridge 6
As in *Footbridge 5* except there are three people approaching the bridge. We all step onto it at the same time.

Suppose the three of us were to pick ourselves up and go on our way, leaving the struggling children behind us, each of us claiming: 'Well, it wasn't *my* fault.' If the children were old enough to do so, they could legitimately call after us: 'You got us into this mess. Now get us out of it.' Filled out, this would amount to the following: 'You all knew what would happen if you all stepped onto the bridge, you saw the signs in time to decide to do otherwise. Any two of you could have prevented the harm—the harm you brought about between you—by waiting a couple of minutes. But you didn't wait: you [plural] went right ahead and broke the bridge. This gives us a special claim on you, over and above the claim we would have on any other set of individuals who could save us from this situation.'

The third objection is as follows. In scenarios such as *Footbridge 1–6*, the boundaries of the potential collectivity are clearly defined. In many other cases, however, contribution to harm does not involve some all-or-nothing action, such as stepping onto the bridge. Rather, it is a matter of doing too much or too little of something. Climate change is such a case. So, insofar as it is the individuals splashing too much rather than their being in the water at all that puts the child at risk, is *Swimming teenagers*. But then an account is owed of where to draw the line of membership. If there is no appropriate cut-off point for inclusion as one of those collectively responsible, people whose contributions are comparatively tiny could become members of potential collectivities held weakly collectively responsible for hugely significant harms. At the extreme, they could become so merely by existing. A member of a South American rainforest tribe with minimal carbon footprint would be a member of the potential collectivity responsible for environmental harm;

someone quietly doing his hydrotherapy stretches at one end of the lake would be among those weakly collectively responsible for harm to the child.[33]

I suggest that a person becomes one of the group weakly collectively responsible for harm once her contribution exceeds the amount such that, were everyone contributing only to that level, there would be no harm.[34] This builds on a familiar idea: that the 'cause' of a harm picked out in discussions of responsibility includes not all the actions and events necessary for that harm, but rather the one or two which stand out. As Joel Feinberg puts it:

> A surprising or unusual event has occurred which is a deviation from what is understood to be the normal course of things...We ask what caused the surprising event and expect an explanation that will cite a factor normally present but absent this time, or normally absent but present this time that made the difference.[35]

Consider, for example, the following:

Footbridge 7
The case is as above except the bridge can hold up to four people of an average weight of 70kg. Four people are approaching the bridge and all know this. Each of us can tell by looking at the others that we each have body-weight around or a little below the average. We all step onto the bridge. However, I am carrying a 30kg rucksack. This pushes our combined weight above the limit. The bridge breaks and the children are harmed.

As in the previous cases, the harm results from the combination of my total weight and the weights of you and the other two people, as well as various other factors relating to the bridge being in its state of disrepair in the first place. Nonetheless, there is something about my carrying the rucksack, and so contributing this additional weight, which makes me specially responsible. My carrying the rucksack, to paraphrase Feinberg, is what is 'different this time': it is the 'unusual cause [that] accounts for this unusual result'.[36] Thus, other things being equal, the moral responsibility for this foreseeable harm lies with me.

Now consider:

Footbridge 8
The situation is as in *Footbridge 7* except that you and I are both carrying 20kg rucksacks and each of the two of us knows this.

Combining the reasoning behind attribution of responsibility in *Footbridge* 5 and 7, you and I are weakly collectively responsible for the harm. The additional trigger, or unusual cause, is the combination of our actions, and this meets the twofold predictability condition.

Footbridge 9
As in *Footbridge 8* except that you, I, and one other person are each carrying 15kg rucksacks.

Building on the discussion of *Footbridge 6*, although only two such rucksacks are needed to bring the weight above the limit, the three of us (and not the fourth person) are morally (weakly collectively) responsible for the predictable, preventable harm. It is in precisely the same way, I suggest, that Polluters are weakly collectively responsible for environmental harm. Section (iv) will fill this out.

Firstly, however, having defended this expanded notion of negative moral responsibility, we can turn to the question of duties. Recall the first of the two moral principles taken as starting assumptions in Chapter One: the no-harm principle. This assigns each moral agent an individual duty not to cause foreseeable and reasonably avoidable serious harm. Given the possibility of weakly collective responsibility for just such serious harms, we are in a position to collectivize this.

> *Collectivized no-harm principle*
> A set of human beings have a moral duty to organize themselves as necessary to prevent serious harm (deprivation of fundamental interests) to another human being or human beings resulting from the predictable aggregation of their avoidable individual acts.[37]

'Predictable' is used in the same twofold sense here as in the threefold condition for weakly collective responsibility: it is predictable to the individuals both that the actions in combination will cause the harm, and that others are relevantly similarly motivated to act. 'Avoidable' is taken as requiring that the agents have alternative actions available to them which would not deprive them of fundamental interests. As Chapter One discussed, there is also generally a secondary duty to compensate (or attempt to make it up to the victims) in cases of failure to abide by the no-harm principle.

(IV) CLIMATE CHANGE AND COLLECTIVE HARM

Section (iii) having defended the notion of weakly collective harm, this section applies it to the climate change case. Firstly, however, I must respond to a more general objection to those raised above.

On this objection, which is a wider version of that dismissed in section (ii), we go too far in applying concepts of moral responsibility to cases such as climate change: the notion of negative responsibility simply loses its moral traction. According to Dale Jamieson, much of what is distinctively 'moral' disappears in the move from paradigm cases of harm, such as Jack stealing Jill's bicycle, to those where there is great distance (in space or time) between victims and agents, where the latter are no longer so clearly identifiable, and where many moral agents are involved.[38]

There is more than one way to respond to this. According to Jamieson: 'The view that morality is involved is weaker still, perhaps disappearing altogether for some people, if we vary the case on all these dimensions [time, distance, number of agents, etc.] at once.'[39] What is hardest to deny in this is that we are generally less morally motivated to adjust our behaviour in the face of such harms. However, following Stephen Gardiner and recalling section (ii), we can again point out that our actual behaviour does not necessarily track our moral convictions.[40]

Secondly, it is not clear that changing most of the factors highlighted by Jamieson would absolve perpetrators of harms—especially severe harms—from general moral condemnation. The harm principle does not limit itself to cases where the victims are (geographically or temporarily) close to the agent, or to where there is a clearly identifiable victim. Nor is it generally taken to do so. To reinforce this point, consider the following.

Bomb here
For fun, Jake throws a bomb into a shopping centre near his home. Several people are killed.

Bomb there
For fun, Jake packages up a bomb, picks a shopping centre in China at random, and posts it there set to go off on arrival. Several people are killed.

Or, to borrow from Henry Shue, compare:[41]

Landmine now
For fun, Henry plants a landmine on the Fingerlakes Trail which is set to explode next week. Henry knows the trail is in frequent use. The bomb explodes and kills a boy scout.

Landmine later
For fun, Henry plants a landmine on the Fingerlakes Trail which is set to explode in 100 years' time. Henry knows the trail is in frequent use and has no reason to suppose it will cease to be so between now and then. The bomb explodes in 100 years' time and kills a boy scout

All these actions are ruled out by the no-harm principle. What Henry and Jake do is wrong because it is reasonably foreseeable that severe harm will result from their actions. This does not change because they do not know exactly who will be killed. Nor, in *Bomb there*, does the fact that Jake's victims are far away from him render his behaviour morally permissible. Nor, as Shue argues in rather more detail, does the mere fact that the future victim of Henry's landmine has not yet been born permit Henry to perform the act that will, in due course, predictably deprive him of his fundamental interests. Rather, as Shue puts it, it is 'obviously totally wrong for anyone to have a hobby of planting even land-mines that would explode only in the distant future'.[42]

Among the variables identified by Jamieson, what does seem to make a significant difference is the involvement of other agents: the fact that some harms are done not by an individual in isolation, or even by intentionally cooperating with others; the fact that, unlike Jake's, our actions in the climate change case are harmful only in combination with those of others.

However, recalling Chapter One, this is exactly the challenge to which I am responding. It is a reason not to attempt to account for the harm (or the correlative duties) thinking only in terms of individual responsibility, but that does not dictate abandoning the notion of moral responsibility altogether. Rather, it is precisely my motive for moving from individual to weakly collective responsibility. The individual's connection with the harm has changed, but the harm is still being done: it is being caused by that set of individuals taken together. (We might further add that that set, being global, can no longer be straightforwardly considered 'distant' from those harmed.) My aim, accordingly, has been to isolate the possibility of such combined harms, use small-scale examples to consider how our core moral notions most consistently expand to such cases, then come back with this expanded theoretical apparatus to the case of climate change.

Now consider Polluters, which set includes those emitting above the level such that, were all to emit at that level, climate change would be made no worse, and who could avoid so doing without sacrificing a fundamental interest. Recall the three-part condition for weakly collective responsibility, beginning with the two predictability conditions. Although alarming numbers continue to deny it, all but the worst-off emitters can reasonably be expected to be aware of the scientific consensus on anthropocentric climate change.[43] As Chapter One laid out, this consensus is confirmed by reports from respected institutions. Many of these reports are accessible online through the most basic search.[44] Moreover, while not universally reflected by the media, it is acknowledged by those outlets whose content can reasonably claim factual authority: those newspapers, for example, which have come to be known for their higher ratio of accurate reporting to conspiracy theory, of text to headline space, and of both to photographs of minimally clad women.[45] We are also aware of how others live, in the developed and increasingly in the developing world: that they share our tastes for such polluting luxuries as fast transport, holidays in the sun, and out-of-season produce. Finally, on the avoidability condition, these are luxuries. As section (ii) has already pointed out, if all or most of us changed our consumption patterns (and at rather less effort if we did so collectively), the harm could be prevented.

The corresponding weakly collective moral duty is threefold: to mitigate and enable adaptation to climate change, and to compensate where neither is possible. As with section (ii)'s appeal to the collectivized principle of beneficence, mitigation and adaptation are defended as two ways of complying with the no-harm principle: that is, of preventing the harm to the individuals. To illustrate this at the smaller scale, recall *Swimming teenagers*. The weakly collective duty is not to harm the child. If this is not fulfilled by not all splashing about in the water in the first place (mitigation), then it might be by getting the child out once the danger is apparent (adaptation). In repeated cases, it would be necessary to design a collective-level system to make sure either that there were never more than a certain number of swimmers in the water at any one time (mitigation), or that the teenagers could carry on with their actions without the child being harmed (perhaps by sectioning off part of the lake or employing a permanent lifeguard). In the climate change case, as Chapter One has already outlined, both mitigation and adaptation are needed.

As also was outlined in Chapter One, compensation is distinct in that it does not prevent the harm. Rather, it attempts to make up for it in some way. In *Swimming teenagers*, in direct parallel to standard thinking in individual harm cases, if the child was seriously injured and the teenagers were weakly collectively responsible (because the foreseeability and avoidability conditions were met), then the duty would be to attempt to compensate in some way, perhaps by funding medical care. In the climate change case, given the inevitability now of some serious harm, the weakly collective duty assigned to Polluters includes compensation.

(V) PRACTICE AND PRINCIPLE

We are coming to the close of Part One. I have offered a threefold defence of a weakly collective moral duty to tackle global climate change. The Young are required to act together to mitigate climate change insofar as it will impact seriously on them. The Able are required to act to mitigate and enable such adaptation to climate change as will prevent it doing serious harm, no matter when it was caused. Polluters are required to stop worsening climate change, to enable adaptation to that caused (avoidably and predictably) by current generations which cannot now be prevented, and to compensate where harms are now inevitable. These are weakly collective duties of each collectivity or potential collectivity to the victims of climate change.[46]

The Able and Polluters include almost all in the developed world and some in developing countries. The two potential collectivities overlap very substantially. However, The Able excludes those in Polluters whose standard of living is sufficiently low that they could not take on extra burdens or stop polluting without incurring morally significant costs: that is, without serious (albeit temporary) interference with the exercise of a central human functioning. These, obviously, are especially likely to be in the developing world. The Able would also include any 'green rich' individuals whose emissions were too low to be in Polluters but who nonetheless met the conditions for duties of beneficence to apply.

The Young overlaps significantly with The Able but is not a subset of it because some of those with a fundamental interest in tackling climate change are sufficiently badly off not to be in The Able. Obviously, The Able is not a subset of The Young: it includes older generations in the developed world on whom climate change is unlikely to impose serious suffering, as well as those in the developing world for whom mitigation could not now make any significant difference. The Young overlaps with Polluters but is neither a subset of Polluters (many in Polluters are in older generations) nor a set of which Polluters is a subset (the likely victims of climate change include many whose own emissions are minimal).

The three arguments are complementary but largely independent. As I explained in Chapter One, this is theoretically important. To return to the mountaineering analogy, anyone leading a climb is advised to secure herself to the rock by at least two separate, trustworthy belays before entrusting her own or her partner's weight to the rope. In doing the same here, I have endeavoured to build a moral case for collective action on which it is multiply safe to rely in outlining correlative individual duties.

The reader who rejects the incorporation of risk into the capabilities model of human flourishing, on which Chapter Two relied, could not on those grounds reject the twofold argument of this chapter. As Chapter One explained, our fundamental interests in retaining (at least) the opportunity for life, health, bodily integrity, practical reason, and affiliation, could be defended on a much sparser framework: basic needs, including some basic conditions for autonomy. Indeed, so uncontroversially central to human life are the areas undermined by climate change, that even a rational or ideal preference model of flourishing could be substituted throughout this chapter.[47] Unlike Chapter Two, the arguments from collective ability to aid and weakly collective harm do not rely on the more controversial view that something—loss of a central capability—can be contrary to a person's fundamental interest even if she doesn't regard it as such.

The principle of beneficence is a common thread between two of the three arguments (hence the qualified 'largely independent', above). However, there are two senses in which they come apart. Firstly, the minimal collectivized weak principle used in Chapter Two was a much weaker—and harder to reject—version. Secondly, this chapter need not, as Chapter Two did, appeal to overall impact on one's life to determine whether the cost condition is met. Even those who reject the principle of beneficence altogether would be faced with the arguments grounded in the no-harm principle: a moral intuition so strong and so widely shared that it is hard even for the most avid libertarians to deny. On the other hand, those unconvinced by my expansion of the notion of collective responsibility for harm, because they insist that the attribution of negative responsibility requires a single entity to whose intentional action the harm can be traced, could not on those grounds reject the arguments based in collective ability to aid, or the principle of moralized collective self-interest.

If all three arguments are reliable, as I have tried to show that they are, most of the global affluent have two and many have three grounds for taking seriously the demands of weakly collective climate duties. From these, individual duties follow at two levels: those incurred within a fairly allocated collective scheme to tackle climate change; and those incurred by an individual in the absence of collective action. Part Three will address the currently under-considered question of what these latter are. This project will not go into detail on the first: on what a fair distribution of burdens would look like as part of a collective scheme to fulfil a weakly collective duty. Although it is generally couched in terms of states, rather than individuals, there is already an extensive literature on the distribution of burdens in the climate change case.[48] However, the remainder of this section will anticipate and alleviate a practical, related concern: that, in identifying three overlapping but non-identical global-level collectivities or should-be collectivities, each with a different weakly collective duty, I have complicated the picture so as to make it impossible to calculate, never mind achieve, even an approximately fair distribution of burdens.

My response is twofold. Firstly, the fact that it would be complex in practice to calculate an exact division of burdens does not tell against the moral case for assigning the weakly collective duty. There are several steps between moral theory and filled-out policy proposals, in climate ethics as elsewhere.[49] Secondly, a fair collective scheme within each of the three collectivities in the climate change case could reasonably be approximated by one overall global scheme. The appropriate division of duties would, moreover, be broadly in line with the trend of existing philosophical discussion on the fair distribution of burdens.[50] I will sketch my reasons for this view.

Polluters have primary responsibility for ensuring that climate change is not worsened, and for enabling adaptation to, as well as compensating for, the harm for which current generations are responsible. By this I mean that the full weight of complying with this duty falls in the first instance on them.[51] This is in line with the no-harm principle, which is itself the plausible intuition behind the widely defended Polluter Pays Principle.[52] The Able then have a weakly collective duty to prevent or compensate for the rest of the harm, with a duty also to pick up the tab for Polluters if they fail to act.[53]

This leaves two organizational options. One is for the two potential collectivities (which become collectivities when they act together to pursue the morally required end) to act as separate sets, fairly distributing duties within each according to familiar factors such as contribution to harm (for Polluters), cost of compliance, and so on. Most members would, of course, be assigned duties by both. However, a fair distribution of burdens within Polluters is highly unlikely to require net sacrifice by those who are not also in The Able: that is, those for whom such sacrifice would amount to a morally significant cost in the terms of section (ii), so long as there is some alternative scheme under which others bear greater but still not significant burdens.[54] Accordingly, a single collective scheme at the level of The Able could achieve both ends in practice, with the distribution of burdens factoring in the primary responsibility of Polluters for some part of the harm, by assigning greater burdens to those who are members of both sets.

Now factor in The Young. It might be argued that, as those who will reap the advantages of climate change mitigation, they have primary responsibility for bearing its costs. (This does not, of course, apply to the costs of mitigation which will benefit only as-yet unborn future generations.) However, this is clearly implausible when it comes to the harm for which Polluters are responsible. To say that those who are also in The Young should pay more than others in Polluters is to claim that those who have contributed to actions which have also harmed them should be required to pay more to prevent or compensate for that harm (because they would benefit from compensation or prevention) than those who contributed to it but were not themselves harmed. Consider the following.

Chemicals
A group of teenagers recklessly emit dangerous chemicals into a school, impairing the health of students. Some but not all of those teenagers are pupils at the school.

To take seriously the line of argument above would be to require this subset to bear all (or at least more than an otherwise equal share of) the clean-up costs because it is in their own interest that the action be taken. This would be a rather bizarre turning of morality on its head.

With regard to The Able, the situation is less clear-cut. The argument would be, presumably, that to require The Able to pick up the tab for such mitigation as would benefit The Young, when The Young themselves could afford to do so, would be to go unreasonably beyond the demands of the principle of beneficence. Consider the following.

Drowning man 1
A man is drowning and cannot save himself. I could save him, but it would ruin my dress.

Drowning man 2
As in *Drowning man 1* except he could save himself by sacrificing a limb.

Drowning man 3
As in *Drowning man 1* except he could save himself with some considerable effort: he would so exhaust himself that he would have to spend several days in bed.

The principle of beneficence clearly dictates that I save him in the first two cases. In the third, however, a more demanding version of the principle would be needed than that on which this project has drawn. Moreover, it is no longer intuitively so clear that I have a duty, as a bystander, to save him. Can a parallel case be made for the claim that, insofar as those responsible are beyond reach (that is, excluding that harm which Polluters have a negatively grounded duty to clear up), The Young rather than The Able should bear the burden of mitigating climate change, so long as doing so does not itself require any of them incurring serious harm (sacrificing a central capability).[55]

I would resist this claim, while conceding that those in The Able who are also in The Young might fairly be required to bear *some* additional burden. The first reason for resisting the claim is that it relies on a doubly collectivized principle of beneficence: one where the victims—in this case The Young—can be taken as a harmed collectivity to which we owe the duty. (That is, the duty would be to the collectivity rather than to its individual members.) This is not what has been defended here: rather, the weakly collective duty is ultimately a duty (of all) to each harmed individual. The Young and The Able both have a weakly collective duty to each individual in The Young. Moreover, fulfilment of this duty would overlap with some of the actions demanded by duties of The Able to others as-yet unborn. There is no reason why one or the other should automatically be required to incur the full costs of fulfilling *that* duty, any more than two people who have both promised the same thing to a friend should each consider themselves excused because the other has the same duty.

A second reason for resisting the claim is that the principle of beneficence might be more demanding than I have hitherto suggested. It might, for example, extend to the requirement to save others from significant (albeit not serious) harm, if one can do so at only trivial cost to oneself. This would give me a duty to save the victim in *Drowning man 3*, and The Able a duty to spare The Young from the full, heavy cost of preventing the harm to themselves. Thirdly, the collectivized principle of beneficence, in the climate change case, might be supplemented with a more controversial principle on which those who have benefited from past actions which have led to climate change (that is, all those currently living in industrialized nations) have a special duty to bear its burdens because they would otherwise be objectionably free riding.[56]

Whether or not this argument is rejected in theory, however, we are likely in practice to end up with the same overall outcome. Suppose we accepted the view that The Young (in effect, for fairness of distribution within The Young, the subset which overlaps with The Able) have primary responsibility for mitigation of such harm as will seriously affect them and cannot be attributed to Polluters. The Able must then take on the remaining costs. However, those who are also in The Young will now be in a more vulnerable position than those who are not, precisely because of the costs they have already been assigned within that collectivity. Thus, they will be less able to bear additional burdens, and fairness is likely to dictate that they be allocated a smaller share of the costs of fulfilling *this* collective duty.

On the other hand, if it is accepted that others in The Able share the duty of preventing harm to The Young, and The Young are treated as a subset in this overall collective scheme, the fact that they benefit from the scheme will mitigate against any burdens they are required to bear, affecting the net cost of compliance the other way, and so making a case for them to take on some additional costs. Either way, a situation is reached in which some additional burdens (but not the whole burden) are assigned to those in The Able who will benefit from climate change mitigation.

CONCLUSIONS

This chapter has presented the second and third arguments for the weakly collective duty to act on climate change: a duty grounded in collective ability to aid requiring The Able to act on mitigation and adaptation; and a duty grounded in weakly collective responsibility for harm requiring Polluters to act on mitigation, adaptation, and compensation.

I have also indicated that all three weakly collective duties could be fulfilled in practice via one collective scheme at the level of The Able. This collective scheme, moreover, fits established lines of thought on the fairness of balancing ability to pay and polluter-pays considerations in distributing the burdens of tackling climate change. Naturally, the individual focus will necessitate some revision to the theoretical debate on the fair distribution of climate burdens, which is often couched in terms of states. However, it will be by no means necessary to start again from scratch.

Rather, these chapters have plugged a key moral gap—expanding moral thought to establish the case for taking action in the first place—and, I hope, enabled the debate to continue from a firmer footing. Parts Three and Four will turn to further theoretical gaps: what the individual's primary moral duty is as things currently stand, and the predicament each is left in, as a moral agent, by continued collective failure. Firstly, however, I wish to consider how the model just defended might expand to accommodate moral duties to non-human animals, and acknowledge the further complications therein encountered.

Part 2

Pushing the Boundaries
Duties to whom?

4

Harming and Protecting Non-Humans

What else is it that should trace the insuperable line? Is it the faculty
of reason, or perhaps, the faculty for discourse?...[T]he question is not,
Can they reason? nor, Can they talk? but, Can they suffer?...The time
will come when humanity will extend its mantle over everything which
breathes.[1]

Jeremy Bentham

[G]iven the likely planetary effects of climate change, one might also
expect to find a third area of ethical debate: questions about the impact
of climate change on the nonhuman world directly. But on this subject,
very little has so far been said.[2]

Clare Palmer

Let us begin with some obvious points. Firstly, sentient non-human animals can flourish or not flourish.[3] Like ours, their lives can go well or badly.
They can, to some degree, experience them as doing so. At the very least,
as Bentham has it, they can suffer: they can feel pain and there is reason to
believe that some adult mammals experience such aversive states as fear or
desire.[4] Correspondingly, they can be said to have certain fundamental interests of their own. What exactly these are—and the extent to which they vary
across species—remains very much a matter for debate, but they include bodily health (or at least avoiding severely painful physical suffering) and some
freedom of movement.[5]

Ecosystems and species might also be said to have interests, but their flourishing is of a different kind. There is a sense in which an ecosystem, with its
many interconnected functionings, has integrity.[6] However, it is harder to
extend to it that notion of dignity widely considered central to the moral significance of individuals. Nor can it be claimed that a species or ecosystem
suffers in the experiential sense that sentient beings suffer.

Secondly, it is not only humans who are or will be affected by climate change. According to the International Panel on Climate Change (IPCC), it is likely that climate change and such connected disturbances as flooding or drought will break down the resilience of many ecosystems within this century. The 2007 Report states with medium confidence that some 20 to 30 per cent of plant and animal species are at greater risk of extinction if global average temperature increases by more than 1.5–2.5°C.[7] The Stern Review warns of '15 to 40% of species potentially facing extinction after even 2°C of warming' and of 'major effects' of ocean acidification on marine ecosystems.[8]

Associated individual deprivations can be inferred. Barring a one-off meteor-strike, a species is not eliminated without prolonged suffering by individual animals. If polar bears, mountain gorillas, or Asian elephants face habitat and prey decline, beneath this headline loss lie countless instances of individual starvation and diseases associated with inadequate diet.[9] If human societies suffer food loss or extreme weather conditions, domesticated non-human animals, generally bottom of the list for aid, will suffer some of the harshest effects.

With this in mind, recall Part One, which defended weakly collective duties to act on climate change adaptation, mitigation, and compensation. (To reiterate, the 'weakly' qualified only the sense in which the duty was collective, not its moral salience: fulfilment would require a number of individuals to organize to achieve the required end.) I offered three largely independent but complementary arguments, appealing to: moralized collective self-interest, via a non-intentionalist account of what it means for a collection of individuals to constitute a collectivity; collective ability to aid; and weakly collective responsibility for harm. These gained their moral force from the impact of anthropogenic climate change on the fundamental interests of those least controversial of all moral subjects, individual human beings.

This leaves us with two interesting possibilities. The first is that of non-intentionalist collectivities whose members include non-humans. The second is that at least some non-human individuals, perhaps even species or systems, are moral subjects: that their suffering or deprivation, like ours, matters, and that we have climate duties not only to each other but also to them. This chapter explores these possibilities.

Section (i) expands the non-intentionalist model to include at least sentient non-human animals as members of collectivities. The remainder of the chapter considers expanding the no-harm principle and the principle of beneficence beyond the human, in general terms and in the context of climate change. I begin with the philosophically compelling idea that both should be expanded to include individual, sentient non-humans. However, the highly problematic implications of this move, taken in isolation, force a further one: either the more contested expansion of interests-based duties further still (to species and systems), or the acknowledgement of differently derived, but at least as compelling, duties to protect them. This is so in general terms (sections (ii) and (iii)) but even more so in the climate change case. Exploring this possibility in the light of the arguments of Part One (sections (iv) and (v)), we are left, in the end, with a set of conflicting reasons for collective action, all of which are either morally salient or salient in some other, incommensurate, way. Because we should (more than ever) undoubtedly do *something* but we cannot now do *everything*, we will need a way either of defending some hierarchy of moral significance, or of trading off incompatible ends against each other.

(I) NON-HUMAN COLLECTIVITIES

The non-intentionalist model, defended in Chapter Two, made the following claim:

> A set of individuals constitutes a collectivity if and only if those individuals are mutually dependent for the achievement or satisfaction of some common or shared purpose, goal or fundamental interest, whether or not they acknowledge it themselves.

A broad understanding of 'common or shared' allowed for both genuinely shared goals—two or more persons committed to doing something together—and individual goals, purposes, or fundamental interests which could only be secured together. Chapter Two further argued that at least younger generations of humans count as members of a 'collectivity of humanity', sharing a fundamental interest in climate change mitigation. Drawing on the possibility of a broader, largely passive, collectivity with the potential for an active subset, it allowed for expansion to include future generations.

This model lends itself to the inclusion of non-humans, all the more so since it was defended against traditional, intentionalist accounts in part on the basis of its ability to include what Peter Singer might call 'marginal case' humans: infants and those with severe intellectual disabilities.[10] It could account both for collectivities entirely composed of non-humans, and for those including both humans and non-humans. Given the current focus on the potential moral duties of co-members of certain collectivities—a question which can arise only if at least some of those members are moral agents—I am primarily concerned with the latter. However, for completeness, I will briefly expand on the former.

Non-human animals are often mutually dependent for the achievement of some purpose or fundamental interest. A community of chimpanzees is mutually dependent in much the same way as a community or family of human beings: irrespective of the (still debated) extent to which they can formulate and share intentions, individuals rely on one another for the fulfilment of basic needs or interests. Moreover, sets of sentient, non-human animals can meet the three criteria for collectivityhood cited in Chapter Two.

Consider a pack of hyenas stalking a lion.[11] Indefinitely many combinations of individual action could lead to the same outcome at group level, so the collectivity does something distinct from what its individual members do. Because no hyena achieves the collective end except as one of these coordinating actors, there is a sense in which the significance of what each does cannot be brought out without reference to his part in the collectivity. Moreover, the collectivity would remain if an individual fell behind and left the others, while another joined them, so the collectivity can survive changes in membership.[12]

Turning to the second possibility, there are many ways in which we depend on our interactions with non-humans. As Cynthia Townley puts it, '[a]nimals can and do make important cooperative contributions to human cultures and societies, to our general and personal well-being'.[13] However, it is important to be clear. Our relying on non-human animals is not enough to make us-and-them a collectivity. Nor would the arbitrary decision of humans to 'count' some non-humans as members be sufficient. Recall Chapter Two's example of the family. The baby, or the person with severe intellectual disabilities, counts as a member not simply because the rest of the family decide that she is so. (If that were so, what is to stop them arbitrarily assigning membership to anyone, however distant or unwilling?) She is a member because of mutual dependence: a positive family atmosphere is in all of their interests, including hers.

There are parallel cases involving non-human animals. Consider the family cat. Even if she cannot formulate and share goals, a secure family life—one of mutual well-being—is in her interest, and it can be part of the shared goals of the others in the collectivity that her life go well. Moreover, this collectivity can satisfy the three conditions, above. As with the all-human family, what it 'does' is nebulously defined, but there is a sense in which the household, through various interactions, achieves a smooth-running, mutually contented communal life. Moreover, it is only in the context of this pattern of relations that certain actions of members make sense: for example, a cat-owner's decision to buy a house well back from the road. Children could grow up and leave, or further animals be introduced, and the collectivity remain.

At a broader level, some economic ties between humans and non-humans are sufficient for them to constitute collectivities: some sustainably run or organic farms, for example, where animal flourishing is a component of the farmer's goals.[14] However, this does not extend to all such relationships. Unless a convincing case can be made for its being in his interest to improve their welfare, the factory farmer and the animals unfortunate enough to be farmed by him do not constitute a collectivity, any more than the playground bully constitutes a collectivity with his victims. He may depend on them for his own selfish ends, but neither the relationship nor the fulfilment of those ends is in their interest.[15]

Collectivities need not be restricted to cases where it is part of (or necessary to) the goal of the human members that the non-humans' interests be satisfied. They might be mutually dependent through the fundamental interests of each. Consider an area of rainforest threatened by loggers, which includes both an indigenous tribe and many non-human animals. Preserving the rainforest is a common interest in the same way that the goal of equal rights for women is common to all women: it is an end which, if achieved, is achieved for all within that society or state, even if it is actively pursued by only a subset.[16] This is so regardless of whether the tribe members care directly about the survival of the non-human animals.

In obvious analogy with this, the 'collectivity of humanity' bound by a mutual fundamental interest in climate change mitigation might be expanded to include at least some sentient non-human animals. However, this is less straightforward than it might seem. Certainly, as I began by pointing out, climate change will undermine the fundamental interests of very many sentient non-humans. However, as acknowledged in Chapter Two with respect to humans, the fact that it will undermine many of our fundamental interests does not guarantee that the positive effects of action to mitigate it (which have a forty-year-plus timescale) would come soon enough to secure them.[17] Most non-human animals have considerably shorter lifespans than ours.

Thus, the set of those individuals with a fundamental interest in climate change mitigation may not include the majority of individual sentient non-humans alive today. However, again in parallel with Chapter Two, it might be extended to include at least some future sentient non-humans. These, along with future and younger generations of humans, would then constitute a largely passive collectivity, with current younger generations of humans potentially an active subset.

This 'some' is an important caveat. As Clare Palmer argues, individual members of some species might flourish better in a warmer world.[18] The chances are that being a polar bear in 2060 will involve greater deprivation than would have been the case had we acted more effectively on climate change. But being (say) a brown rat could involve *less* deprivation. This does not affect the case for collectivityhood, where the collectivity includes only those future non-humans who do suffer such deprivations as a result of climate change. However, it could affect attempts to defend climate change mitigation on the basis of collective ability to aid (or even not to harm) individual non-human animals. I will return to this in section (iv).

I have one more possibility to raise before moving on, based on the more controversial notion (to which I will return in section (ii)) that species and ecosystems have fundamental interests in a relevantly similar way to us. This could mean extending the notion of collectivityhood still further. Given that so many non-human species and ecosystems are threatened by climate change, this would certainly make the expansion of the collective self-interest argument section (v) easier. Moreover, it is in many ways an attractive idea: the systems of the natural world are built up around interdependence. Moreover, ecological ethics, such as that defended by Aldo Leopold, revolve around the idea of our interdependence with non-human life in general.[19]

I do not rule this out. However, I have reservations, and will not attempt any such move here. It would take the notion of the collectivity well beyond the sense in which it is understood in the philosophy of social science debate with which Chapter Two engaged. Whether human or non-human, the assumption so far has been that members of collectivities are bound by interests and experiences that are in a recognizable sense interests and experiences *for them*: that they, in other words, are in some way aware of experiencing.

For now, I return to the realm of the sentient, for whom the expansion both of the non-intentionalist model and of moral concern seems most obvious, and will embark on the latter task.

(II) HARM, BENEFICENCE, AND NON-HUMAN ANIMALS

There are at least two strong reasons for extending the no-harm principle and the principles of beneficence to non-human animals: not, of course, as duty-bearers, but as moral subjects to whom such duties are owed. One is specific to the interests-based framework of this book; the other is more general.

We have much in common with non-human animals, as I stressed in opening this chapter: a capacity for both dignity and suffering, a potential to thrive—and experience that thriving—in various central ways. Indeed, on the relatively uncontroversial model adopted in Chapter One—of the moral significance of individual human flourishing and of certain central interests or capabilities as prerequisites of such flourishing—it seems so natural as to be unavoidable to extend moral concern to sentient non-human individuals.[20] However, even outside this particular philosophical approach, it has proved all but impossible to pick out some feature shared by all human beings that would entitle them to equal moral status without also entitling at least some non-humans to the same. In Jeff McMahan's terminology, these are, respectively, the 'equality problem' and the 'separation problem'.[21] The bar, in terms of intelligence, consciousness, or some other capacity, has to be set low enough to include human infants and those with severe intellectual disabilities, without including any adult non-human mammal. The claim that this is indeed impossible is made by Singer as the argument from marginal cases.[22]

Implicitly acknowledging this, separationists (as we might call them) have focused instead on the relational component of our moral concern. In the wonderfully titled 'Eating Meat and Eating People', Cora Diamond points out that our reluctance to treat other humans in certain ways can't be reduced to a reluctance to harm them.[23] If it were, we might be willing to eat humans who have died by accident. But of course we find the very idea repellent.

A number of recent relational accounts have tried to distinguish between our duties to one another and to non-humans by appeal either to the kind of interaction we have with all other humans or to a certain necessary dependence.[24] However, these tend to reject only positive duties to non-human animals, rather than deny duties not to harm them in certain central ways. This is an important point for present purposes. Moreover, difficulties arise even in this relational context. As Townley argues, we have ties of communication as well as economic and familial links with non-humans, and it is not clear that individuals do necessarily depend primarily on others of their own species.[25] So recalcitrant are such obstacles that we might reasonably doubt, with McMahan, whether the equality and separation arguments can ever simultaneously be solved.[26]

As this summary suggests, there are strong reasons to accept that we have moral duties not to undermine, and if possible to protect, the fundamental interests of sentient individual non-humans. (I should stress, however, that this chapter is concerned with exploring the implications of this natural move, rather than with offering a comprehensive defence of a point already covered extensively by others.) It might seem tempting to stop here: to quit while we're ahead, or at least while we are still in the space of intuitive plausibility and philosophical consistency with the two moral principles taken as read at the human level.

However, unfortunately for this strategy, intuitive plausibility pulls both ways. Exploring the implications of extending these principles to individual non-human animals, without also acknowledging some duties to (or at least regarding) species or ecosystems, we come up against consequences about which many have intuitions every bit as strong, but in the opposite direction. In other words, we will either have to swallow some repugnant consequences, or not only return to the problem of marginal cases but also stretch the sphere of moral concern further still. (The results will be equally counterintuitive if we cannot find some way to justify prioritizing some *human* over individual non-human interests. On this latter, however, it is at least arguable that our intuitions should be taken with a pinch of salt: being humans, we may be biased.)

Let us consider the two collectivized principles (no-harm and beneficence) in turn.

Collectivized no-harm principle
A set of human beings (moral agents) have a moral duty to organize themselves as necessary to prevent serious harm (deprivation of fundamental interests) to another human being or human beings (moral subject(s)) resulting from the predictable aggregation of their avoidable individual acts.

Predictability, recall, is twofold: it is reasonably foreseeable to the individuals both that the actions in combination will cause the harm, and that others are relevantly similarly motivated to act. 'Avoidable' is taken as requiring that the agents have alternative actions available to them which would not deprive them of fundamental interests.

As with individual or strongly collective versions of this principle, extending it to sentient non-humans would demand wholesale change in current behaviour and institutions. Much of the suffering imposed on non-humans is unnecessary to secure our own fundamental interests.[27] Indeed, in some instances the reverse is true. For example, widespread factory farming worsens climate change, damages human health through excessive meat consumption, and undermines animal welfare. However, there are some cases, notably medical testing, where some animal suffering (although almost certainly considerably less than is currently imposed) can be necessary to securing a fundamental human interest.[28] Faced with these, there are two alternatives. One is to appeal to the same reasoning generally used in applying individual or strongly collective versions of the no-harm principle in the human case, where it is taken to trump the principle of beneficence. Then we could simply rule out any such testing. To avoid this conclusion, it would be necessary to argue for the priority of at least some positive duties to humans over negative duties to non-humans. Quite apart from its other difficulties, this would necessitate a return to the problem of marginal cases.[29] However, I will not make this point in detail here, since it arises at a much wider level in the context of climate change.

Now recall the two forms of the collectivized principle of beneficence.

Collectivized weak principle of beneficence
A set of human beings (moral agents) have a duty to cooperate to prevent the serious suffering of another human being or human beings (moral subject(s)) if they can do so at minimal cost to each.

Collectivized moderate principle of beneficence
A set of human beings (moral agents) have a duty to cooperate to prevent the serious suffering of another human being or human beings (moral subject(s)) if they can do so at less than significant cost to each.

'Serious suffering' was read relatively conservatively as including the permanent loss of some fundamental interest: the opportunity or capability for continued life, bodily health, bodily integrity, practical reason, or affiliation. 'Significant' was filled out, as a placeholder, as involving serious (even if temporary) disruption to the exercise of such a central human functioning. (For example, suffering a debilitating but short-lived ailment, or being required to delay one's education by a year.)

Extending these to sentient non-human animals, we face a dilemma. The principles of beneficence, as they stand, demand action to prevent serious human suffering whatever the cause, or at least so long as it isn't the sufferer's own fault. Recall the following from Chapter Two.[30]

Easy rescue 1
On his way to work, Peter passes a pond in which a child is drowning. He could easily stop and save the child, although it would slightly damage his clothes to do so.

Whether the drowning child fell in by accident or was thrown in by a fortune-hunting uncle, Peter should pull him out. He should do so even if the child was chased into the pond by a wild boar.

Correspondingly, subject to the cost condition, we would have a weakly collective duty to prevent the serious suffering of non-human animals not only when it results from human negligence or cruelty, or natural disaster, but also if it is inflicted by other non-human animals. Consistent application of the collectivized principle could demand constant intervention between prey and predator. As Nussbaum—who comes close to biting the bullet on this—puts it, we could have a duty 'to police the animal world'.[31] She suggests corralling predators, and painless extermination to control prey numbers.

Thus, a step hard to resist in itself (from the moral significance of fundamental human interests to that of at least some comparable non-human interests) has taken us to a wildly counterintuitive conclusion. There are four possible ways out.

One is to reject the principle of beneficence for non-human animals altogether. That is not to say that we must deny any positive duties to non-humans. Rather, in line with some of the most recent accounts, duties of some humans to some non-humans would be defended by appeal to specific relationships between them, and these would include strong positive duties to domesticated animals.[32] Section (i)'s expansion of the non-intentionalist model of collectivities would be a first step.

This is a tempting way out, but it is hard to defend given the relatively uncontroversial starting point of this monograph. The principle of beneficence to humans, taken as a duty of any human moral agent to any other human being, is by no means thus curtailed. Moreover, the interests-based flourishing model serves to emphasize commonality between humans and at least some other animals. To defend maintaining the principle for (all) humans and rejecting it for (all) non-humans, one would, again, have to resolve both the separation and equality problems.

The second alternative is to acknowledge the prima facie case for a positive duty to intervene, but avoid actually defending such a policy in one of two ways.[33] We might argue that fulfilling the duty would do more harm than good: it is either impossible (by the nature of predator flourishing) or too costly, so it is not required in practice.[34] To justify this move to weighting interests across individual animals, we would have to explain that in moving beyond the human we had entered a realm in which the potential claims of moral subjects outweighed the ability of moral agents even collectively to fulfil them. It thus becomes necessary to find a way of deciding between them. Such sum ranking might then be defended as the least unfair way. This has some appeal, but remains intuitively very discomforting, since it would only be our inability to do so (or do so at non-significant cost) that stood between us and a moral duty to sanitize the natural world.

An intuitively compelling version of this strategy points to the dependency of individual animals on those very systems within which many of them suffer. If (say) the gazelle would not be living that kind of life at all, if it weren't for the complex set of interconnections within which tigers regularly eat gazelles, then this might be used as a reason not now to interfere to save it. This would be a reason grounded in the interests of the individual gazelle.

This, however, rests on a misunderstanding. The fact that an individual's very existence (and so possibility of flourishing) depends on a certain system having been developed and maintained up until now, does not make it in his fundamental interest, now, to do or suffer whatever is best for the system. Consider a human analogy.

Bob and his state
A citizen of a state, Bob, has benefited from its policies, which give him the opportunity for a full, flourishing life. A more powerful state, with more (although not unbearably) restrictive policies, is attempting to seize sovereignty. While Bob's state might be able to defend itself successfully, this would cost the lives or health of almost all its young men and women, and certainly those who, like Bob, are physically rather weak.

It can be simultaneously true that the preservation of his state until now has been a precondition for the kind of life Bob leads, and that it would not now be in his best interest, as an individual, that it be defended.[35]

It is similarly problematic to appeal to the fundamental interests of current individual non-humans to reject 'policing nature' policies, especially if we were to accept the view that death itself (as opposed to painful death) is not the same kind of fundamental interest loss as it is for humans.[36] Moreover, to anticipate section (iv) and recall Chapter One, we cannot assume that individual, not-yet-existing animals have a fundamental interest *in coming into existence and flourishing*, rather than simply in enjoying various central capabilities or basic needs if they happen to exist. Thus, while apparently appealing to individual animal interests, this response actually draws on the view that it is valuable that there continue to be flourishing animals, and so (as a prerequisite for this) assigns significance to preserving species or systems.

Alternatively, we might appeal to human interests. In general terms, it is obvious that humans rely on maintaining ecosystems: we are part of many of them.[37] As was discussed in Chapter Two, some environmental protection is needed to secure fundamental human interests. Attempts have been made to expand Nussbaum's list to include a specific environmental capability or meta-capability, while in environmental ethics Bryan Norton has highlighted the importance of diversity for human productivity.[38] However, it is a far cry from this to the claim that protecting every species or ecosystem is necessary to securing human interests. Even allowing Nussbaum's other species as a fundamental human interest—which itself goes beyond anything in Chapter One—a further argument would be needed to show that all intervention to protect prey from predator would be bad *for us*.[39] Even aside from this, such contingency is, again, disturbing.

The third response is to curtail the collectivized principle of beneficence. This could take two forms. One would demand assistance only if the suffering resulted from human action, whether past or present, individual, collective, or weakly collective; the other in all cases where the suffering wasn't caused by other non-human animals.[40] The boundaries are, in any case, blurred by climate change, which raises questions as to which—if any—weather events can now truly be considered 'natural'. Building on Chapters Two and Three, fulfilling even this weakly collective duty might require establishing institutions to protect animals from such harms.

Note that this does not simply collapse into the weakly collective harm argument, as the potential collectivity assigned the duty is not negatively weakly collectively responsible for all the harm. However, by the same token, it could be difficult to defend. Both versions of this suggestion take us a long way from our relatively uncontroversial starting point: the moral 'badness' of individuals being deprived of fundamental interests, because of the moral significance of individual lives going well. The suffering is, after all, just as bad for the individual animal regardless of what imposes it. To meet this challenge it would be necessary to do two things. One is to explain why being harmed by some human, aggregation of humans, or human institution is sufficient to put an animal in a relationship with any other human such that the human has a positive duty to aid the animal if she can at reasonable cost to herself. The other is—again—to explain why our duties to other humans are not limited in this way. (That is, to resolve the problem of marginal cases.)

In any case, not one of these three responses has got at what is really behind the negative intuitive response to Nussbaum's proposal of 'policing nature'. That is, that such a policy is in fundamental conflict with something else often held to have significance: not destroying species or ecosystems. This brings us to the fourth response, below.

(III) HARMING AND PROTECTING SPECIES
AND SYSTEMS

Even before we consider climate change, expanding our model beyond the human has (to borrow Stephen Gardiner's terminology) yielded something of a 'theoretical storm'.[41] We not only lack robust moral theories: we also lack clear starting principles like those taken as read in relation to humans in Chapter One. Instead, on the one hand, we have the philosophical consistency of extending these principles to individual sentient non-humans. On the other, we have some fairly strong intuitions against which we can test these expanded principles. Unfortunately, section (ii) put the former into sharp conflict with the latter. Accordingly, we are pushed into going further still.

This could be done in two ways. One option is further to expand the interests- or capabilities-based flourishing model. The other is to appeal to some other reason to preserve species and systems, independent of but powerful enough to count against those two moral principles.

I will begin with the first option, by drawing extensively on David Schlosberg.[42] He argues that it is arbitrary to draw the line at sentient individuals. Systems and species also have interests and can be harmed, and this is of moral significance. Systems, he argues, are 'living entities with their own integrity; atomising nature into isolated animals devalues a form of life, and the way that this form of life flourishes'.[43] Consider his example of a river system.

> Water, a primary good, is increasingly taken from the river for agricultural and urban use. The effect is a serious impingement on the functionings of the river—to support fish species and native flora, or to supply silt to beaches that support other wildlife on the riverside.[44]

At species level, prey and predator flourish in interconnection with one another. Predation, maintaining numbers at levels suitable for flourishing in that habitat, is necessary for both.[45]

However, there remains at least one significant challenge for this approach, and two objections. The challenge is this. Ecosystems are constantly evolving, in themselves and in interaction with humans. While we also do a great deal of damage, at least a part of this latter interaction is positive. Many systems evolve successfully, or even come into existence, in response to our actions. At the extreme, ecosystems can develop even on landfills. More generally, many areas now heralded as sites of great biodiversity would not be as they are without the influence of centuries of human agriculture.

The point is not that proposals such as Schlosberg's are unaware of this, or are appealing to some fixed set of interests (some notion of the system 'as it is now') to justify attempting to hold time still, or separate humans artificially from nature. Quite the reverse. There is no contradiction, as Schlosberg himself points out, 'between growth, change, evolution, or diverse paths on the one hand, and the telos and integrity of a system on the other'.[46] The notion of humans as simply one part of a wider natural system is central not only to Schlosberg's approach, but also to much of the environmental ethics on which he draws.[47] Rather, the point is a practical one: the challenge is to provide an account of the central functionings of ecosystems which could adequately capture this scope for evolution (whether human-initiated or not), whilst picking out as impermissible some human interactions with systems. We need a way to criticize the dam which threatens the central functionings of Schlosberg's river ecosystem, without dismissing as 'maimed' or unnatural all systems which have been significantly influenced by humans.

If Schlosberg is right, this challenge can be met: by drawing on a combination of ecological science, sympathetic imagining, and traditional knowledge to produce a sensitive, filled-out account.[48] However, should the line prove too fine to walk in this way, another possibility would be to focus not on preserving (or at least not harming) ecosystems themselves, but something else, such as populations within species.[49] The claim then would not necessarily be that populations themselves have ultimate moral value. It could be that their survival is the best 'hallmark' of whether the flourishing of the system—or species—has been undermined.

There is, then, reason to be optimistic that this challenge could be met. However, the first objection is more fundamental. This expansion of the interests- or capabilities-based model has taken us a very long way from the relatively uncontroversial claims with which we began. This chapter began from the commonality of human and non-human individuals. (It has been taken as read throughout that humans are moral subjects.) However, as we move beyond the sentient, and beyond individuals, any common ground starts to look rather thin.

Certainly, something bad is done to Schlosberg's river system, but in what sense is it bad *for it* that the water is removed? Schlosberg may have shown that this is a sense different from that in which (say) two extremely cold winters in a row were bad for Edinburgh's roads, but that in itself does not render it morally comparable with the sense in which it is bad for an individual seal (or person) to be choked by oil. (It is not even clear that it is bad for the system in the teleological sense often appealed to in ecological ethics: the sense—to which I will return below—in which it is bad for a plant to be cut down because it has a biological interest in fulfilling its potential as a plant.[50]) Rather, with the appeal to interconnectedness, it looks closer to the sense in which it is bad for an Edinburgh ice-cream business when Scotland has yet another wet summer. But nothing has been said here to defend the moral significance, *in themselves*, of the interests of human collectivities, or corporations.[51]

The third difficulty is that such an expansion would not automatically rule out duties to police nature. It sets another moral claim against those of the individual animals. It does not render them compatible. On the contrary, the conflicts are already well known between doing what is best for individual animals and for species, as are those between either and securing human interests.[52] As with human–non-human conflict, either an account must be given of why systems and species should be prioritized, or we must resign ourselves to being outside the situation comfortably assumed in Part One: of broadly compatible, mutually fulfillable, collective moral duties.

Schlosberg, in the context of his expansion of capabilities justice, is happy to accept this.[53] For me, however, it is a reason to stop and take stock. If expanding the interests-based model in this way cannot yield an outcome without incompatible demands, even at the collective level, then given how much it stretches the original, uncontroversial model to go this far, we might want to consider alternative means of accommodating our strong intuitions about the value of species and ecosystems. These appeal not to interests-based duties to species and systems, but to some other moral (or even aesthetic) reason to protect, or at least refrain from destroying them. This would be incommensurable with, but could act as a constraint on, our moral duties to individuals.

Again, there are various options. One in-between possibility would be to appeal to the need to protect species and systems indirectly, via the inherent value or moral significance of even non-sentient organisms. The point would be that while the 'merely living' (to use Brian Baxter's phrase) do not have the potential for experienced flourishing (or suffering) that would give us duties *to them* of the same kind as we have to other humans, there is a teleological element to their life: a sense in which it has a purpose, and can go better or worse, and its doing so is of moral significance.[54] However, these interests can only be protected via the species (or at least the population). As Baxter argues:

> [N]o individual specimens of [merely living] species possess particular ambitions or purposes, different from those of any other member of the species... The projects of individuals are interchangeable, and so it makes straightforward sense to say that the individuals themselves are interchangeable or fully replaceable. The giving of moral priority to the group over the individual is... fully justifiable.[55]

In other words, given the lack of distinction between what is good for (say) this particular mollusc and for molluscs as a population or species, we avoid the difficulties associated with appealing to the interests of individual sentient animals to justify protecting systems and species.

Finally, significance might be assigned directly to the preservation of species and systems, but in a different sense to that assigned, in Chapter One and above, to the flourishing of human and non-human individuals. They might be said to have intrinsic value even if they do not have interests in a relevantly similar way to those of individuals: to have value *in* themselves even if not *for* themselves. This significance looks less like that of the avoidance of great suffering by a human (or dog), and more like that assigned to the preservation of a work of art, a beautiful building, or some geological feature such as a mountain. There is considerable debate as to whether such value is still, in a sense, anthropocentric (being conferred by the human observer) or whether humans only discover it: whether or not, as Holmes Rolston III has it, we merely 'carry the lamp that lights up value'.[56] However, on either variant, on such an account we could have a duty not to destroy, and/or a duty to protect, systems or species. This duty would be of a different kind to those to individual humans and animals, but might be of incommensurate importance.[57]

It is beyond the scope of this project thoroughly to commit to one or other of these alternatives, or to either as opposed to Schlosberg's expansion of the capabilities model. Nor is it necessary to do so. The point is that if we are to avoid hugely counterintuitive implications of the expansion of moral concern to non-human animals, we will have to adopt one of these three strategies. This will involve acknowledging reasons to act that are potentially as significant as those given by the no-harm and beneficence principles as they apply to non-human animals (or at least differently so). We would then have to find a way of balancing these different ends against one another.

For now, however, let us return to the problem of climate change. Part One applied the collectivized no-harm principle and principles of beneficence to defend duties to organize to secure mitigation, adaptation, and compensation. We have now to consider the implications, for this, of extending the sphere of moral concern. Here, too, however, the dangers of focusing only on individual, sentient non-humans become clear.

(IV) WHAT'S IN A NUMBER? MITIGATION AND THE NON-IDENTITY PROBLEM

Having highlighted a general failure in the literature ethically to evaluate the impact of climate change on non-humans, Palmer ends her own attempt to do so with the wry observation that, having considered the subject more closely, it 'seems less surprising' that everyone else has been so silent on it.[58]

In particular, she raises two challenges to appealing to harm to individual non-human animals as grounds for mitigating climate change, the first of which resurrects a frustrating philosophical niggle that I earlier assumed away as far as humans were concerned. The reasoning is as follows. Many individual non-human animals will suffer severe deprivations as a result of climate change. In parallel with Part One, this seems automatically to give rise to independent but complementary negatively and positively grounded, weakly collective duties to mitigate climate change and enable adaptation where necessary. However, many of those individuals who will suffer the associated deprivations do not yet exist and, crucially, would not have existed at all had it not been for the pattern of human actions which also gave rise to climate change. As Palmer points out, this gives rise to the non-identity problem: deprived as they will be as a result of climate change, these individual animals would not have existed at all without it, so how can they be said to have been harmed?[59] Examining this challenge in this context, I will suggest, it becomes harder still to retain a focus only on our moral duties to individual animals. Rather, we are, as in the general case above, pushed towards the question of duties to (or at least in respect of) species or systems.

Faced with the non-identity problem, it is tempting simply to refer back to Chapter One. I made no claim there to solve the puzzle. Instead I cited the vastly repugnant consequences of taking it seriously and, having done no more than highlight some promising attempts to resolve it, simply assumed that the two relatively uncontroversial moral principles that I took as starting points could retain their force if reformulated to avoid it.

These consequences are just as repugnant in the non-human case: we could impose any suffering on future individuals, no matter now horrible, so long as in the process we a) changed who those individuals are and b) did not render their lives so utterly dreadful as not to be worth living at all. The only difference is that we do not have to look to the realm of the bizarrely hypothetical—or to such historical abhorrences as Nazi policies—to find plentiful examples. They are, sadly, all around us. Many domesticated animals are bred to meet human requirements or tastes, in a way which causes them considerable suffering but which also determines which individuals come into existence. Consider show dogs, milk cows, or laying hens, at least some of whom will have lives which, though deprived of some fundamental interests, are still worth living.

Accordingly, it seems natural to make a parallel move, assume that we can count the deprivations imposed by climate change on future non-human individuals as relevantly unacceptable, and move on. However, the non-identity problem is peculiarly problematic in this context, because it combines with Palmer's second objection (a point I also raised in section (i)). She points out that, while a great many future individual non-humans undoubtedly will be denied fundamental interests as a result of climate change, there are a great many others for whom the reverse will be true: life as a member of some species might be substantially better than it would have been without climate change. For example, there may be some one-horned rhinos denied fundamental interests, but there may also be (quite possibly many more) brown rats who have all their interests met.

Thus the choice is no longer that implicit in my earlier discussion of the non-identity problem. In Chapter One, the collective-level choice could be treated as analogous to the following.

Future A (continue as we are): Anne, Bertha,…, Yvonne, and Zoe will be born and suffer great deprivation; or

Future B (mitigation): Alice, Belle,..., Yvette, and Zia will be born and flourish.

It is possible that there might be more or less in the second set than in the first, and indeed probable that some of Alice to Zia would still be deprived, but the choice was essentially taken to be one between worsening climate change and bringing about extra individual deprivations, or not doing so, and those deprivations being prevented.

Now, it looks more like the following.

Future A (continue as we are): Rat 1, Rat 2,..., Rat m will be born and flourish, but Rhino 1, Rhino 2,..., Rhino n will be born and suffer great deprivation; or

Future B (mitigation): Rat 1, Rat 2,..., Rat p will be born and suffer great deprivation, but Rhino 1, Rhino 2,..., Rhino q will be born and flourish.

To make matters more difficult, m might well be larger than either n, p, or q.

Given that there are individuals on both sides of the equation who suffer and who would not have existed otherwise, rather more is demanded of our hypothetical way round the non-identity problem. Of the various strategies cited in Chapter One, those which focused on the unacceptability of actively inflicting specific deprivations on individuals continue to dictate against option A. However, those focused on not creating worse states of affairs, or on not making things *de dicto* worse for those in certain relations to oneself, would not.[60]

How might we respond to this challenge? For the argument from weakly collective harm, there are three potential lines of defence. The first clings tightly to the act–omission distinction. On this, all that matters in applying the collectivized no-harm principle is the fact that if we do something (worsen climate change) we will bring about a future (A) in which individuals (e.g. rhinos) suffer great deprivations. We have a duty not to do this. The fact that there will come into being other individuals (e.g. rats) whose interests are secured by our actions cannot count against this duty, any more than preventing serious harms to some would justify inflicting them on others within current generations. This is in line with the letter of the no-harm principle adopted in Chapter One: the duty was not to deprive other humans of fundamental interests, whether present or future humans, regardless of whether they would have existed otherwise. However, it was not taken as read in Part One that the *collectivized* no-harm principle would always trump that of beneficence. Moreover, assuming away the non-identity problem in this context is no longer so obviously in line with our small-scale intuitions, even at the individual level.[61]

Secondly, the non-identity problem rests on the assumption that, even in the worse future, the individuals have lives worth living. For many individual non-humans in a world of worsened climate change, this will not be true.

This cuts off any possible appeal to their being made overall 'better off', through existing at all, to mitigate against the deprivation of fundamental interests through climate change. The collectivized no-harm principle can be applied more straightforwardly to them.

Thus, Palmer's challenges need not defeat the argument from weakly collective responsibility for harm, although they do force it into committing to a narrow harm/benefit distinction which is arguably less plausible at this weakly collective level than at that of the individual. As will become clearer below, this also raises the danger that two arguments treated as complementary in Chapter One could now pull in opposite directions.

Now consider the principle of beneficence. In Chapter One, this was taken to require positive action to secure the fundamental interests of individuals—present or future, and regardless of whether they would have existed otherwise—but not to require creating such individuals simply because they would have secure fundamental interests. Call this latter the *non-creation clause*. This was important to avoid the possibility that, in creating deprived A instead of flourishing B, one also created lots of other flourishing people, whose happy existence might be used as grounds for preferring this outcome.

Here, however, there is a sense in which numbers created must matter. The crucial point, again, is that whichever of the two futures is chosen there will be deprived individuals *who would not have existed otherwise*. In the same generation case, if we can only secure the fundamental interests of some (or at least can only do so within the cost condition), we would standardly be held to have a duty to do so much. The best way of deciding whose interests to secure remains up for debate. Can we, for example, legitimately prioritize those close to us? Should we go for those who can be helped most efficiently, so as to help most? Or should there be some kind of lottery system to give everyone at least the same chance of rescue?

In future generation cases, given that none of the individuals will exist otherwise, parallel reasoning seems to dictate a policy of efficiency: that is, securing the fundamental interests of as many as possible. But precisely because none would have existed otherwise, the way to maximize the proportion with fundamental interests secured is to create lots of those individuals whose interests would be secure. In the non-human context, this suggests a duty to create as many individuals as possible of the relevant species (such as rats).

We might reject this as too flagrant a violation of the non-creation clause, and argue instead that attending to numbers in future generation cases means only attending to the numbers of those who are deprived of fundamental interests. Then, less counterintuitively, neither the total of flourishing rats in Future A nor of flourishing rhinos in Future B is significant, but only the number of suffering rhinos in A and suffering rats in B. Even this, however, does not avert the difficulty.

Palmer's claim is that '[w]e can't tell whether climate change will cause more suffering to non-humans than it will relieve'.[62] Given this, to determine whether there is a weakly collective duty to mitigate on the basis of a positive duty to prevent individual non-human suffering, we would have to compare predicted implications for all predicted members of sentient species (and arguably also of potential species). As Palmer argues, it is difficult to see how such a calculation is possible. At best, then, we would find ourselves unable to defend mitigation because of uncertainty about numbers. At worst, we might have a case against it.

How can this be avoided? Three possibilities present themselves. One, as Palmer suggests, is that greater weight be assigned to more complex sufferers (humans or rhinos, say, rather than rats).[63] There are two ways in which this might be justified. One draws on Singer to argue that, without taking the flourishing of more complex beings to be more important, we can justify prioritizing them because the same objective impact would be worse for them.

> [I]f a choice has to be made between saving the life of a normal human being and that of a dog, we might well decide to save the human because he, with his greater awareness of what is going to happen, will suffer more before he dies; we may also take into account the likelihood that it is the family and friends of the human who will suffer more; and finally, it would be the human who had the greater potential for future happiness.[64]

Two parallel points can be made here. Firstly, quite apart from the possibility—left open—that death in itself is not a fundamental loss for a non-human, the same physical impact could deprive a more complex being of more fundamental interests. A tarantula deprived of its home and food would suffer various health effects; a dog so deprived would do the same, but might also pine for its companions (human or non-human). A human in the same situation would suffer in both these ways, but also experience the thwarting of ambitions and plans of life, and suffer vivid anxiety about what was happening to his loved ones. Secondly, it is more likely, as we move up the scale of complexity, that the death or suffering of one individual could impose a fundamental interest loss on another. It is hard to believe that rats, for example, are marred for life by the loss of one of their young in the same way that a human or a chimpanzee mother would be.

The alternative is to argue that while all serious suffering by sentient individuals is morally significant, that of the more complex beings matters more. That is, even if the impact on the individual were exactly the same, it would be morally worse for it to happen to a human than to a rhino, and to a rhino than to a rat. This would, however, require further defence: not least, a response to the separation and equality problems.

The second possible way out is to appeal to the threat of abrupt, or even runaway, catastrophic climate change.[65] It seems incredible to claim that, under such a disaster scenario, life would not be significantly worse for the majority of sentient individuals. This is especially so if we needn't concern ourselves with all—or even all sentient—organisms that will ever live: that is, if we needn't factor in the possibility of new species of flourishing, sentient individuals evolving after millions of years. As John Nolt argues against Palmer, 'our moral responsibility is limited by our capacity to produce, recognize and anticipate harms and benefits resulting from our actions...At most, we can knowingly affect biodiversity over a few million years.'[66] What could happen millennia after a global catastrophe can hardly justify us in knowingly bringing that catastrophe about now, any more than the fact that he might thereby discover a rewarding career as a painter would justify me in breaking a footballer's leg, or even exposing him to a significant risk of it.

(Part One did not rely on the significant risk of such catastrophic change. It appealed to the near-certainty of widespread loss of central capabilities or fundamental interests rather than to the risk of much worse, and more widespread, impact. However, the no-harm principle (individual and collective) could plausibly be extended to rule out not only causing others to lose a fundamental interest, but also exposing them to an unchosen risk of losing all of them. The principles of beneficence might be extended to require protection against such risks.)

However, as in section (ii), neither of these responses fully addresses one crucial element of our unease about this possibility. Calculations across individual lives ignore the underlying fact that some of those individuals are of a species (one-horned rhinos) whom anthropocentric climate change is likely to render extinct. They ignore the intuitively compelling possibility that securing the fundamental interests of the various individual rhinos could matter more (or matter in a different way) because of the implications for the species.

The third response, then, is to appeal to this significance, whether through an expanded interests-based model, or by appeal to some other moral (or other) intrinsic reason to preserve species and systems. In climate change, as in the general case, we are pushed to this by the repugnance with which we greet the implications of a focus only on individual non-human animals.

Arguments in terms of species and systems appear to avoid the non-identity problem because, unlike individuals, they could last over the time frames in question.[67] Undoubtedly, between us we are destroying species. Biologists have warned of a mass extinction of the kind 'previously...seen only five times in about 540 million years'.[68] Even focusing only on climate change, our combined actions put many currently existing species at high risk of extinction. Beneath the headline IPCC predictions are specific examples cited by the Worldwide Fund for Nature, such as one-horned rhinos, orang-utans, sea turtles, American pikas, or many Australian frog species.[69]

In terms of positive duties, the situation is complicated by the possibility of new species evolving to replace those lost. Two points appear to count in favour of a weakly collective duty to mitigate climate change. Firstly, parallel reasoning to that in the individual case, above, could avoid appealing to such potential new flourishing species. The idea would be that we have a duty to protect species, but not to create new ones just because they would have their interests protected, or have intrinsic value, and especially not to do so at the expense of destroying already existing species. However, this distinction need not transfer from individuals to species or systems, especially if our reason to protect them is not grounded in duties to them, via the expanded interests-based model, but appeals to some other moral or aesthetic significance. The idea of 'making up' for the suffering of one person (or cat) by creating lots of happy people (or cats) is particularly unattractive because this would by no means make it up to that suffering individual. This would not apply with species or systems.

Secondly, following Nolt as above, we can take issue with the appeal to this possible-but-far-distant future of increased numbers of species and flourishing systems. Biodiversity loss is going to be with us for (or quite possibly outlast us by) a very long time: quite probably those millions of years which, as Nolt rightly notes, should mark the outside of our reasoning.[70]

This section has served to reinforce the danger of limiting our expansion of the moral sphere to individual sentient non-humans. It is already clear that we cannot, even between us, do all that we have moral reason to do. Fulfilling our weakly collective moral duties will require balancing different claims against one another. Moreover, our strong intuitions suggest that in some cases this will amount to meeting the claims of individual animals only insofar as is possible within the context of securing those of species and systems. The next section will reinforce this conflict. Having highlighted collective moral claims that are by their nature incompatible, we will now consider those that are practically so, because of insufficient resources.

(V) TOO MANY VICTIMS

Consider more generally the application to the climate change case of weakly collective duties not to harm, and to protect, non-human individual animals, and of parallel duties regarding species and systems, whether or not these are duties *to them* in the same interests-based way. (Note moreover that following section (iii), a duty to protect species and systems might amount to a duty to protect populations from severely detrimental human impact.)

The collective self-interest argument is quickly reiterated here, given the groundwork laid in section (i). Chapter Two defended the following:

Principle of moralized collective self-interest
A set of human beings (moral agents) who are mutually dependent through a common fundamental interest have a weakly collective duty to cooperate to secure that interest, so long as this is possible without those individuals having to sacrifice some other fundamental human interest.

This appealed to the collectivized weak principle of beneficence, on which there is a duty to organize to prevent the serious suffering of others if this can be done at minimal cost to each. Because in such cases the set of active duty-bearers is the same as those facing the deprivation, it was suggested that this minimal cost condition must be met. It is in each of their interests to secure the common end, and it can hardly be a non-minimal cost to an agent, in a morally significant sense, to do something that is to her own overall advantage.

If this convinced in Chapter Two, it should do so again. Although non-human animals would be passive members of the collectivity, the moral significance of protecting their fundamental interests would add weight to appeal to the principle of beneficence. (The same point could be made regarding species, populations, or systems, were the notion of collectivityhood to be stretched thus far.) The problems of section (iv) do not arise, because by definition precisely those included in the collectivity are those whose basic interests would be secured by climate change mitigation.

Things are less straightforward when it comes to the arguments from weakly collective harm and collective ability to aid. As section (iv) showed, a duty to mitigate can be defended on the basis of the no-harm principle to humans, individual animals, *and* species, as well as on that of the collectivized principle of beneficence to humans and species. Recalling Chapter Two, this is a reminder of the extent to which our own interests are inseparable from—because dependent on—showing at least some concern for the natural world. After all, as we are too often in danger of forgetting, we are simply one part of it. Although the argument from collective ability to aid non-human individual animals makes a less clear-cut case for mitigation, this result is so much at odds with central intuitions as to count, in this instance, in favour of prioritizing duties to species or humans.

When we turn to adaptation, however, matters are more difficult. Even our negative—and still more so our positive—collective moral duties are limited not by what needs to be done, but by our capacity, even collectively, to do it. The duty would be to enable adaptation to such climate change as cannot now be mitigated: adaptation by individual sentient animals on the one hand, species or systems on the other.[71] The idea, recalling Chapter One, is to prevent now-inevitable climate change from undermining the relevant fundamental interests. It is hard to know what this would mean in the case of species or systems. In particular, there is a lively debate going on in ecological ethics on the strengths and weaknesses of a nature restoration approach.[72] However, it might require attempting (if possible) to save certain ecosystems from destruction, providing alternative habitats for populations where theirs had become irreversibly hostile, and in the last instance intervening actively to preserve a species, if necessary in captivity, until sufficient habitat could be renewed. Just to make matters more difficult, this last gives rise to further conflicts: captivity itself could undermine the fundamental interests of individual non-humans.

Following Chapters One and Three, on the argument from weakly collective harm, it is also arguable that duties to compensate would be owed to individual animals, where adaptation could not prevent the loss of the fundamental interests or central capabilities. This would have to mean boosting functioning in another central element of their life, or in some way partly offsetting the loss of an interest. (Thus, for example, zoos could be as well managed as possible, and individual animals given inadequate-but-better-than-nothing substitutes for their opportunities in the wild. The ball on the string for the Bronx Zoo tiger, which so impresses Nussbaum, might fit this category.[73]) However, it is not clear that this would play the same role as compensation as in the human case. Among humans, there is an element of shared recognition of a wrong—at least arguably, a significance to being offered compensation over and above its practical impact—which does not apply here. Moreover, species and systems, which lack the experienced element of flourishing, are hardly the kinds of entities to whom compensation can be offered.

Given these prima facie duties, three points should be made. The first reinforces the problematic implications of extending our moral concern only to individual non-human animals. Without a duty *also* to protect species and systems, even a curtailed principle of beneficence could mandate mass-scale interference in the non-human world. It might turn out that individual non-human animals are best enabled to adapt to climate change through protecting populations, but it need not. Suppose individual non-humans could best be spared these deprivations by controlled extermination of certain species (through euthanasia or birth control). If we are unwilling to accept such policy implications then, in the climate change as in the general case, it would be necessary either or both to reject any such general duty to non-humans (necessitating a return to the problem of marginal cases at its least tractable) or to make the more controversial expansion to species and systems.[74]

The next two points follow from the fact that fulfilling these duties will be extremely difficult. This is so even if we restrict ourselves to the argument from weakly collective responsibility for harm. In the human case, the weakly collective duty was taken to be broadly collectively fulfillable. However, whether we are dealing with a duty only to some current generations of non-human animals, or to all of them, the costs of adaptation will be very great. Compensation—if possible or appropriate—would impose further costs. The same applies to whatever is possible by way of enabling adaptation of species or systems. Even higher costs follow from the argument from collective ability to aid, where the duty extends to providing adaptation aid to those individuals, species, and systems (or perhaps populations) put in hazard by any climate change, no matter whether those who caused it are long dead.

From this, we can make the second point. Both the no-harm argument and the collective ability to aid argument as regards species can be used further to weaken the allegedly economic arguments, such as that previously offered by Bjørn Lomborg, for focusing only on enabling adaptation to climate change.[75] These start from the claim that what matters is not climate change itself, but its negative impact on human lives. They then argue that, as adaptation can avoid deprivation of fundamental interests, and is much more efficiently secured than mitigation, it is better to focus on that than attempt to curb emissions.

Such arguments have already been widely discredited: their final premise assumes unacceptable discounting of the moral value of future lives.[76] If, however, adaptation were required to prevent not only the deprivation of fundamental human interests through climate change, but also that of individual non-human animals, and the devastation of species and systems, it would be still harder to make a convincing case for the greater costliness of mitigation. Mitigation will cost the same no matter how many more benefit from it, whereas such additional adaptation aid fast ratchets up total burdens.

The final point applies to both no-harm and ability to aid arguments. Even if we assume that mitigation should be prioritized, extending the moral sphere to sentient non-human animals or species and systems (let alone both) can be expected to render our weakly collective climate duties unfulfillable. Let us begin with the argument from weakly collective responsibility for harm. Even if we went to the wire ourselves in order to do so, it might be impossible to secure adaptation for all.

It can be responded that ought implies can even in rectification cases. While we could and should have avoided the harm, we cannot now entirely negate it, and so are not required to do so. Instead, we must live with our moral failing. We are like the drink driver who disabled a pedestrian and now is unable to do more to help than provide a carer because there are limits to what medical care can do. However, this analogy is only partly convincing. This is not a matter of doing as much as one can for one victim, even if one can't ever truly make it up to him. Rather, it is a case of multiple potential victims, to some of whom we can make it up, and between whom we must decide. We might seek some fair way of allocating these scarce adaptation resources across victims all considered equally entitled, whether human or non-human. This might be by lottery. However, given the sheer numbers of non-humans (growing human numbers notwithstanding), this would be extremely likely to leave many human victims unaided and many species to go extinct.

A parallel point applies to the argument from the collectivized principle of beneficence. Whether this is extended only to individual non-human animals, or to populations, *or* both, protecting all whom climate change would deprive of fundamental interests would be so costly as to be impossible. The collectivized moderate principle of beneficence required coordination to prevent serious suffering if that could be done at less than significant cost to the duty-bearers. This limits what we can be expected to do by way of enabling adaptation. However, we still have the difficulty of deciding between victims.

Where does this leave us? Building on sections (iii) and (iv), three remarks can be made. Firstly, given the inevitable conflict between fulfilling our weakly collective duties to species or systems and to individuals, we need either to justify prioritizing the former (which has proved highly difficult), or to acknowledge that, even at the collective level, responding adequately to the moral reasons we are given to act is, as with Schlosberg's version of capabilities justice, a matter of finding the least bad trade-off between incompatible ends.[77]

Secondly, given the sheer numbers of non-humans, adopting some kind of lottery between individual victims to determine who gets adaptation aid (and perhaps compensation) would in practice mean doing a lot less for humans. If we are unwilling to bite this bullet, we might, again, do one of two things. We might try to defend prioritizing enabling adaptation for humans over non-humans (or at least non-humans *qua* individuals). The Singer-inspired suggestion above—that the same objective loss is greater to humans in terms of fundamental interests—is perhaps the most promising route, but it would not necessarily justify a blanket priority system. Any attempt to claim that the same suffering is worse if it happens to humans would, among other challenges, require returning to the problem of marginal cases.

Without any coherent model on which to defend ranking interests, we would have to acknowledge our prima facie collective moral duties to individual non-human animals, to species or systems, *and* to humans, as incompatible and incommensurate. The best we could then do is attempt to trade them off against one another, as Alan Carter suggests in the general context of anthropocentric, zoocentric, and ecological ethics.[78] (Even this, however, requires a sort of return to the separation and equality problems. If the capacities of some non-human animals—or their relations with humans—are on a par with those of some humans, what could justify this kind of separation of zoocentric and anthropocentric duties? The point, surely, is that they are not separate but are equal.)

Thirdly, the three arguments taken to be complementary in Part One are no longer even broadly mutually fulfillable. It is thus a further challenge to assess how they should be balanced against one another. To give an absolute priority to the weakly collective duty not to harm—something to which

I avoided committing in Part One—would leave little or no scope for tackling (or enabling adaptation to) climate change for which Polluters were not responsible. This, again, would leave a great many victims unaided, human and non-human. As in section (ii), to avoid this we would need an argument for prioritizing at least some duties to aid humans over duties to avoid harming non-humans, or destroying species and systems. Among other things, this too would require grappling with a version of the separation and equality problems.

CONCLUSIONS

When I first planned this chapter, I intended simply to take the first step of expanding our moral sphere to include climate duties to individual sentient non-humans, leaving it open whether to go further still. This quickly proved unrealistic. The implications of even this limited project commit me to taking a stance on precisely the question of the significance of species and systems that I intended to avoid discussing: a stance at conflict with some very strongly held intuitions. To avoid them, it has proved necessary either to expand the same model further still (a move not without its own difficulties), or to defend a different kind of duty in relation to species and systems.

Doing this, we find ourselves with moral (or other incommensurably salient) reasons to act which are incompatible both in their own terms and in the context of the duties to humans defended in Part One. What does this mean? Certainly not that we should give up on the whole project. The impossibility of meeting all these incompatible calls on us in no way justifies us either in doing nothing at all, or in retreating to a realm (the human) where our weakly collective climate duties are at least broadly mutually fulfillable.[79]

Instead, we must rise to the expanded challenge. Even acting collectively, as a global élite, we are limited by what can be demanded of us: by the costs that would be imposed on each of us, or at least by how much it is possible for us to do. Our collective duty now is not only to act, but also to find a way of deciding how to act. This is so not only in practical terms, not only (as is long familiar) in terms of fairly allocating the burdens across duty-bearers within the collectivity, but also in terms of balancing salient but incompatible ends.

In navigating this particular 'theoretical storm', philosophical reasoning may only take us so far. It can, as I have tried to show, make a start.[80] We lack the clear convictions—consensus on moral principles—that we could take as starting points in the human case. However, we have on the one hand philosophically strong reasons (briefly reiterated in section (ii)) for expanding these, and on the other some pretty central intuitions as a constraint on the implications of such expansions.

Beyond this, in the absence of one coherent model able to identify a neatly defined, all-things-considered, fulfillable weakly collective duty, it may be that the best we can do is to take a lead from Carter, and appeal to collective-level indifference curves to identify optimum trade-offs.[81] I would add, moreover, that given that these ends are not only mutually incompatible but likely to become more so the longer it takes to act effectively, we have yet another case for urgency. We must get started all the sooner on the task we now know can never fully be achieved, because to leave it later will be to do it even more inadequately, and leave more victims unprotected.

Against this background, then, the rest of this monograph turns to the position of the individual in the absence of any effective collective attempt: the absence, that is, of collective-level action to fulfil the weakly collective duty, within which she can simply play her part.

Part 3

Climate Change and Me
What I should do when we fail to act

5

Mimicking Duties

It is better to enjoy your Sunday driving while working to change the law so as to make it illegal for you to enjoy your Sunday driving.[1]

Walter Sinnott-Armstrong

If you see the behaviour of the West as clearly wrong, even a moral outrage, you might be drawn to an uncomfortable conclusion...If we are consistent in the application of our moral principles, it is hard to avoid the conclusion that our lives are moral outrages too.[2]

James Garvey

What must I do as an individual facing some morally salient goal which should be—but is not—being pursued collectively? What should I do as one of two dozen uncoordinated beach-goers watching a child struggling in the water whose rescue would require most of us to act together?[3] Or as one of hundreds of individuals crowding onto a weak bridge that will, if it collapses, injure children swimming in the river below, or all of us, or both? What, most pressingly of all, must I do as one of those billions of persons whose actions in combination are worsening climate change, who could by organizing themselves not only cease this harm, but alleviate that done by others before us?

I start here from the duty defended in Part One: a weakly collective duty to organize as necessary to prevent such harms. In the climate change case, Polluters were assigned mitigation, adaptation, and compensation duties on the basis of weakly collective responsibility for harm. The Able were assigned mitigation and adaptation duties, on the grounds of collective ability to aid. The Young were assigned a narrower collective duty to mitigate climate change, via the argument from moralized collective self-interest. Following Chapter Four, these could extend to adaptation and mitigation duties to non-human animals, as well as duties to, or at least in respect of, species and systems.

This is something *we* should do: a duty we have, as a collectivity or potential collectivity, to the victims of climate change. Given this, the question, 'What should *I* do?' arises at two levels. One is as part of a fair collective scheme (formal or informal) to fulfil the duty. The other is in the absence of any such collective endeavour. I address only the latter here. There is already an extensive literature on what constitutes a fair distribution of the burdens of climate change mitigation, adaptation, and compensation, albeit one generally focused on states rather than individuals.[4] Moreover, from the point of the concerned moral agent, the second—comparatively under-considered—question is actually more urgent.

I consider three possible kinds of individual duty:[5]

Mimicking duties
Duties to do what would be required of one as part of a fair collective scheme to fulfil the duty.

Promotional duties
Duties to attempt to bring about the necessary collective action.[6]

Direct duties
These fall into two subsets...
   Protecting duties: duties to protect the interests at stake
   Mitigating duties: duties to mitigate the harm directly

...and two versions within each subset:
   Individual version: fulfil the duty acting on one's own
   Sub-collective version: fulfil the duty acting in combination with a
      like-minded subset.

At first sight, it appears natural that individuals have promotional duties. Without such demands on individuals, would not the weakly collective duty be meaningless, because it could never be fulfilled? However, this comes up against a commonly held perception in the climate change case: the perception that our primary (perhaps our only) moral duty as individual agents is to cut our own emissions. This often equates to the idea that individuals have only to do their 'bit' in securing the overall end. On this reasoning, I should take the train, turn down the central heating, buy local fruit and vegetables, insulate my flat, remain vegetarian, and so on, because what is required (perhaps all that can be asked) of me is that I do what would be my share if we were all doing as we ought.

It might even be argued that the 'natural' conclusion above is mistaken, because some weakly collective duties could be fulfilled without any strongly collective action. This would be so if each individual played her part, acting only as an individual, and these actions combined to bring about the required collective-level result. Accordingly, if we could fill out the common perception with a plausible philosophical defence of individual mimicking duties, promotional duties might be unnecessary.

This chapter responds to this view, clearing the ground for Chapter Six, which defends promotional duties as primary. It argues that mimicking duties are neither exclusive nor primary. Section (i) rejects the claim that they are exclusive. It points out that there are many weakly collective duties where strongly (at least intentionally) collective action is required for fulfilment. It also rejects one possible ('fair shares') defence of such exclusivity. The rest of the chapter focuses on cases—of which climate change mitigation is of course a central one—where aggregate individual fulfilment of mimicking duties could at least partially fulfil a weakly collective duty. It will consider a number of possible philosophical cases for such individual duties, concluding that none succeeds in defending them as primary in the context of the weakly collective duty.

In section (ii), the claim is rejected that we are individually, directly responsible for harm through climate change, and so acquire an individual duty to cut emissions by appeal either to act-consequentialist reasoning or to the individual no-harm principle. Section (iii) rejects a rule-consequentialist argument, on which an individual has a mimicking duty because if everyone fulfilled such it would bring about the best overall consequences.

Section (iv) reviews Aaron Maltais' appeal to fairness to future cooperators in a collective scheme.[7] Section (v) assesses virtue-based arguments. Section (vi) considers appeal to Kantian reasoning: to the categorical imperative on which an individual should act only according to maxims (rules for conduct) which she can consistently universalize. Maltais' argument is accepted as a limited case for mimicking duties, but not as giving them priority over promotional duties. On the last two possibilities, insofar as they defend such duties as primary, these theories also do so in so rigidly ideal-world or narrowly character-focused a way as to raise doubts about their relevance in the actual—very much non-ideal—situation in which we find ourselves. However, a character-based case for mimicking is left open when there is nothing else that the individual can do.

(I) EXCLUSIVITY AND 'FAIR SHARES'

For individual mimicking duties to be exclusive—to be all that is required of the individual in the face of unfulfilled weakly collective duty—the collective end must be achievable through aggregated individual mimicking actions. There are some cases where this is possible, including climate change mitigation. However, there are many others where it is not. These are cases where collective action in a stronger (at least an intentional) sense is required.

Indeed, in some situations, it is not even clear what mimicking could amount to. There are some individual actions which can only be explained—which only make sense *as actions*—as part of a collective enterprise to which they contribute. Recall Chapter Three's *Beach rescue*, summarized in opening this chapter. A collective solution might involve several of the holidaymakers rowing a boat out to save the child, but how could an individual imitate this alone? By sitting in the stationary boat pushing an oar in a rowing movement? Such a performance would be utterly meaningless, taken as an individual action.

The same can be said of the actions making up certain collective attempts to respond to climate change. Consider such adaptation efforts as flood-prevention measures or providing new homelands for displaced communities. In most adaptation or compensation cases, the nearest an individual could get to 'mimicking' would be by trying directly to compensate or aid victims of climate change. However, these actions are exactly what is involved in fulfilling direct duties, and can be morally salient only insofar as they are such: that is, insofar as they can be expected actually to make a difference to the victim. Otherwise, they would not only be practically useless, but would be so far from actually replicating what would happen in a fair collective scheme as to be even symbolically nonsensical. (I will return to direct duties in Chapter Six.)

Thus, even if they could be defended as primary, individual mimicking duties could not be exclusive. If they were, the weakly collective duty would indeed often be doomed to non-fulfilment. However, there are two supporting points to make and one potential objection to address before we can leave this section.

The supplementary points are as follows. Even regarding emissions cuts—a glaringly obvious mimicking action if ever there were one—the situation is not straightforward. Even if the overall result (mitigation) could be secured by aggregate individual emissions cuts, securing it efficiently requires collective action. For example, coordination is needed to develop renewables or energy-efficient technology. This is significant because of the greater burdens imposed on each individual if she acts on her own. Anticipating Chapter Six, it might be unreasonably demanding to expect some individuals to cut their emissions sufficiently in isolation (because the cost to them is too high), while contributions to a collective effort would be by no means so demanding. (This applies particularly to those in The Able and The Young.) Again, then, leaving the fulfilment of the weakly collective duty to the fulfilment of individual mimicking duties could render it effectively meaningless.

Moreover, the flipside of the same point is that an individual cannot assume that mimicking what would be required of her by such a fair collective scheme equates to reducing her own emissions to a level such that, if all emitted, climate change would be made no worse. (That is, assuming that the cost of compliance would be at least one factor in determining a fair distribution of burdens within such a scheme.) This is important because many of the arguments considered in this chapter, if they did convince, would do so only to this latter extent.

The objection is this: mimicking duties must be exclusive, even if this does render the weakly collective duty unfulfillable, because anything else is unfair on the duty-bearers. The objector makes his case by appeal to Liam Murphy's compliance condition, according to which an individual cannot be expected to take on others' shares of moral duties on top of her own.[8] The idea here would be that, in being required to fulfil promotional or direct duties rather than do what would be her part in a fair collective scheme, the individual is being expected to pick up the moral tab for others who have failed to cooperate, and this is unfair.

Chapter Six will reject the compliance condition. However, even if it were taken to limit the costs that can be demanded of us in cases of collective failure to fulfil weakly collective duties, the objection here would not hold. Even if we accepted that an individual cannot fairly be asked to do more under partial than she would under full compliance, it need not require her to do exactly the same thing as she would under a fair collective scheme, no matter whether it will have any effect at all in isolation. Murphy himself is clear on this.[9] The condition should be taken as capping the cost to the individual of fulfilling the individual duties she acquires correlative to the weakly collective duty, whatever those duties turn out to be. It does not make a case for mimicking duties in particular.

Having rejected the claim that mimicking duties are exclusive, we can turn now to cases where the arguments above do not apply: that is, where mimicking actions are available and their performance, in aggregate, would secure the overall end. In the climate change case, asserting the primacy of such duties equates to the claim that, as individuals, we should prioritize cutting our own emissions over fulfilling promotional or direct duties. This taps into a widely attractive idea. I will, accordingly, consider some ways in which its appeal might philosophically be filled out.

(II) INDIVIDUAL HARM

Throughout this book, climate change has been discussed as a 'new harm'.[10] Part One expanded the notion of collective moral responsibility to accommodate cases where each individual neither caused nor prevented harm, but harm was being caused—or at least could be prevented—at the collective level. It was implicitly assumed that we couldn't motivate individual emissions cuts either by appeal to the individual no-harm principle, or by appeal to the direct consequences of individual behaviour. In other words, it was taken as read that my turning up my heating or my neighbour driving to work makes, in itself, no difference to the suffering brought about by climate change.[11]

However, this has been questioned. John Nolt has estimated that the average American is responsible through her emissions for the 'serious suffering and/or deaths of two future people'.[12] This suggests that individual emissions cuts might be defended either on individual consequentialist grounds or by appeal to the individual no-harm principle.

Nolt reaches this figure as a proportion of the total harm caused by climate change. He takes an average lifespan of 1960–2040 and an increase in atmospheric concentration of carbon dioxide from 317 ppm to an estimated 450 ppm over that period, causing at least four billion premature deaths. On the basis that US emissions are about one-fifth of the global total, he calculates that the average individual American will have been responsible for about one two-billionth of that.[13]

As it stands, two points can be made against this as a defence of the primacy of individual duties to cut emissions. The first concerns only the appeal to consequentialism. Even if we accepted Nolt's reasoning, this needn't be the last word from a strictly consequentialist viewpoint, because it needn't follow that the individual would bring about greater net good by refraining from harm. Suppose (albeit implausibly) that in failing to curb her carbon footprint our American was not maintaining a luxury lifestyle for herself. Instead, suppose she was saving all the money she could to donate to Oxfam, thereby saving hundreds from starvation. Thinking only in terms of maximizing human flourishing through her own behaviour, she might still be justified in continuing these emissions.

This is an important feature of the distinction between the individual and the collective-level situation. From the fact that a long-term collective solution to global poverty would require (and so cannot be treated as a reason not to take) effective action on climate change, it does not follow that an individual, taken in isolation as things currently are, could not do more good in terms of saving people from extreme poverty than she does harm through climate change.[14] Suppose she faces a choice between the two, perhaps because she is deciding where to allocate all the resources left after securing her own fundamental interests. Strictly consequentialist reasoning would not dictate the emissions cuts. In other words, mimicking, insofar as it could be defended, could not be assumed to have priority over direct duties.

I include this argument for completeness. However, in the wider context of this book, it is likely to be undermined. The individual no-harm principle was accepted as a starting assumption in Chapter One, and I left open the widely held view that this takes priority over any positive duty to confer benefits.

The second counter-argument is this: if four billion people are seriously harmed by current emissions, and we can treat the average American as having caused one two-billionth of those emissions, it need not follow that that American has, herself, caused those deaths. In many cases, individual actions do not cause harms in themselves, but operate only as what we might call *harm ingredients*. These (like the flour, eggs, sugar, and butter that make a cake) do nothing towards the overall result unless they are brought together in a certain way. Consider the distinction between three men each of whom shoots one woman, and three men each of whom presses a trigger switch, which in combination set off a bomb to kill all three women. Such reasoning, in the climate change case, is in danger of ignoring this kind of distinction. It is not that each individual's emissions actually kill another two people; rather, in combination our emissions destroy a great many people.

However, the argument can be reformulated to avoid this, by appealing to expected rather than actual consequences. Even if individual actions bring about harm only in combination, there must be some level or threshold of such contributions at which the harm is triggered.[15] Or—as seems more plausible in the climate change case—there might be various subsidiary harms triggered at a number of thresholds along the way. Both Avram Hiller and Shelly Kagan appeal to the chance of triggering such thresholds, the former specifically in the context of climate change. The argument, very roughly, is as follows. Suppose a harm H will come about after some total number x of individual contributions, and increase again after $2x$ individuals, and so on. As an individual, you don't know what others will do, so you assume that you have a chance of one in x of being the xth individual, who triggers the harm.[16] Accordingly, you have a chance of one in x of causing harm H, and your action has an expected disutility of H/x. As Kagan puts it: 'Do I make a difference? I might.'[17]

I will reject this as a defence of mimicking duties in the climate change case. However, we need firstly to be clear on the cases in which it is convincing. Consider the following paraphrased version of Kagan's own example.[18]

Chicken-eater's dilemma
Shelly wants to eat a delicious chicken. However, he is a strict act-consequentialist. He knows that the torture and death of a chicken is a greater harm (to the chicken) than the benefit he gets from eating it rather than some vegetarian dish. So, if his choice were to lead directly to the torture and death of the chicken, he would refrain. However, he also knows that this is not the case. Rather, he knows that only when exactly 25 chickens have been purchased will his local butcher order another 25 chickens to be tortured and killed. Thus, he knows that his decision to buy a chicken will only result in more chicken deaths if he happens to be one of exactly 25 (or 50, 75, 100...) purchasers. There is a 24 in 25 chance that his decision will make absolutely no difference to how many chickens are tortured and killed.

According to Kagan, the act-consequentialist does not buy the chicken because there is a 1 in 25 chance of being the trigger for 25 chickens to be tortured and killed. This equates to an expected disutility of one chicken death, which has been assumed to be greater than any benefit from eating the chicken.

Transferring this reasoning to the climate change case, it might be argued that, although any given individual cannot know she will impose death or severe suffering on two people, she can calculate the expected outcome of her actions to be that two people die or suffer. Thus, she has a primary duty to curb her own emissions. However, there are three potential difficulties with this argument. The first is a difficulty for act-consequentialist defences of mimicking duties. The second (which can be resolved) is a problem for appeal to the no-harm principle. The third is a problem for either.

Firstly, there is a disanalogy between Kagan's example and the climate change case. *Chicken-eater's dilemma* began with the assumption that the benefits of eating the chicken are outweighed by the harm to the chicken. It was taken as read that, if his choice were to lead directly to torturing and killing the chicken, Shelly would be wrong to make that choice. In the climate change case, we start instead from the collective-level balance of good and harm. The assumption is that, overall, all those in the relevant set would do more good by mitigating climate change than by not doing so.[19] However, this renders the argument vulnerable to the first point made above against Nolt, because the collective-level assumption need not transfer to the individual level. Thinking only as act-consequentialists, we cannot simply assume that an expected disutility of two deaths rules out individual emissions. It might be that by continuing to emit, an individual could prevent more than equivalent suffering elsewhere.

Perhaps this can be avoided by appeal to the individual no-harm principle. The idea then would be that severe harm cannot be justified even as a means of preventing suffering elsewhere. However, the no-harm principle, as stated in Chapter One, does not impose a blanket ban on risk. As Chapter Two filled out, it would rule out exposing individuals to significant, ongoing risk to life, health, bodily integrity, affiliation, or practical reason, because this would effectively undermine the capability (or secure opportunities) to enjoy those functionings. But it would be an impossibly demanding principle which forbade all exposure of others to *any* risk, even of the most severe harms. If I can never take even a one in a billion chance of causing someone else's death, I can hardly do anything at all. I can never drive my car, or even my bicycle. I can never eat a packet of Revels in a public place, in case a person sitting near me has a severe nut allergy. Because the chance that my emissions will kill anyone is so small, this seems to count against appeal to the no-harm principle in the climate change case.

There is another version of the no-harm principle which would apply in such threshold cases. This is a negative-duty version of Derek Parfit's claim that it is dangerous to neglect small chances of making a very big difference. According to this principle, I have a prima facie duty not to take even a small chance of imposing severe suffering on a big enough number of people. Although this was not stated as a starting assumption, it is sufficiently compelling that I would not wish to rest my argument on its denial. As Parfit puts it: 'It may be irrational to give any thought to a one-in-a-million chance of killing one person. But, if I was a nuclear engineer, would I be irrational to give any thought to the same chance of killing a million people? This is not what most of us believe.'[20] In this case, the expected outcome of two deaths is based on a very small chance of causing very many deaths. Thus, this objection can be largely set aside.

However, the final point counts against both act-consequentialist versions of the Kagan/Hiller argument and appeals to this kind of expanded individual no-harm principle. Recall *Chicken-eater's dilemma*. The argument rested on the individual's having an equal chance of being one of any number of chicken-buyers, and so a 1 in 25 chance of being pivotal for the next batch of harm. Suppose, however, this were not the case. Kagan himself argues that, given reliable evidence that there will be (for example) 66 other purchasers, act-consequentialism would not count against the purchase.[21] He would know that, in practice, his action would make no difference to the number of chickens killed.

Two factors, in combination, strongly suggest a parallel conclusion in the climate change case.[22] First, drawing from Maltais, the system is so complex that it can effectively be treated as overdetermined (that is, as if there are more potential emitters than would be needed to tip any given threshold). Although there is a statistical correlation between overall polluter inputs and harmful outcomes, the system is far too complicated to be assessed as straightforwardly analogous to the case of the three men pressing their triggers for the bomb, or the original *Chicken-eater's dilemma*. As Maltais reasons against Hiller, we can question the claim 'that when my emissions cause an increase in the global mean temperature from 2.99999999896096°C to 3°C there is a small but normatively significant probability that this change will cause a large number of deaths'. He argues:

> For example, the impacts flowing from a strengthened greenhouse effect are not just the result of the rate of warming and the global temperature peaking point, but also the result of this temperature stress persisting over time. Thus the effect of reducing the peaking point by a billionth of a degree and slowing the rate of warming by a fraction of a second may be to only faintly delay the harmful outcomes warming of 3°C would cause over time. In other words, the effect of reducing my emissions could be to trivially expand the range of time over which human induced global warming will be harmful as opposed to potentially reducing the harm global warming will cause.[23]

Secondly, each individual is aware of others being motivated by their self-interested desires to perform the acts that would do harm in combination. Accordingly, the individual has every reason to believe that not only are there sufficient potential emitters, but that there are enough *actual* other emitters for her action to have only the kind of impact envisaged by Maltais.

Because the case is, in effect, overdetermined, each individual has reason to believe that, were all (or most) others to act in the relevant way, her actions would not trigger any extra harms. Because of the numbers involved and what she knows about others' motivations, she can assume that, were she to continue to emit at current levels, she would be one of just such a set.[24] (Recalling Chapter Three, it is that same combination of features that makes the attribution of weakly collective responsibility particularly appropriate, rather than individual, or even Larry May's shared responsibility.[25]) Like Shelly in the adjusted *Chicken-eater's dilemma*, in theory the individual could appeal to the chance of being pivotal to the death of further persons (or chickens). However, neither has reason to believe it to be empirically possible that they will make a difference. As Maltais puts it, 'simply conceiving of individual emissions as triggering harmful climate thresholds for the purpose of calculation is not an argument for the claim that an individual's emissions can actually have this type of threshold effect'.[26]

This counts against appeal to individual harm to defend mimicking duties, whether via the no-harm principle or on individual consequentialist grounds.

(III) CONSEQUENCES AND IDEAL RULES

Section (ii) backed up the common-sense view that we can safely regard our individual emissions as making no difference to the harm done. However, precisely because of the role of individual emissions cuts in a collective mitigation effort, a globalized rule-consequentialism looks like a more promising defence of mimicking duties. On this reasoning, the appropriate moral rules for individual conduct are those general compliance with which would maximize overall well-being. This is the focus of this section.

Under this heading, I will consider Dale Jamieson's argument that we should adopt certain 'green' character traits because this would, in aggregate, mitigate climate change.[27] His reasoning is as follows. Because it would be better if we all reduced our contribution to global emissions, all of us should do so. However, the way to motivate this as an individual agent is to detach oneself from calculations of individual consequences and think instead in terms of character traits, or virtues.[28]

However, the difficulty with Jamieson's argument is the same as with rule-consequentialism in general: it only works, in its own consequence-driven terms, if everyone else is similarly motivated. To bring this out, consider two possible situations, in only one of which would adopting 'green virtues' be rational. The first is a world in which all humans are genuinely motivated to act on climate change (or at least enough of them to achieve mitigation, adaptation, and compensation). They are concerned about the problem, prepared to make sacrifices, and aware that others are similarly motivated. They are deterred only by the so-called rational altruist's dilemma. This is the quandary facing any individual who knows that her action, taken in isolation, will make no perceptible difference and that she could do perceptible good by devoting herself to some other worthy cause, but that the overall results of everyone acting on this reasoning would be very bad.[29]

Jamieson's suggestion avoids this particular collective action problem. If each individual changes her motivation patterns by cultivating a character of caring about mimicking actions for their own sake, each will act without calculating the immediate consequences. This will bring about better consequences in combination. Each individual knows this and, knowing that others will also be looking for a way out of the dilemma, has reason to be optimistic that they will do the same. Thus, she might rationally seek to change her own character.

So the argument is plausible in this situation. However, it is so, I suggest, only because the demands of rule-consequentialism overlap with those of a collective or cooperative consequentialism: that is, a theory on which an individual ought to do what would bring about the best results in combination with those others similarly motivated.[30] This is not the case in the climate change case, because our world is *not* one of rational altruists.

Instead, the second possible scenario is more accurate: many individuals would not be motivated to cut their individual carbon emissions even if others did. Jamieson makes the point that, in actually motivating oneself to act in collective action problems, one must not fixate on the likely behaviour of others. This is true, insofar as such fixation is all that stands in the way of a collectively successful outcome. But his proposed detachment from what others can be expected to do is also a weakness so long as he is making an ultimately consequentialist case for non-consequentialist reasoning. This very strategy of detachment only works if everyone, or nearly everyone, does it, and each individual will know this.

In this way, Jamieson's argument falls foul of the partial compliance objection, a familiar complaint from the literature on rule-consequentialism.[31] We might, therefore, turn to that literature for a way round the difficulty. However, as I will show, attempts to adapt rule-consequentialism to avoid the objection do so only at the expense of the case for mimicking duties.

One option is to abandon the focus on *ideal* rules in favour of something akin to Richard Miller's actual rule utilitarianism. This requires the individual to act in accordance with only those best-consequence-promoting rules which are actually practised in her society.[32] This avoids the partial compliance objection at the level of any given society. However, it would have to be reformulated to a global level to avoid it in cases such as climate change. Moreover, it does not defend most mimicking actions in the climate change case, because (unfortunately) they do not correspond to existing social practices.

Alternatively, we might retain ideal rule-consequentialism, but amend it. One possibility is to adapt it to permit non-compliance in dealing with non-reciprocators. This would avoid a specific version of the partial compliance objection: that an individual might, as Brad Hooker puts it, be required to do something that, *'because others are not complying, would be harmful or inconvenient to [her] and beneficial to the very people who are not complying'*.[33] However, insofar as it avoided the problem above in the climate change case (by classing the rest of the world as non-reciprocators), it would also make it permissible not to fulfil mimicking duties.

Moreover, the objection raised against Jamieson was a different one: that fulfilling mimicking duties in a situation of partial compliance will result in a worse outcome overall. To avoid this, we might adapt rule-consequentialism to enable individuals not to comply with any given rule if obeying it would clash with the aim of preventing great harm.[34]

This caveat can be understood more or less broadly. Narrowly, it focuses on the direct impacts of each individual's compliance (or non-compliance). Richard Brandt uses the example of attempting to uphold a rule against race discrimination in apartheid South Africa. There, individual compliance might plausibly provoke 'serious social harm', and indeed great harm to the individual.[35] This is not straightforwardly analogous with fulfilling mimicking duties in the climate change case: it is unlikely that turning down my heating in isolation will cause great harm, although there may be some mimicking actions which could do so. (Consider, for example, cycling to work on a fast road full of cars.[36])

However, given ultimate concern for consequences, it is unclear why the consistent consequentialist should take into account only the harm done by complying with the rule. Rather, in parallel with points made in section (ii), she should also consider the harm that could have been prevented by devoting the same effort to some other act instead. An example would be using the money saved by taking a cheap flight rather than an expensive train to sponsor a child in a flood-stricken country. Interpreted more broadly to include such alternatives, the caveat excludes mimicking duties and demands direct duties instead.[37]

Indeed, it seems inconsistent not to interpret the caveat more broadly still: as permitting individual non-compliance whenever, because of partial compliance, there is an alternative set of *overall* actions with better overall consequences. The levels cannot neatly be separated, because an individual whose ultimate moral concern is consequences would be irrational not to factor into her calculations the impact she could have on whether others follow these hypothetical rules. In considering how she might prevent great harm, she has to take into account not only a) the harm that might result from her compliance in a situation of partial compliance and b) the harm that might be prevented by her acting in some other way instead, but also c) the harm that might be prevented by devoting her energies, instead, to securing collective action and persuading non-compliers to cooperate. The consequentialist case could then be for promotional rather than mimicking duties.

With this in mind, let us return to Jamieson's argument. Undoubtedly, great harm would be prevented if nearly all individuals could become motivated to reduce their emissions. This would be so whether it were achieved by widespread adoption of an environmental virtue ethic, a variant on a major religion, or whatever else worked. However, as an individual, concern for consequences isn't going to motivate me to prioritize changing my character if I genuinely don't believe sufficient others will do so to achieve this overall good. I will instead be motivated to do what I can to bring about positive consequences, myself or with those similarly motivated, by fulfilling either direct or promotional duties.

Having rejected the rule-consequentialist case for mimicking duties, in general and as underlying Jamieson's argument, this section will end by briefly acknowledging a related line of reason. This is presented as a case for consequentialists to cut individual emissions but, I will argue, is liable to exactly the same objection as was just made. James Garvey defends mimicking by calling for consistency between what an individual demands of large polluting states such as the United States and what she is prepared to do herself, as a big per capita polluter. 'If you are a utilitarian with good consequentialist grounds for thinking that the world's biggest polluters ought to take strong action on climate change, then maybe consistency demands that the everyday choices in your life must be much more green.'[38] Or, as he puts it in slightly different terms elsewhere, because we see the behaviour of the West as a moral outrage we must, on consistency of principle, see our own behaviour as also outrageous.[39]

However, this is not a conclusive case for mimicking actions so long as it derives all its moral force from consequentialist considerations. In purely consequentialist terms, there is a vast gulf between the US, which is polluting disproportionally and could make a significant difference by cutting emissions, and me. It is true that I am also polluting disproportionally, but (unlike the US) I could not directly change the consequences by cutting my emissions. Thus, the moral outrage is appropriately directed collectively, at me and those relevantly like me, because between us we are causing harm. It is appropriately directed at me only insofar as I fail to respond appropriately to that situation. But the appropriate reaction, on consequentialist reasoning, will not be that which makes no difference. Concern for consequences, collective or individual, does not render me inconsistent in failing to make a sacrifice that would help no one.

If Garvey's argument is to defend mimicking duties—if it is even to rule out Sinnott-Armstrong's provocative suggestion of driving a gas-guzzler on a sunny afternoon while campaigning for the institutional changes that would make that very driving illegal—it must be read as more than an appeal to consequences. It must be read, instead, as incorporating direct concern for one's own moral character.[40] I will return to this possibility in section (v).

(IV) PLAYING BY FUTURE RULES

This section considers a recent defence of mimicking duties in the context of climate change: a hybrid of appeals to fairness and to ideal rules. Although Maltais, whose argument it is, considers the case ultimately overridden, it is worth considering here in its own terms. It can defend mimicking duties in the climate change case. However, it does not show them to have priority over promotional duties. (Nor, as Maltais has subsequently clarified, is it intended to do so.[41])

The argument is restricted to cases where the relevant harm results from the over-use of some specific, finite resource. The reasoning is as follows. Any collective response to climate change must be constrained by a safe global emissions budget. Any individual's emissions must be part of this total whether they happen before or after the collective scheme is introduced. Thus, it is unfair of me to emit excessive greenhouse gases now. As Maltais puts it, 'it would be unfair if I...flagrantly exploited my comparatively large capacity to emit and my temporal position of not currently being subject to constraints'.[42]

The claim is not that the individual wrongs her future cooperators by reducing the amount they will later have to divide between them, and so reducing the quality of life each will be able to enjoy within the new budget. Such an argument would rely on the possibility that individual consequences make some perceptible difference: a line of argument which Maltais himself has ruled out, and which was excluded here in section (ii). Rather, Maltais points out that *within* a fair collective scheme an individual would have a duty to reduce her own emissions even if it didn't make any difference in isolation. Without such correlative individual duties, the overall scheme would not be viable.

We might well respond by asking why this should make a difference now. Why should anybody play by the rules of a game that hasn't started yet? Because, on Maltais' reasoning, the individual who does otherwise is deliberately (or at least knowingly) exploiting her temporal position. She is exceeding what will be her fair entitlement when the scheme comes into place, and so taking unfair advantage of those who come later. To make the point, consider the following.

Before rationing
Augustus is on a long and arduous hike in a remote area with 99 others. The terrain has proved difficult and the weather unexpectedly hot. In order to keep all healthy and avoid the danger of fights breaking out over resources, they would shortly have to agree to pool all the food and water they have with them and ration it out strictly. Augustus overhears some of the others beginning to plan such a scheme. These are charismatic, natural leaders who can be expected quickly to secure general agreement. He immediately drinks the remaining contents of his own water bottle.

We can assume that the drink makes Augustus feel better, but that distributed across 100 people it would make no perceptible difference to the sufferings of each. The point, then, is not that Augustus has harmed the others by reducing the water available to each under the future scheme. Rather, he has taken unfair advantage of his future cooperators by drinking more than would be assigned to him by the fair scheme he can expect to come into force.

However, such reasoning in the climate change case does not succeed in defending mimicking duties as having priority over promotional duties. This claim rests on two related points. Firstly, the question of an individual's 'fair share' within the prospective collective scheme cannot be treated as fixed independent of whatever she does before the scheme comes into force.

This applies even while we focus only on emissions cuts. Little has been said about what a fair collective scheme would look like. However, as section (i) noted, there is no reason to assume it will involve equal emissions. On the contrary, it is plausible (and in line with dominant discussion in the literature on distributing burdens) that one determining factor would be previous emissions.[43] The same might be true of Augustus: if his share under the future fair scheme would be reduced to allow for what he has already drunk (or at least what he has drunk since knowing the scheme to be necessary), then he gains no advantage by his action.

This pulls two ways. Interestingly, it gives rise to a self-interested variant of Maltais' argument. If I believe that a scheme will shortly be introduced on which I will have an emissions allowance *and* that this allowance will go up or down in inverse proportion to my current emissions, then it is to my long-term disadvantage to emit wastefully now, given the decreasing marginal utility of additional emissions at any given point.

However, it also counts against the case for mimicking as having priority over promotion. To some extent, Maltais himself accepts this:

> [I]n one sense I am happy to say that an obligation to promote the adoption of a global budget that takes past emissions into consideration is the primary duty...If I think a collective scheme will take my personal past emissions into account...[m]y decision to continue emitting unrestrainedly now is...just a choice about when and how I would like to be constrained by the budget.[44]

For Maltais, however, it is questionable whether an individual can really 'do their fair share of remaining within a safe budget by *only* waiting for the collective scheme', because those in developed countries have probably already used up their fair share of the global emissions budget. '[W]hen I emit at unrestrained levels I am increasing the amount I owe (i.e. emissions debits), not decreasing the amount I will have left in the future budget.'[45] Returning to Augustus, the point is twofold. If he actually believes that drinking the water now will deprive him of it in the future scheme, it is implausible that he will do it. (Correspondingly, as Maltais points out, it is unrealistic to believe that those who do act in this way with emissions are thus motivated.) Moreover, if we suppose he has a lot of water in his bottle, Augustus might be drinking so much now that to take it fully into account in the future distribution would mean giving him a negative entitlement. This would be impossible in this case and in general would probably be overruled: whatever the conditions for a fair collective scheme, they are likely to include not depriving individual cooperators of fundamental interests. So drinking his water now makes it impossible for him to do his fair share.

Returning to the climate change, however, this counter-argument is weaker. There is more to an individual's contribution to a fair collective scheme than personal emissions reductions. Against this point, *Before rationing*, to which Maltais' reasoning neatly transferred, becomes an inadequate analogy for climate change. An individual can, at least to some degree, 'pay' her emissions debt by funding emissions reductions by others.[46] (That is, by providing resources such that they can reduce their emissions without bearing the costs themselves.) Moreover, for Polluters and The Able, fulfilling the weakly collective duty will also involve assigning adaptation and (for Polluters) compensation duties. Greater burdens can, accordingly, be assigned there. The claim is not that overall we could make up for failure to mitigate climate change by enabling adaptation. This was denied in Chapter One. However, there are ways other than (or at least alongside) emissions reductions in which any given individual can do *her* share. To both of these we might add a third point: that collective schemes are likely to make the necessary emissions reductions personally less costly.

The points just made do not count against Maltais' defence of mimicking duties, so long as they can be fulfilled alongside promotional duties. However, mimicking need not have priority over promotion even if the latter requires predictably higher individual emissions than a fair scheme, introduced now, would have permitted.

The second response to Maltais' argument is as follows. We cannot, like Augustus, be sure that a fair collective scheme is on its way. Maltais himself ultimately rejects the argument on the grounds that there is no reason to believe the collective scheme will come into force.[47] However, I would make a slightly different point. Of course, it is true that certainty that there will be no scheme counts against the argument: an individual violates duties of fairness to no one in failing to abide by rules to which no one will ever sign up. However, *un*certainty as to whether there will be a future scheme counts not so much against all mimicking, as in favour of promotion. To prioritize considerations of fairness to future cooperators in a scheme which may or may not be introduced over taking such actions as might help to introduce it, is very peculiar reasoning. Were it the case that a business-as-usual emissions approach by an individual now would undermine *all* possibility of her doing her fair share in the overall scheme, then mimicking duties might be defended. (Or at least, the individual might offer a 'damned if I do, damned if I don't' explanation either for mimicking or for promoting.) However, as I have argued above, this is not necessarily the case.

Having rejected the possibility that Maltais' argument can uphold mimicking duties as primary—because it does not give them priority over promotional duties—it is worth now considering direct duties. Do such considerations of fairness to future cooperators give mimicking duties priority over direct duties? I suggest that they do not, for reasons which—if convincing—also reinforce the discussion above. However, this point is made only briefly here because to some extent it anticipates the rejection of the compliance condition in Chapter Six.

In appealing to considerations of fairness among duty-bearers, this section has gone beyond the starting principles laid out in Chapter One: the no-harm principle and the principle of beneficence. It has done so uncontroversially enough. For most people (and on most philosophical views), considerations of fairness do have moral significance. However, it would have to go a great deal further to justify prioritizing fairness among duty-bearers over meeting the needs of victims, which is exactly what would be necessary to defend mimicking rather than direct duties. Although significant in themselves, considerations of fairness cannot be seen in isolation. In particular, they cannot be seen as separate from the situation of those very victims whose suffering is what prompts the future collective scheme in the first place. In that wider context, the individual who must choose between alleviating that suffering and being fair to future cooperators has reason to prioritize the former.

This section has identified a case for mimicking duties, but not as primary. This curtailment is important. It applies obviously in exceptional cases, such as flying round the world as a necessary part of promoting collective action on climate change. (Al Gore is the inevitable example.) However, it also applies more generally. We can safely assume that there is some limit to the demandingness of these individual duties. Such limits were built into the moral principles in Chapter One and I will return to them in this context in the next chapter. For now, the point is that, given some 'cap' to what an individual is morally required to do, then except insofar as mimicking is a means of fulfilling promotional or direct duties, she will have to choose where to distribute her efforts between them.

(V) MIMICKING AS A VIRTUE

This brings me to the last two possible cases for mimicking duties: by appeal to virtue ethics or the Kantian categorical imperative. It is worth stressing, however, that my degree of engagement with these arguments is curtailed by context before I even begin.

In taking the individual no-harm and beneficence principles as starting points, this project began with the presumption that expected consequences *matter*, at least at some level. The discussion in Part One was motivated by the further, intuitively compelling conviction that global-scale, terrible consequences must have moral weight with us, even if standard moral theory cannot explain why. Now, because the two starting principles can each be defended on more than one moral theory, it is worth considering what different philosophical approaches have to say about the individual's dilemma. However, the moral significance of the collective-level challenge remains in the background. The following sections will not show that there is no potential virtue ethics or Kantian defence of mimicking duties (although, as I will indicate, this is far from straightforward). Rather, I will argue that insofar as they can promote such duties as primary, these theories do so in so narrow, individual-, or character-focused a way as to appear irrelevant in the weakly collective context.

This section returns to the possibility left open in section (iii): that we should fulfil mimicking duties for the sake of our own moral characters. The consistency to which Garvey appeals would then be in line with something like Jonathan Glover's 'Solzhenitsyn Principle': "'Let the lie come into the world, even dominate the world, but not through me.'"[48] The same idea—that I should not be a part of what brings about harm, even if it would happen anyway without me—could also be found in Jamieson's virtue of 'mindfulness':

> A mindful person would appreciate the consequences of her action that are remote in time and space. She would see herself as taking on the moral weight of production and disposal when she purchases an article of clothing (for example)... Mindful people would not thoughtlessly emit climate-changing gases.[49]

As section (iii) argued, we need to look beyond ultimate moral concern for consequences in order to make a convincing case for individuals to develop these virtues. Instead, the argument would draw on the Aristotelian idea that we cannot flourish fully as human beings without being true to some kind of moral ideal.[50] 'Mindfulness', in this sense, is similar to the alleged virtue of integrity, to which Marion Hourdequin appeals in her defence of mimicking duties and which, she argues, 'requires a certain synchrony between personal and political action'.[51]

However, a virtue theory which advocated only a narrow concern for one's own moral integrity, satisfied by performing mimicking actions regardless of the actual situation, would be neither convincing nor appealing. As Bernard Williams argues, acting for the sake of your own integrity in this way looks suspiciously like moral self-indulgence.[52] If a great harm requires a collective solution, it is at best disingenuous—at worst repugnant—to wash one's own hands, morally speaking, and leave the resulting catastrophe to unfold. A more sympathetic model would take into account the possibility of collective as well as individual action. But in so doing, it would no longer clearly advocate mimicking duties, and certainly would not advocate only such duties.

Consider the following, based on the *Footbridge* cases of Chapter Two, and summarized in opening this chapter.

Weak bridge
A bridge can only hold 50 people safely. Hundreds of people are pushing onto it. If it collapses it will do serious harm to those on it, and to children swimming in the water underneath.

Consider an individual in this crowd. Mindfulness would connect her rushing onto the bridge with the harm to the children. On a narrow interpretation of the virtue approach, her only duty is to dissociate herself from that harm, presumably by waiting her turn. However, opting out might require her to get so far out of the crowd that she would have no influence on anyone still in it. She would then appear to have washed her own hands of the ensuing harm at the expense of actually doing something to stop it. Equally, zooming round smugly on a bicycle while failing to engage with the political process or otherwise promoting collective-level change looks like trying to save one's own soul while letting the rest of the world go hang. Even if it were bad *for the* individual to act in a way which in aggregate causes harm, it is hard to resist the idea that she has duties here to more than her own moral self. She has responsibilities to others.

Were there no alternative—if it were an exclusive choice between the harm without her and the harm with her—I am not ruling out the Solzhenitsynian view that the individual agent should detach herself from it in order to live with herself. Intuitively this is compelling, although it has been criticized.[53] I will return to such questions in Chapter Seven. Rather, I am suggesting that where there is an alternative—where a much better situation could be brought about by collective action—it is an implausible moral theory which limits her duty to such separation.[54]

In fact, as I will show below, such a reading would be unfair to most virtue ethicists, who are well aware that we act within a social context.[55] Once the collective element of environmental problems is fully acknowledged, considerations of what it means to be a virtuous human being do not provide a clear-cut defence of mimicking duties.

Virtue ethicists have a choice: appeal to the traditional virtues to address peculiarly environmental problems, or introduce new environmental virtues. On the former, it is worth noting that at least some immediate concern for consequences is introduced by the virtue of benevolence. This motivates the virtuous person to do what is to the advantage of others.[56] However, as sections (ii) and (iii) made clear, beneficence does not ground a clear-cut case for mimicking duties.

On the latter, development of specifically environmental values has taken two main forms.[57] On the first, specific duties to nature or to the environment are defended. However, the idea that she should respect the environment or respect nature is no more clearly action-guiding to the individual, in this context, than the fact of the collective-level harm to humans done by climate change. Unless the requirements of virtue ethics are interpreted in only the narrow sense above, it is unclear what—if anything—an individual can do to be virtuous if she lives in a society which is not set up to show respect to nature. (In Chapter Four, where weakly collective duties to non-humans were defended, the question of what *I* should do, as an individual in the current situation, remained open.)

Virtue theorist Rosalind Hursthouse acknowledges this. She points out that 'being rightly orientated to' nature seems either to rule out almost everything about modern society or yield only 'the obvious prohibitions that even the palest green environmentalist is already living in accordance with'.[58] There are a few things we can take as read: don't buy tropical caged birds; don't set fire to the Australian bush.[59] But such blindingly obvious restrictions correspond to prohibitions on direct harm. They are of little use when it comes to our day-to-day activities.

Perhaps the environmentally virtuous individual should give up all practices which in combination are harmful to nature. But can she? As Hursthouse points out, it may be impossible, given the way Western society is structured, genuinely to exhibit the environmental virtues within it. To exclude oneself altogether from society would be to prevent oneself from exercising other virtues. This leaves the individual not with a clear-cut path of action, but in a dilemma. As things are, *eudaimonia* (true well-being or flourishing) 'is beyond my grasp'.[60] Accordingly, insofar as Hursthouse recommends action, this is action, by individuals or motivated groups, to change society. In particular, she recommends inculcating environmental virtues in our children, with the idea that they will, in time, develop a way of life within which they can exercise those virtues. In other words, the defence is not of mimicking but, in the first instance, of promotional duties.

The second way in which virtue theorists have responded to this problem is by shifting their focus from specific behaviour types to an alternative virtue: judgement, based on practical wisdom. This, as defined by Trachtenberg, is 'the ability [of an individual] to discern the salient features of a particular situation and to choose the political action that will best advance his or her environmental values'.[61] Put like this, it might seem that appeal to judgement doesn't so much resolve the problem, as push it back onto the individual. Precisely the difficulty with which I am trying to grapple is that of knowing *how* to bring about certain results (whether advancing one's values or avoiding harm) when one's own action, in isolation, neither caused nor could prevent them.

Viewed more sympathetically, however, two points can be made. Firstly, there is an important—and true—observation here. Whatever overall strategy is proposed (whichever of direct, mimicking, or promotional duties are defended), it would be unrealistic for a general level account to attempt to dictate to each individual exactly what she could most effectively do, in the circumstances. Within the general guidelines, to some extent she will have to use her own judgement. Secondly, the appeal to judgement, in Trachtenberg's approach, can be narrowed down. Then, it can in no way be construed as a defence of mimicking duties. Rather, he is concerned with the individual as a green citizen. He is defending political actions: actions to change the way things are done, either to put an end to a deleterious way of life (promotional actions) or directly to secure some environmental goods.

(VI) KANTIAN CONTRADICTIONS

Our final possible defence of mimicking duties appeals to the idea that an individual should not live by maxims (or rules for conduct) which she cannot consistently will as universalized. This is the first formulation of Kant's categorical imperative.[62]

The idea is this: in producing greenhouse gas emissions through the pursuit of luxury goods, an individual is following a maxim which she cannot consistently will that everyone else should live by as well. This maxim would be something like 'consume as much as you can' or 'don't conserve finite resources'. Thus, in living by such implicit rules—in driving an SUV, for example, or taking repeated transatlantic flights—the individual is 'making an exception of [herself]'.[63] She could not justify this in terms of the rational humanity that (for Kant) is supposed to be the source of all moral value. As Garvey puts it: 'The very fact that the maxims are themselves part of an unsustainable order means that they could never be universal laws, never part of consistent worlds, never in keeping with the moral law.'[64]

In response to this, I have three points to make. Firstly, it is not universally agreed that high-emitting individual behaviour does actually violate the categorical imperative. Garvey may be adamant that it does, but Sinnott-Armstrong considers it just as self-evident that it doesn't. On his reasoning, a maxim such as 'expel greenhouse gases' is universalizable because it is no contradiction even if the aggregate consequences are bad.[65]

The dispute hangs on a distinction between logical and practical contradiction. If everyone emitted greenhouse gases at the rate of (say) a middle-aged resident of Texas, the consequences would be disastrous. But does this render it a contradiction to will that everyone be permitted to do so? Compare such scenarios to the following classic Kantian case.

False promise
For personal gain, an individual contemplates making a promise she knows she will not keep.[66]

This cannot be universalized without contradiction because, were everyone to make false promises when it suited them, there would be no reliable institution of promising and her own plan could not succeed. There would be a contradiction in universalizing the maxim whether the world were one of two people or of upwards of seven billion, and whether its resources were finite or otherwise. With carbon emissions, by contrast, universalization is problematic only in a finite world of high enough population. This seems to make it a different kind of contradiction: one which depends on contingent considerations. It is only because of these external facts that the individual knows that she can only adopt the maxim 'don't conserve finite resources' so long as not everyone else is doing so as well.

On at least some readings, the categorical imperative would exclude maxims where the contradiction is practical.[67] This suggests a way round Sinnott-Armstrong's argument. However, on such readings, a subsidiary difficulty arises: that of how far the Garvey reading of the imperative has to move away from the core Kantian idea of conclusions drawn solely from internal reasoning, towards appeal to actual consequences. (I say 'subsidiary' because my third point, below, stands independent of it.) It seems that this process must either rule out too much else as well, or have to apply a wealth of contingent details: details not only about the situation others are in, but also about how they can be expected to act.

This is an important point in the weakly collective context in general. After all, there are many acts which are perfectly harmless (even beneficial) if only a few do them but disastrous if many people do. Recall *Weak bridge*. If sufficient numbers rush onto the bridge, great harm will be done. This is the case whether the attraction on the other side is a meet-and-greet by the latest boy band, or a new type of beetle. Now consider the maxim: 'Cross weak bridges.' Suppose, in determining whether this is universalizable, we appeal only to the negative consequences of everyone crossing the bridge. Then the answer is no in either case. However, from the point of view of the individual motivated to cross, there is a huge difference between the two. Hundreds of others would throng onto the bridge to get to the boy band, but only a handful couldn't care less about the beetle, and no harm would be done even if she and they all rushed onto it.

To avoid being hugely, unnecessarily restrictive, the Kantian inclined to Garvey's interpretation of the imperative would have to frame maxims with in-built (more or less explicit) appeal to facts about how others can actually be expected to behave. 'Cross bridges which can only support the weight of 100 people when 100 people are already expected to cross it at the same time' would be ruled out, as would 'Cross the bridge if you want to see a boy band'. The equivalent in the climate change case would be something like: 'Don't consume finite resources for non-essentials if there is reason to suppose that others will do the same.'

This seems far indeed from the core Kantian idea of appeal to pure, internal rationality. Moreover, the more social the imperative becomes, the harder it is to see why the individual should cling to what is left of the core appeal to pure rationality. If the application of the imperative must appeal to as many contingent factors as this to avoid ruling out too much, why should the individual not go further still? Why should she not factor in not only how other people are motivated to act, but how they actually will: that is, whether they, too, will follow these hypothetical rules? In other words, a parallel partial compliance objection arises to that made against rule-consequentialism in section (iii).[68]

However, in the climate change case there is a response to this objection. Perhaps the Garvey reading of the imperative needn't go so far as this, because maxims permitting luxury emissions fail the universalizability test given only general knowledge. This includes practical knowledge about our finite planet and growing population, as well as general facts about human motivation (or human nature). However, it need not include predictions about how particular other people will behave.[69] To mix my analogies, we can take it as a general fact that this is a boy band rather than a beetle situation.

We are left, however, with the third (and most substantial) point against appeal to the Kantian imperative in this context. That is, that Kant's is very much an individual-focused, ideal world moral theory. As John Rawls puts it:

> Kant is concerned solely with the reasoning of fully reasonable and rational and sincere agents. The CI-procedure is a schema to characterise the framework of deliberation that such agents use implicitly in their moral thought. He takes for granted that the application of this procedure presupposes a certain moral sensibility that is part of our common humanity.[70]

However, this is not a world of fully motivated, fully rational agents. Why, then, should we adhere to a rigidly ideal world approach in making our individual moral decisions, rather than respond as effectively as possible to the actual situation?

This point can be made at two levels. The first is internal to the Kantian project. In section (iii), I questioned why individuals should adhere to those rules that would have the optimum consequences if everyone else complied with them, given that a) others are unlikely to do so, and b) the individual acting in isolation may have no positive consequences at all. The parallel point here, against the Kantian, is that in rigidly adhering to rules justified for a world of 'fully reasonable and rational and sincere agents' rather than attempting to bring about collective-level change in a world which is nothing like this, we fail adequately to respond to some very probable, very terrible outcomes. These are terrible not only in terms of aggregate well-being, but also in terms of preserving the conditions for that very rational humanity which is so central to the Kantian project.

The second level is more general. As even contemporary Kantian Christine Korsgaard acknowledges, the theory's indifference to actual consequences can, in some cases, be a weakness:

> The advantage of the Kantian approach is the definite sphere of responsibility. Your share of the responsibility for the way the world is is well-defined and limited, and if you act as you ought, bad outcomes are not your responsibility. The trouble is that in cases such as that of the murderer at the door it seems grotesque simply to say that I have done my part by telling the truth and the bad results are not my responsibility.[71]

This acknowledged individualistic focus leaves Kantian thinking struggling to get a grip on the real questions at stake in climate ethics. As Jamieson puts it: 'If our primary concern is how we should act in the face of global environmental change, then we need a theory that is seriously concerned with what people bring about, rather than a theory that is (as we might say) "obsessed" with the purity of the will.'[72] A rigidly individually and internally focused approach is all the more inappropriate given the moral significance associated, from the very start of this book, with very serious negative consequences and the potential *collectively* to respond to them. There is even more reason, like Jamieson, to eschew as a guide to individual action an approach so entirely opposed to the view 'that the business of morality is to *bring something about*'.[73]

CONCLUSIONS

This completes the first stage of my defence of promotional duties as primary. I have considered a number of ways in which the widespread appeal of mimicking duties might be explained philosophically. I have argued that none succeeds in defending such duties as exclusive or even primary. Broadly interpreted, most arguments which did not fail altogether to convince made a better case for promotional or direct duties. More narrowly interpreted, some traditional theories failed altogether to get a handle on what is at stake in the climate change scenario. They were too narrowly individualistic, too preoccupied with moral character taken in isolation, to be of real use in situations where the only solution is collective. No man is an island, or can consider himself such for the purposes of limiting his moral sphere.

This does not mean we should not do any of the things standardly regarded as 'green'. I left it open that there may be a 'clean hands', character-based case for mimicking duties where it is genuinely impossible to fulfil promotional or direct duties. I also accepted a fairness-based case for mimicking when compatible with them. Moreover, a distinction can be drawn between mimicking *duties* and mimicking *actions*. It may yet turn out that we have a duty to perform the actions that would be required of us by a fair collective scheme not because this can be defended as a duty in itself, but because such actions are a necessary part of fulfilling direct or promotional duties. I will return to this in the next chapter. For now, contrary to widespread perception, the point is this. In making unilateral emissions cuts I cannot consider myself to be doing all that my climate duties demand of me. Moreover, in cases of conflict between mimicking and promotional or direct duties, there is no plausible philosophical case for prioritizing the former.

6

Promotional and Direct Duties

> We hold these truths to be self-evident, that all men are created equal, that they are endowed by their Creator with certain unalienable Rights... That whenever any Form of Government becomes destructive of these ends, it is the Right of the People to alter or to abolish it, and to institute new Government...[1]
>
> *United States Declaration of Independence*

> The reality throughout my lifetime has been, corporations and governments are powerful, and people are weak, and there is nothing you can do to change that. Now that paradigm is starting to shift, and all of a sudden, the world is starting to believe in people power again.[2]
>
> Tim de Christopher, climate activist

The previous chapter began with the question: 'What should *I* do?' This chapter completes my response to it.

Given collective failure to fulfil a weakly collective duty, individual duties fall into the following broad categories. Mimicking duties are duties to imitate what would be required by a fair collective scheme to fulfil the duty. Promotional duties are duties to attempt to bring about the necessary collective action. Direct duties are duties to protect the interests at stake or mitigate the harm directly, oneself or in combination with a like-minded subset. Chapter Five argued that mimicking duties are neither exclusive nor primary: they are not all that can be expected of us as individuals and they do not take priority over promotional or direct duties. This chapter defends promotional duties as primary, supplemented by direct duties.

Section (i) indicates the range of possible promotional actions in the climate change case. It also distinguishes this approach from that of Walter Sinnott-Armstrong, who advocates some promotional duties. Section (ii) defends promotional duties on the basis of effectiveness, fairness, and efficiency. Section (iii) makes the case for direct duties when an individual is unable to fulfil promotional duties or it would be overdemanding to require her to do so, or when she can do so as an effective means of promoting collective action. With this framework in place, section (iv) returns to the question of individual emissions cuts: of whether (and why) we should 'go green' as individuals. It makes a limited consequentialist case for mimicking *actions*, as derivative of promotional or direct duties.

Sections (v) and (vi) comment on the demandingness of these correlative individual duties and on whether this varies across individuals. In the process, I reject Liam Murphy's compliance condition, according to which individuals should not be required to do more under partial than they would under full compliance with moral duties. I also respond to the objection that it is implausible to assign even moderately demanding duties in the climate change case because this is so entirely out of tune with our everyday assessment of our own behaviour.

Before embarking on this, one further point must be stressed. Chapter Four argued that our weakly collective climate duties include duties to non-human animals, as well as duties either to or at least to protect or not to destroy species and systems. This expansion complicates the picture: even collectively, we could reach the limits of demandingness before securing the interests of even nearly all those affected. However, what I say in this chapter will hold as long as it remains the case that the most that could be done towards protecting the relevant interests would be done by acting collectively.

(I) INDIVIDUALS AND INSTITUTIONS

We start here with the weakly collective duty defended in Part One. This is crucial, as will become apparent, in making the effectiveness case for promotional duties. However, it also sets this chapter apart from Sinnott-Armstrong's more limited argument.[3]

Sinnott-Armstrong also argues that individuals should promote collective action on climate change. However, his focus is on state-level change, and his approach is encapsulated by the title of his paper: 'It's Not My Fault'.[4] This chapter begins, by contrast, with the idea that it is *our* fault, or at least our responsibility. In claiming that 'it is not individuals who cause [climate change] or who need to fix it', he glosses over the distinction between individuals in isolation and individuals in combination as collectivities or potential collectivities. I have argued that, as Polluters, The Able, or The Young, we have weakly collective duties to act on mitigation, adaptation, and compensation. That is not to say—even within Polluters—that each of us is blameworthy in a full-blooded, guilt-inducing sense. However, it does mean that we cannot consider ourselves apart from the problem.

According to Sinnott-Armstrong, environmentalists should focus on 'getting governments to do their job to prevent the disaster of excessive global warming'.[5] This highlights a relevant promotional duty but fails, in two ways, to go far enough. Firstly, it underplays the extent to which, at least in many states, the government is *our* government. It is important to be clear here. I am not making the highly controversial claim that we can each be held accountable for all of our government's actions and failures. The point is simply this: if our government is not acting so as to fulfil its obligations, then as citizens we cannot dissociate ourselves from this failure. Even if it were our government's 'job' to tackle climate change, it would be so because, ultimately, that was required of us. The duty, if unfulfilled at that level, would fall back on us.[6]

Secondly, to refer to 'the government's job' is to underestimate the scope of the problem. Existing governments, in isolation, are neither the cause of climate change nor its solution. As collectivities or potential collectivities, The Young, Polluters, and The Able have a global span. It goes without saying that existing institutions, especially states, provide channels through which individuals might effectively promote collective action. However, our collective potential to prevent externally caused harm, or to stop ourselves from causing it in aggregate, goes beyond existing collective-decision-making structures. Because of this, fulfilment of the weakly collective duty could involve changing, or if necessary establishing, decision-making structures.

This can be so even at the small scale. For example, recall the following.

Swimming teenagers
A number of teenagers, all independently, decide to swim in a small lake. They cause so much turbulence between them that a child also independently swimming in the lake is in severe danger of drowning.

To prevent the danger to the child, the teenagers need to stop splashing, or enough of them need to get out of the water. As Chapter Three pointed out, on a one-off basis, if this is possible in time, it will almost certainly be informally organized. However, in repeated cases, some ongoing system is needed reliably to limit the number of teenagers in the water. There may be some established institution which, in the first instance, would be responsible for setting up such a system: probably an agency within the local or national government. To this extent, in parallel with Sinnott-Armstrong, it might be deemed 'its job' to do so. However, the fact of such an institution does not mean that individuals can rest on their laurels. Nor can they necessarily do so even if they have attempted to persuade it to act. If it fails, the duty falls back on them, and requires either changing the institution, or acting collectively independently of it.

Moreover, there is not always such an authority. Suppose the lake is in a remote area on the boundary of several countries, with the teenagers coming from various hamlets in the different countries. Or recall *Easy rescue 5* from Chapter Two, in which various smallholders need to cooperate to protect children from a foreseeable danger. In either case, the necessary organizational structure, formal or informal, needs to be established before the weakly collective duty can be fulfilled.

As Chapter One stressed, I am not committing myself to any particular type of collective action as necessary or appropriate in the climate change case. I have left it open whether the weakly collective duty would best be fulfilled via an effective agreement between states, by giving greater authority to some existing international body, by establishing some stronger global-level institution, or even—at the other extreme—by some global-level agreement between individuals or sub-state collectivities, perhaps coordinated by NGOs or some other voluntary body.[7]

This leaves open innumerable ways in which an individual might fulfil promotional duties. Recall *Weak bridge*, in which hundreds of individuals are crowding onto a bridge that can only safely hold 50 and will, if it collapses, injure those on it and/or children swimming in the river below. An individual might jump onto a wall and shout to the rest to remind them of the danger. She might shout to a policeman, standing at the side, to impose order. She might start by trying to persuade those she knows, or those closest to her, to wait until it is clearer. She and a subset of others might simply pick out random sets of individuals and ask them to wait.

Now consider an individual living in (say) the UK, faced with the problem of climate change. She could campaign and vote for candidates for local and national office who are committed to promoting international and national mitigation and adaptation efforts.[8] In the absence of such candidates, she could stand herself or encourage a suitable candidate to do so. She could petition her local MPs and MEPs to change their policies. She could send emails to the UK Prime Minister, the US president, the UN Secretary General, the President of the European Commission, or the President of China. She could write them open letters in national or international newspapers or on social media sites. She could donate to campaign organizations such as Friends of the Earth. She could sign and circulate petitions, in person or online. She could join or organize marches at international summits. She could write articles, set up websites, and otherwise call for adherents to the kind of norm-changing 'global citizenship movement' suggested by Dale Jamieson.[9] The list is by no means exhaustive, but it serves to illustrate the scope of possible actions.

Having indicated what is meant by promotion, the next section will defend promotional duties as primary.

(II) EFFECTIVENESS, FAIRNESS, AND EFFICIENCY

The appeal to effectiveness is as follows. As Chapter Five pointed out, on the assumption that at least some intentionally collective action is required to fulfil a weakly collective duty, promotional duties follow automatically.[10] If individuals didn't bring such action about, it couldn't happen. The weakly collective duty would be rendered meaningless, because doomed to remain unfulfilled.

To make the point, consider the following:

Broken dam

A dam has broken above an extremely populous and poor area. The resulting rush of water is causing more and more deaths. Concerted effort by most of the other people in the vicinity (bystanders) could repair the dam, rescue those already in the water, and prevent further harm. As individuals, the bystanders can rescue individual victims. However, even if all were to do so, and go on doing so, they would not be able to prevent anything like all the deaths.

Without individual duties to bring about collective action, the collective-level duty will remain unfulfilled.

The same example can be used to illustrate the appeal to fairness and efficiency. Over the long term, very great effort will be demanded of those individuals who go on and on trying to rescue victims from the water (as ever more are swept into it). This is far more effort than they would have to make in a fairly implemented collective plan to mend the dam and provide the necessary support for individuals to rebuild their lives afterwards. Moreover, if only some of the individuals perform such actions, the disproportionate burden on them is prima facie unfair.

So far, so apparently straightforward. However, there are a number of objections to this reasoning, at least some of which have to be taken seriously in the climate change case. Firstly, the effectiveness argument would be undermined if the collective end could be secured by aggregated fulfilment of individual direct duties. This is a parallel claim to that made in the previous chapter about mimicking duties. However, to some extent it is a stronger one: direct duties, unlike mimicking duties, can be defended independently, as protecting individuals from serious harm.

This objection can largely be rejected. There may be cases in which combined performance of direct actions could fulfil a weakly collective duty (often because they overlap with mimicking actions), but in many situations where aggregated individual actions could bring about an overall end, those actions *cannot* be defended as fulfilment of direct duties. As Chapter Five made clear, individual emissions cuts are one such case. Moreover, as was also stressed in Chapter Five, there are many cases of a weakly collective duty in which it is only by acting collectively in a stronger sense that all or even most of the fundamental interests at stake can be protected. In such cases, without correlative individual promotional duties, the weakly collective duty would indeed be meaningless, because destined for non-fulfilment. Indeed, if the overall harm is ongoing and its resolution involves large-scale cooperation, those individuals who fulfil only direct duties will have given themselves a task as relentless and interminable as painting the Forth Road Bridge.[11]

Of course, even in such cases, fulfilling direct duties can be expected to do *some* good (to alleviate some suffering). However, this does not count against the appeal to effectiveness. The point is not directly to compare expected individual consequences, but to reason backwards from what is needed for the weakly collective duty to be fulfillable. The framework defended in Part One enables us to make sense of the demands on individuals as derivative of a primarily collective duty: what *I* should do follows from what *we* owe the victims of climate change.

The second objection is as follows. In some weakly collective situations, a subset of individuals could either mitigate the suffering entirely, or make it up to the victims, on their own. (This might be so even if they could not, in the context of the argument from weakly collective harm, prevent the predictably harmful combination of actions.)

This option changes the dilemma faced by the individual. She might be almost certain that she could achieve the weakly collective end with the help of others she knows to be motivated, but have reason to doubt that a more generally collective solution can be achieved. For example, in *Swimming teenagers*, two of the teenagers might doubt that they could motivate the others in time to prevent the harm by reducing the splashing, but realize they could save the child by swimming across and pulling her out themselves instead.

In such special cases, effectiveness, on the one hand, and fairness and efficiency, on the other, pull in opposite directions. The outcome will almost certainly be unfair, because the distribution of the burdens across those weakly collectively responsible is arbitrarily uneven. (I say 'almost certainly' because it is of course possible, although highly unlikely, that those bearing the burdens will be exactly those to whom a fair collective scheme would have assigned them.) By the same token, it is also likely to be inefficient.[12] The cost to those individuals of saving all the victims will generally be comparatively high, with greater impact on other life projects, ties, and relationships.[13]

To make the point, imagine a variant on *Broken dam* in which half of the bystanders could save all the lives between them if each devoted days to the effort. If the burdens were shared among the potential collectivity as a whole (that is, among all the bystanders), not only would economies of scale be possible, but the sacrifices made by each would be only at the peripheries of their lives. Overall costs would be lower.

In responding to this objection, we must distinguish between direct duties performed by individuals or small-scale subsets and those performed by very large subsets. With regard to the former, the greater the scale, the less likely it becomes that an individual or comparatively small subset could secure the overall end. Moreover, anticipating section (v), there are limits to what can be demanded of individuals in fulfilment of correlative individual duties. To count against the case for a primary duty to promote collective action, not only would the individual or subset have to be able to secure the overall end through fulfilling direct duties, but she or it would have to be able to do so at a cost below that demandingness limit. Again, in ongoing cases, this becomes increasingly unlikely. (Recall the subset, above, in *Broken dam*, and imagine how exhausting this effort would be for the relevant individuals, how incapable they would be of maintaining other projects—even looking after their own children—for as long as they were committed to the rescue.)

The situation is different when we turn to large subsets, which constitute a significant proportion of the overall collectivity or potential collectivity. In the climate change case, a subset would have to be very substantial in order to be able to secure mitigation, adaptation, and compensation on its own, although there is some dispute about just how large. For example, David Victor argues that the most promising route for action on mitigation is via the cooperation of a much smaller set of states than those currently involved in negotiations, while Stephen Gardiner maintains that it would be 'virtually impossible for a group of countries to deliver a global ceiling on emissions without the cooperation of the others'.[14] The kind of global citizens' movement envisaged by Jamieson would not need universal participation to succeed, but it could not do so without being truly global in scope, and including a substantial proportion of Polluters.[15]

In either case, however, the current situation is not relevantly changed from the point of view of the individual moral agent. Were this a subset already full of like-minded, motivated individuals, effectiveness would dictate their taking on the additional burdens to mitigate and enable adaptation to climate change. Anticipating section (v), and in line with developing discussions in the literature on allocating the burdens of tackling climate change, a case could be made for prioritizing this effectiveness (which would actually secure the fundamental interests of victims) over considerations of fairness between duty-bearers.[16] However, this is very far from the situation we are in now. Whether the action is to be at the level of the overall collectivity or at a global sub-collective level—or even at the level of some set of ten or twenty states—*that* action still needs to be brought about. The individual's primary duty remains promotional. (Indeed, as the subset gets closer to the size of the overall collectivity, the line becomes blurred between fulfilment of sub-collective mitigating direct duties and collective fulfilment of the overall duty.)

The third objection combines the first two, arguing that the collective end could be secured through the aggregation of actions of a number of existing sub-collectivities. Each would itself be taking strongly collective action to fulfil a direct duty, but doing so independently of the others. In the climate change case, the idea would be that the overall ends (mitigation, adaptation, perhaps even compensation) could be secured through the combined actions of a handful of states (or, in the case of the European Union, of groups of states already set up for collective action). Promotion of global-level action would, accordingly, be unnecessary. This might be reinforced by appeal to the fact that certain individual states (say, the US, or China) are such high emitters that, in theory, they could secure a large proportion of the overall emissions reductions necessary to mitigate climate change simply by cutting their own emissions.[17]

As a case against the primacy of promotional duties, this can be questioned at one level and rejected altogether at another. Firstly, recalling Gardiner's scepticism about effective cooperation by a small group of states, there is reason to doubt the empirical claim, at least as regards mitigation. As he points out, the flipside of the potential of individual states to make huge emissions cuts is their potential to undermine cuts achieved elsewhere simply by increasing their own emissions.[18]

Secondly, even if aggregate state action could secure the overall end, and could be defended independently as fulfilling a direct duty, then—again—all that would have changed from the point of view of the individual is the relevant collective level, *not* the case for promotional duties. Unfortunately, no state can be regarded as representing a like-minded subset of individuals, all eager to fulfil sub-collective direct climate duties. Rather, there is a first stage needed to get to the point of action—whether on mitigation, adaptation, or compensation—by each of the relevant states. Individual promotional duties remain necessary to fulfilling the weakly collective duty.

The final objection is this: effectiveness at the collective level doesn't automatically equate to effectiveness at the individual level. In the last chapter, mimicking duties were rejected at least in part because their fulfilment by individuals can be expected to make no difference. Cannot a similar case be made against promotional duties? Can I, as one individual, really do anything to increase the chance of collective action, especially if that action has to be at the global level? If not, why should I be required to waste my effort in this way, especially if I could instead perform some direct action which would at least do some positive good? This objection concedes that without such correlative duties the overall end would be unachievable (and so the weakly collective duty meaningless), but points out in return that if individuals can make *no* difference through promotion, then even the assignment of such duties would do nothing to remedy this.

This can be rejected. There are important differences between mimicking and promotion. Firstly, in the case of individual emissions cuts, others' actions were taken as fixed independent of our own. I considered appeal to the chance of triggering some threshold for harm, and rejected it on the grounds that we will hit this threshold regardless of the actions of any one individual. Now, however, it is more rational to appeal to the small chance of making a big difference, because one of the factors to be taken into consideration is that of changing the behaviour of those others.[19]

(A quick clarificatory aside: it will, of course, be pointed out that individual mimicking actions might also be expected to influence others. This is true. However, insofar as they are defended on these grounds they are defended only as a means of fulfilling promotional duties. I will return to this in section (iv).)

The second distinction between the cases is related to the first. Promotional actions, unlike many mimicking actions, are not throw-away acts: one-off bets, the consequences of which, win or lose, are to be assessed in isolation. Even if they don't succeed straight off, they can still contribute to a stockpile of impetus for collective change. Thus, they are less like losing bets and more like money put in the bank which, even if it doesn't immediately enable you to buy what you want, can be a part of a successful attempt to do so later. They can be added to, complemented, and improved, both by the individual and by others.

Recall *Weak bridge*. If an agent slips out of the crowd and walks away, she's made her one-off sacrifice and can only stand by to see whether it turns out to be pointless. If she tries instead to alert the crowd to the problem, she can cajole others until either something happens or it is too late. (Moreover, in ongoing cases, there is no natural cut-off point at which her attempt has failed.) She can try other strategies to add to her influence if one isn't proving sufficient. If others join in, they can build on her efforts, the combination becoming greater than the sum of its parts. As the range of promotional actions available in the climate change case brings out, parallel reasoning applies here.

To these we might add a further, practical, point. It can hardly be denied that *some* individuals influence what happens at the global level. Individuals do change history: often, admittedly, for the bad, but sometimes also for the good. However, the objector has a response to this, which concedes the odd exceptional case but maintains that most of us are in no position to change history. We are 'ordinary individuals', not the UN Secretary General, or the Pope, or the President of China, or even the head of Greenpeace or Oxfam.

I do think that more might be expected of individuals already in such positions. I also allow that there may be some individuals with no influence, for whom direct duties take priority. I will return to both these points in later sections. However, for most of us in Western democracies, in reasonable health, with at least ordinary abilities and a reasonable education, this response fails. Imagine if the young Barack Obama or Nelson Mandela had reasoned thus! Imagine, in the climate change context, if Caroline Lucas, the first British Green Member of Parliament, had done so. If bringing about change requires so-called ordinary individuals to seek such extraordinary roles, then promotional duties could be fulfilled by trying to achieve this.

There are two possible counter-arguments to this. On the one hand, it might be pointed out that the individuals I just listed, even if they did acquire their position through their own efforts, were (or are) exceptional in their talents. But most of us are not like that. We are not even the kind of uniquely charismatic or already influential individuals who could spearhead a movement to change behaviour at the global level. Nor are most of us at an unusual advantage, in terms of influence, for some other, unrelated reason: we are not most of us rock stars, or actresses, or Premiership footballers.

On the other hand, the objector might appeal to the cost of taking on such roles.[20] Again, anticipating section (v), there are limits to what can be demanded of us in fulfilment of our moral duties. However, seeking to become a public figure amounts, in effect, to making the pursuit of these ends one's life's work. The costs of taking up a public position are also high in other ways, especially in terms of intrusion into one's own personal life. This is so whether or not the role adopted is in an existing, formalized institution. Once in the public eye, one can expect to have personal decisions scrutinized and lifestyle choices—even one's religion or sexuality—examined and criticized by an unsympathetic media. This is likely to be all the more costly for those whose way of life is outside the dominant model in their society. At a comparatively mild level, consider the media furore over the 'outing' of British politician Peter Mandelson, or the fact that the current leader of the British Labour Party, Ed Milliband, was not married to his long-term partner. In 2012 a spokesman for US Republican presidential candidate Mitt Romney resigned after only a few weeks, allegedly because of conservative reactions to his sexuality.[21]

Indeed, bringing the two points together, some individuals have a skill set such that it would be peculiarly arduous to stand for public office or otherwise seek a leadership role. Consider King George VI's stammer; an individual with a choice about taking on the position might understandably decline if he had such an obstacle to overcome.

I agree that these are significant costs, and will return in Chapter Seven to the potentially still far greater costs of some promotional action. However, to avoid the objection here it is only necessary to show that there are many ways in which individuals can contribute meaningfully to promoting collective action without incurring unacceptable costs. To do this, it is important to be clear on what is being asked. I do not claim that all individuals are duty-bound to try to hold public office and implement green policies. Promotional duties could be fulfilled by promoting or aiding the election of those who will use their position to promote action on climate change. Nor are we all required to devote our lives, as some have done, to climate action. So long as there are some who are ready, willing, and appropriately motivated to take up such roles (within or beyond existing institutions), for most of us it will be sufficient to support them.

Indeed, it will often be more efficient to do so. Naturally gifted orators could better and more efficiently achieve promotional ends by campaigning for political or social change than those who are by nature shy and retiring. However, these latter could still write letters, sign petitions, commit publicly to a global citizenship movement, or at the very least contribute financially to campaign organizations. (Anticipating sections (v) and (vi), that is not to suggest that all those who are naturally gifted orators must give up their lives to green politics or follow activists such as Tim de Christopher into the dock in pursuit of environmental ends. Rather, the point is that there are efficiency as well as demandingness grounds for not requiring all of us, including the constitutionally unsuited, to seek public careers.)

This completes the appeal to fairness, effectiveness, and efficiency in defence of promotional duties as primary. I end the section by making another (I hope obvious) clarificatory point. The claim here is not that, all things considered, an individual must always prioritize promotional over all other duties, including her interpersonal and other moral duties. Chapter Seven will reinforce this. Rather, it is that, in the context of this weakly collective duty, the individual acquires moral duties, and her primary such duty is promotional.

(III) DIRECT DUTIES

Having defended promotional duties as primary, this section will briefly consider the circumstances under which individuals might also incur direct duties. I am concerned here not with those cases (discussed in section (ii)) in which the sub-collectivity fulfilling the direct duty is large enough to secure the overall end. The focus, instead, is on when individuals or small subsets should attempt to aid victims or mitigate the harm directly. Accordingly, I begin with the proviso that the discussion applies only to cases (unlike, say, *Beach rescue*) where there is scope at this level for preventing or alleviating the suffering of victims. Clearly, climate change is one such case.

The most obvious case for direct duties is, of course, where the necessary collective action is impossible, or impossible in time. In such cases, all individuals must turn to second-best responses. However, in such cases there would be no weakly collective duty. Chapters Two and Three have already made the point that global-level action on climate change is not collectively impossible. Ignoring this possibility, then, I will outline two scenarios in which there is a weakly collective duty but certain individuals might nonetheless acquire direct duties.

Firstly, to return to a point highlighted in section (ii), there may be some individuals who cannot or should not be expected to contribute to bringing collective action about. Two possible cases emerge. The individual might genuinely and reasonably believe that she can do nothing by way of promoting collective action, but could do some good in isolation. In *Weak bridge*, a man universally reviled as untrustworthy might recognize the risk but know full well that no one will listen to him. Then, his best response would be to rush to the aid of the children below the bridge. Alternatively, promotional activities might be disproportionately costly for a given individual, because of the position they are in or their own abilities. Then, anticipating section (v), it could be overdemanding to perform any promotional acts but not necessarily so to fulfil direct duties. Perhaps—to use a particularly extreme example—our individual in *Weak bridge* is fleeing an assassin who is also in the crowd. To draw any attention to himself would cost him his life, but he could quietly attempt to get individual children out of the water.

Bringing the two together, an example in the climate change case would be an individual in a totalitarian regime who knows that any criticism of his government's current policy would cost him his life or liberty, to no effect, but who could nonetheless do some direct good by spending time helping the victims of a tsunami. It is worth stressing, however, that these are exceptional cases. In more developed states, even the shyest (and all but the poorest) individuals can sign an email petition, and most can do considerably more, at relatively little cost to themselves.

Secondly, it may be possible both to fulfil promotional duties and to perform direct duties. Again, there are two possibilities. Suppose an individual has done all she can by way of promotion and still has some effort to spare within (anticipating section (v)) the limits of demandingness. In *Weak bridge*, an individual might shout to alert everyone else to the problem, suggest that those in a particular part of the crowd should wait their turn, then lose her voice. Then, perhaps, she should rush down to get as many children as she can out of the water.

Given the range of available promotional actions, it is hard to see how this could occur in the climate change case in general, although it might do so for some special case individuals. However, the second possibility, which is relevant here, is that fulfilling direct duties is one way of promoting collective action. Then, if it is as effective as other methods, there is reason to favour it, because direct duties can be defended independently, by appeal to the individual principle of beneficence. By conspicuously assisting the victims of an environmental disaster, a celebrity might at once do good herself and alert public attention to the need to tackle climate change.

(IV) BACK TO MIMICKING: MOTIVATION AND HYPOCRISY

Chapter Three rejected a number of defences of mimicking duties as either primary or exclusive. This included rejecting appeals to consequentialism, at two levels. Now, however, we are in a position to return to the question, with a limited consequentialist case for some mimicking actions.

It is worth being clear from the start about just how limited this is. The case for mimicking actions is derivative of promotional duties: not a defence of mimicking as a duty in itself. The fact that the action concerned is one the individual would perform under full compliance with a collective scheme is, when relevant at all, only indirectly so. (Relevant because that fact itself might play a part in motivating others to act.)

There are two versions of the claim that mimicking can be part of fulfilling promotional duties. On the milder version, it is the most effective means of fulfilling some promotional duties. On the stronger version, it is a prerequisite to any such promotion, because without it the individual would be a hypocrite. I will begin with the latter, where, again, it is important to distinguish three levels of the argument. On the first, there really is morally problematic inconsistency in such behaviour. However, appeal to consistency as a case for prioritizing mimicking duties was rejected in the last chapter, on both consequentialist and character-based readings.

At the second level, this is an extreme version of a point made by Marion Hourdequin: the claim that it is psychologically impossible for the individual to campaign for collective action on climate change whilst continuing to live a high-emitting lifestyle herself.[22] Were this the case, mimicking would be a universal prerequisite for fulfilling promotional duties, because any promotional duty which conflicted with mimicking would fail the test of 'ought implies can': that is, that an individual cannot have a moral duty which it is impossible to fulfil. Certainly, such apparent inconsistency could be psychologically problematic. However, the stronger claim is, on the face of it, implausible: people do campaign on climate change and ratchet up their own emissions in the process. (As in Chapter Five, Gore is the obvious example.)

At the third level, the argument appeals to the negative impact of perceived hypocrisy. Rightly or wrongly, publicly promoting systematic change whilst continuing to maximize your position within the old system tends not to improve public opinion either of you or of the worthiness of your goals. Consider the criticism of UK government ministers who stress their commitment to improving the state school system whilst sending their own children to private schools.[23] Imagine how effective an individual's promotional efforts would be if she pushed herself to the front of the crowd in *Weak bridge*, all the time yelling out that only fifty people should be allowed on at once. Thus, whether or not there is morally relevant hypocrisy involved, the impact of its perception on the success or failure of attempts to promote collective change provides a consequentialist case for some mimicking actions.[24]

This is an important consideration. However, it is not so universal as to rule out any successful promotion without mimicking attached. The extent to which it will be a factor in the climate change case will vary. Those more in the public eye (those very individuals of whom, I will suggest in section (vi), more promotional success might reasonably be expected), who are likely to have their actions overhauled by an often unsympathetic press, can least afford to ignore the consideration of perceived hypocrisy. However, even for them there does seem to be a trade-off. (Once again, consider Al Gore.)

Returning to the milder claim, there are cases where an individual could best promote collective action by performing mimicking actions. This might operate in two ways: either by prompting sufficient other individuals to commit to acting together, or by prompting existing institutions to change policies. In the former case, this could be because, by making a sacrifice herself, the individual sets an example, and makes it more likely that others will do so. Alternatively, conversely, taking the action might be the best way to show others that it is actually comparatively easy or pleasant to do so, and motivate them in that way.

However, it is highly unlikely that quietly performing any or all mimicking actions will be effective. We might draw a distinction here between *private* mimicking actions (turning down my heating in isolation, for example) and *public* ones (for example, conspicuously refusing to fly and explaining my reasons at any opportunity). As with direct duties, we might also distinguish between those mimicking actions performed only as an individual and those that contribute to some sub-collective effort. In larger-scale cases, it becomes increasingly unlikely that even public individual mimicking actions, taken in isolation, would be an efficient means of promotion, unless the individual were exceptionally popular or influential. However, an individual might perform mimicking actions (private or public) as part of intentionally collective action with like-minded others.

In performing these actions, an individual would be playing her part in collective action, rather than thinking only in terms of her impact as an individual. To draw an analogy, consider the difference between my quietly deciding, in isolation, to refrain from buying the products of a company whose environmental or other policies I find repellent, and my doing so as part of a coordinated boycott, knowing that as a collectivity we might have sufficient impact to provoke a change in policy. In the latter case, what I do is explicable as part of the collective action, and is motivated by its being such.[25]

In the climate change case, such cooperative efforts could be a means of bringing about changes in policy by existing institutions. For example, a widespread effort among individuals visibly and vocally to re-use carrier bags might prompt a change in policy on their issue by supermarkets or governments, and—still more importantly in this context—increased awareness at that level that unnecessary emissions are to be taken seriously. Equally, they could be a means of promoting collective action at the wider collective level. This is particularly relevant in the case where collective action might bypass state institutions altogether, for example taking the form of a global citizens' movement.[26]

Once such a scheme was effective at the global level, an individual, cutting her own emissions, would of course be fulfilling a correlative duty of the first kind identified in Chapter Five: doing her 'share' of fulfilling the weakly collective duty. However, in committing to such a project at an earlier, smaller-scale stage, her action would be part of intentionally collective action by that smaller collectivity: action intended to bring about global-level action.[27] Performing mimicking actions (cutting her own emissions) would be part of this: the idea being that as a smaller-scale collectivity, they could then show commitment and gain momentum.

Even among like-minded individuals, there might be rational altruist motivation difficulties in getting such a scheme going. However, given that these are like-minded others, there would be a (cooperative) consequentialist case for finding ways round these. (Perhaps via Jamieson's suggestion of developing green character traits or by emphasizing other considerations, such as the independent health benefits to the individual of a greener lifestyle.)

Thus, mimicking can be a means effectively to fulfil promotional duties. However, the reverse situation might also arise, in which adherence to mimicking duties limits an individual's scope for promotional activities more than it improves their effectiveness. Recall *Weak bridge*. Perhaps the individual could best promote an effective response if she sets an example herself, by getting back out of the crowd and publicly showing willingness to wait her turn. But equally, if she retreats in this way, she may no longer be in a position to get the attention of the others and bring about any collective-level change. In the latter scenario, perhaps, after all, as Jamieson puts it in the climate change case, 'the best strategy for a utilitarian agent would be hypocrisy'.[28]

One final point, before moving on to considerations of demandingness. It is at least theoretically possible that an individual might also be required to perform mimicking actions as a means of fulfilling direct duties. There are two possibilities. One is that mimicking actions happen to be involved in fulfilling *protecting direct* duties. Recall *Swimming teenagers*. If two of the teenagers drag the child out of the water and take her to hospital, they stop swimming themselves. However, clearly it is not integral to the justification of these actions, which contribute to a smaller-scale collective endeavour to save the child's life, that they mimic (indeed, go beyond) what would be required as part of a fully collective effort to fulfil the overall duty.

Alternatively, mimicking might be among the most effective means of fulfilling sub-collective *mitigating direct* duties. Assume for now that emissions cuts at the level of the state or another subset would at least make a difference to the harm done through climate change: in other words, it would save lives. Then individuals could have a duty to make such cuts as part of such a sub-collective effort. However, following the discussion of sections (ii) and (iii) and above, this would be the case only if a) the sub-collectivity could do nothing to promote wider collective action, b) fulfilling such duties could render the global-level action unnecessary, by achieving the overall end without it, or c) this was an effective means of bringing about wider-level action.

Thus, an individual may have a duty to perform at least some mimicking actions. However, this consequence-driven argument is restricted to those actions which are means effectively of fulfilling promotional or direct duties. Moreover, it is likely to be limited either to public mimicking actions, or to those which are part of some sub-collective effort either to offset the harm directly or to promote wider collective action.

(V) THE LIMITS OF DEMANDINGNESS

I have now indicated what an individual's moral duties are, as derivative of an as yet collectively unfulfilled weakly collective duty. Nothing has yet been said, however, about how much we are required to give up in fulfilling such duties, or how they may vary across individuals. The next two sections will take some first steps towards remedying that omission.

In line with the relatively uncontroversial moral principles that were the starting point of this monograph, I take it as read that there are limits to the demandingness of these correlative duties: to what individual moral agents can be blamed or even criticized for not doing. In the case of members of The Young and The Able, as I will briefly fill out, these limits might consistently be drawn from whatever is accepted as such in individual beneficence cases. However, I leave it open whether the limit for members of Polluters should be taken from the individual no-harm principle, or be set in line with beneficence cases.

I will then respond to two key objections to this approach: that it is unfair because it could demand more of an individual than would be expected of her in full compliance with a fair collective scheme to fulfil the weakly collective duty; and that the assignment of such duties in the climate change case is too much at odds with how we tend to evaluate our own behaviour.

For members of The Able, we might consistently set the limit of demandingness in line with the moderate principle of beneficence. This principle was, after all, the basis of the argument from collective ability to aid. This would require individuals to fulfil promotional and perhaps direct duties up to the point of giving up something of moral significance themselves.[29] Using the apparatus of the interests- or capabilities-based account of human flourishing, Chapter One offered a working suggestion of a 'morally significant' cost as one as involving serious interference, even on a temporary basis, with the exercise of a central human functioning. These central functionings were taken to include life, health, bodily integrity, affiliation, and practical reason. This cost would be significant even if the individual were not permanently deprived of the relevant capability (which would count as serious suffering). Examples included a severe but temporary illness or incapacity (say a broken leg), or the temporary disruption of a central relationship (for example, being separated for a few days from one's young child).

Turning to The Young, matters are less straightforward. There, the weakly collective duty was grounded in the collectivized weak principle of beneficence, which had its own minimal cost condition. Chapter Two argued that this condition would be met for members of The Young so long as collective action would not cost them a fundamental interest or central capability. This was because overall the collective action, which would *secure* them a fundamental interest, must be to their advantage. However, it would be disingenuous simply to transfer that reasoning here. There is a distinction between what can reasonably be demanded of an individual as part of a collective effort to secure something that is also in her own interest and what can be so when she is being asked to promote something which, though it would be to her overall advantage if successful, might still not happen.

Returning instead to the original weak principle of beneficence, individuals, insofar as they are members of The Young, would be required to incur only minimal costs in fulfilling promotional or other duties. But even then, many would be required to perform promotional actions. It is barely an effort at all to sign an Internet petition, post the same on Facebook, or email one's MP (especially since existing sub-collective groups such as Friends of the Earth will send the necessary links and suggested text direct to one's inbox).

This leaves Polluters. Their weakly collective duty, being negatively grounded in a collectivized no-harm principle, stands independent of appeal to collectivized beneficence or moralized self-interest. Moreover, building on what I believe to be strong intuitions in small-scale cases, it seems that more might reasonably be demanded of individuals in cases of weakly collective harm than collective ability to aid. For example, compare the following.

Car crash bystanders
A car has fallen into a bog, entirely through natural causes. It is very slowly sinking. I am one of a number of bystanders on the scene. By cooperating, we could rescue the driver at only small effort and risk to ourselves. I have pleaded with the other bystanders to cooperate. I have suggested a viable scheme for getting to the car. I have produced a rope and tied it to my own car to get things going. However, because of general confusion, and some disinclination among some others, I have so far failed to persuade them. It might be that, with more persuasion, they would agree. However, I am already exhausted from trying. If I continue in my efforts, or attempt to save the victim on my own, I will make myself ill for some days, and miss my sister's wedding.

Car crash participant
The situation is exactly as in *Car crash bystander* except that I and some of the others on the scene (although not the victim) are weakly collectively responsible for the harm. (Perhaps we all drove a little too fast, knowing both that if others did the same this would be dangerous and that many other drivers were likely to think in the same way.)

In *Car crash bystanders*, it might be rejected as overdemanding to require me either to continue my promotional efforts or to attempt to save the victim on my own. (At least, the comparatively moderate starting principles accepted in Chapter One do not require me to do so.) In *Car crash participant*, however, I am negatively connected to the harm. Accordingly, it seems reasonable to ask more of me either in promoting collective action to save the victim from what we have brought about, *or* in acting directly to save her if I could do so.

But how much more? Should we simply borrow the limit of demandingness that was written into the no-harm principle in Chapter One? That is, the level at which, by not causing the severe harm, the individual would suffer equivalent deprivation herself? This was also taken as the avoidability condition for membership of a set weakly collectively responsible for harm. (It is, in fact, relatively generous to the harmer: we often think we should not impose severe harm even to save ourselves from the same.) In line with the treatment of the cases of moralized collective self-interest and ability to aid, this looks like the consistent response.

However, further intuitive considerations pull the other way. In parallel with the discussion above, there is a difference between demanding some sacrifice of an individual within an effective collective scheme (that is, if she can be sure her action actually is part of preventing the overall harm) and demanding it of her in promoting something which might not happen despite her best efforts. In other words, extreme demands on each individual look less reasonable now we are considering harms which not only have been caused only weakly collectively, but are also only collectively fully avoidable. The boundaries start to blur between individual positive and negative duties when they are filtered through the weakly collective level in this way.[30]

I leave open this question. Nothing hangs, for the purposes of the overall argument, on whether the limit for members of Polluters is set at the point of morally significant cost, at comparable harm to that that would be suffered by the victims, or somewhere in between.

However, there are two particularly salient objections to my approach which do need to be addressed here. The first is that it is unfair to set limits in line with the individual principles in this way, because in some cases it will demand more of the individual than would a fair collective scheme to fulfil the duty. This objection draws on Murphy's compliance condition, which he defends in the context of duties of beneficence. Murphy's reasoning is that morality—or at least beneficence—is a collective project, and an individual cannot be expected to take on others' shares on top of his own.[31]

I have two points to make against this argument. Firstly, there are reasons to question the compliance condition even in the context for which it was originally designed. Secondly, even if it were accepted in the kinds of beneficence case Murphy has in mind, there are, at least arguably, further grounds to reject it in weakly collective harm cases.

Murphy defends his compliance condition in cases of a great many victims and a great many potential benefactors, many of whom fail to do anything to help. The condition limits what morality demands of the individual, in such cases of partial compliance, to what would be required of her in full compliance. His defence appeals to the 'natural thought'...

> that it is objectionable to expect agents to take up the slack caused by the non-compliance of others. We should do our fair share, which can amount to a great sacrifice in certain circumstances; what we cannot be required to do is other people's shares as well as our own.[32]

However, we can agree that it is unfair that some agents duck out of doing their share in morality as a 'collective project' without concluding that other duty-bearers are entitled to act as though nothing had changed.[33] Rather, the situation has to be evaluated as it now is. This is, of course, morally second-best, but even in such second-best situations some available outcomes can be more or less (un)fair than others. To put this another way, the cost of the moral default (the failure of some to act as they should) now has to be assigned somewhere. This means, in practice, that it must be divided between the victims, as the cost of going unaided, and the other potential beneficiaries, as the cost of picking up the tab. If the cost to those victims will be a very serious deprivation, while the cost to other potential duty-bearers would be comparatively insignificant, then it seems arbitrary—not to say *un*fair—simply to assume that those victims should bear the costs.[34]

Consider the following, set up to fit the kind of situation Murphy has in mind.

Contrasts
There are 1,000 very rich people and 1,000 starving people. The situation of the latter is the result of a freak natural disaster and the rich people are not to blame. The only way for the rich people to save the lives of the poor is through the transfer of resources from individuals to individuals. If all do this, each rich person saving one poor person, the cost to each benefactor would be equivalent of giving up his second daily cup of Starbucks coffee. However, half of the rich people fail to do anything to help.

The 500 who have failed altogether to help have undoubtedly behaved badly. They have wronged both the 500 victims, who will now starve unless someone else steps in, and the other duty-bearers, who are left with more victims in need of help. This is not in dispute. However, in evaluating what should happen now, Murphy focuses entirely on questions of fairness to the latter, and ignores the former. According to the compliance condition, the burden of this moral default should be borne entirely by the 500 victims, who will starve, rather than by the 500 remaining rich people, at the price to each of another cup of coffee.

Murphy has a response to this, but it is one that I, at least, find puzzling. He appears to regard the objection—the greater cost to victims—as not relevant at this level of discussion, because we have moved from the question of overall duties to victims, to that of what can be demanded of individuals in cases of non-compliance. 'Although', he argues, 'the victims of noncompliance…are worse off than they would be under full compliance, this is not unfair to them in the sense of fairness embodied in the compliance condition.'[35] Their plight is the result of agents not complying, not a problem with the principle of collective beneficence in the first place.

This appeal to one narrow sense of fairness (fairness between duty-bearers) seems itself to beg the question. If our duties (in this case our weakly collective duties) are originally grounded in the moral badness of the severe suffering of other moral subjects, it is hard to see how that suffering can be altogether irrelevant in determining an appropriate response, even when there is only partial compliance.

Murphy adds that the victims, unlike the other duty-bearers, are not being asked to take on 'responsibilities that rightly belong to others'.[36] However, in this context, such reasoning seems almost a mockery of their plight. Consider, for a moment, the rich duty-bearers grumbling about this kind of unfairness (the unfairness, in the case above, of giving up two hazelnut lattes rather than one) while victims starve. Now consider a couple of doctors, bickering over professional etiquette while their patient, untreated, bleeds to death on the table between them. To say to the starving victim, 'This isn't about you: no one is asking you to pick up the tab for others', seems as inadequate a reflection of what is morally at stake as it would be for the doctors to say to the patient: 'This isn't about you: you're not the one being expected to assist a junior colleague.' How can it not be *about* him, when it is his fundamental interests that will be lost?

In rejecting this reasoning, it is important to reiterate what I am not doing. I am not claiming that the individual's primary duty, in cases of collective failure to fulfil a weakly collective duty, *is* always to go on aiding victims directly, herself. Section (ii) made this clear. *Contrasts* was designed as an exceptional case where strongly collective action is not only not necessary, but impossible. Nor does rejecting the compliance condition mean accepting that there are no limits at all to what the individual can morally be required to sacrifice, right up to the point at which she is as badly off as those she is trying to aid.[37] This section has already suggested some alternative such limits. The claim is, rather, that to set that limit according to what the individual would have had to do if others had acted as they ought, but did not, is to render her moral duties too detached from the situation she is actually in. In the process of adjusting to that non-ideal case, this amounts to giving all consideration arbitrarily to the duty-bearers, and entirely ignoring the needs of the victims.

Thus, there are reasons to reject the compliance condition altogether. However, a second point can be made in the context of Polluters. Even if the compliance condition were accepted in beneficence cases, it still looks implausible to draw the line between the claims of duty-bearers and victims entirely on the side of the former if the basis for assigning duties in the first place was that those duty-bearers are (weakly or strongly) collectively responsible for the victims' plight. Suppose the situation is as is described in *Contrasts* except that the 1,000 victims are starving because the 1,000 rich persons, through predictably aggregating actions, caused pollution which destroyed their environment with acid rain. The default of the 500 looks even worse than in the original case, and the refusal of the remaining half—their plea of 'it's not fair' as justification for leaving 500 victims to starve—looks even less convincing.

Having rejected the compliance condition, it is worth re-stressing a point made in Chapter One. Neither the monograph as a whole, nor even most of what has been said in the last two chapters, hinges on this. Even if my argument in this section were rejected, the defence of promotional and direct rather than mimicking duties would still hold.[38] Moreover, whichever of various limits canvassed here are accepted—whether we are required to incur minimal, less than significant, or up to comparable costs to ourselves in promoting collective action on climate change, or whether we should take on only the burdens we would in a fair collective scheme—very much more would be required of most of us than we are doing now.

However, this immediately prompts the second objection: that, however plausible all this would be in small-scale cases, or even in in-between scenarios like *Contrasts*, it is too counterintuitive to defend relatively demanding individual duties in cases like climate change. Many people don't think of themselves as doing anything wrong in failing altogether to promote collective action on mitigation, adaptation, or compensation. Still more feel not remotely guilty for not continuing to do so up to the point of morally significant cost to themselves. This is very different from how they would feel had they failed to promote a rescue of someone drowning 50 metres away.

My response, which echoes points made briefly in Chapter Three, is to question this reliance on how we actually behave (and our own lack of self-condemnation).[39] Rather, we should ask whether differences in response to these kinds of cases can consistently be linked to salient variables in the situations themselves, or even to differences in how, at bottom, we actually regard them. Are they not, in fact, better explained by individually or socially developed mechanisms of denial?

According to Peter Unger's collation of moral reactions to hypothetical cases of severe suffering, none of those criteria which might potentially be decisive in deciding between cases—factors such as physical proximity, social proximity, informative directness, experiential impact, urgency, emergency, or causal focus of aid—can consistently explain differences in response.[40] Instead, he argues that we have developed psychological tricks to separate cases: projective separation of some victims from others, and subconscious attachment to 'protophysical' principles, which turn out on examination to be empty of even physical (never mind moral) substance.[41]

This taps into a familiar phenomenon. Faced with widespread conflict between our beliefs, desires, and values, we need to adapt one or the other of them if we are to escape cognitive dissonance. To give the standard example, faced with scientific evidence of the link between smoking and cancer, the heavy smoker must either quit, live with the knowledge he is killing himself, or convince himself that the science cannot be trusted.

In the climate change case, recent sociological research provides evidence of psychological mechanisms of denial. Faced simultaneously with increasing empirical evidence, and the inconvenience to themselves of responding to that evidence in a manner consistent with their own general moral views, privileged agents find ways of convincing themselves that the situation is not as it seems.

This does not necessarily involve denying the science itself (although, of course, there is also evidence of just such widespread denial, particularly in the United States).[42] In Swiss focus groups conducted by S. Stoll-Kleemann, Tim O'Riordan, and Carlo C. Jaeger, respondents 'were alarmed about the consequences of high-energy futures, and mollified by images of low-energy futures. Yet they also erected a series of psychological barriers to justify why they should not act either individually or through collective institutions to mitigate climate change.'[43] In Kari Marie Norgaard's study of the Norwegian town of Bygdaby, it is not that the residents do not understand climate change, or even that they do not care about it. Rather, 'these qualities are acutely present but actively muted in order to protect individual identity and sense of empowerment and to maintain culturally produced conceptions of reality'.[44]

This, Norgaard argues, is a reflection of a general trend.

> [Climate denial] is an outcome of a world where for millions of people a keen moral socialization and a belief in equality collide with more information about the vast inequality of economics and life chances of people than ever before ... Widening gaps in global income and increases in international trade ... lead to the displacement of environmental and social problems across national boundaries, onto other people (and species), and across time (through extinction, sea-level rise, and future weather scenarios) and space (through melting polar ice caps, floods, food scarcity, and disease in tropical nations). Under these conditions, the kinds of contradictions between values and actions that Bygdaby residents face become simultaneously more visible and further obscured.[45]

Faced with such contradictions, individuals and societies find ways of blocking or denying the situation, rather than attempting to bring about an effective collective-level response. Thus, for example, as Stoll-Kleemann et al. summarize their findings:

> From the viewpoint of changing their lifestyles of material comfort and high-energy dependence, they regarded the consequences of possible behavioural

shift arising from the need to meet mitigation measures as more daunting. To overcome the dissonance created in their minds they created a number of socio-psychological denial mechanisms. Such mechanisms heightened the costs of shifting away from comfortable lifestyles, set the blame on the inaction of others, including governments, and emphasised doubts regarding the immediacy of personal action when the effects of climate change seemed uncertain and far away.[46]

For these reasons, I set the objection aside. How we are motivated to act and to evaluate our own behaviour on a day-to-day basis can be a poor reflection not only of what we should be doing, but also of how, if we were honest with ourselves, we would think we should respond. In the face of global climate change, this is even more than usually the case.

(VI) DIFFERENT DEMANDS?

Let us begin with a distinction: between what can be *demanded* of an individual, in the sense of the limits of impact on her own life that she must accept in fulfilling a duty, and what can be *expected* of her. I am taking this latter to refer to what she could achieve within those limits.

This section is not concerned with whether more can be demanded of those who are also Polluters than of those who are in only The Able or The Young. The discussion of differential limits, above, has already covered this. The question here is whether more could be demanded of some individuals *within* each collectivity or potential collectivity: either because of their particular skills or because they hold a position of influence or power. Transferring reasoning from backward-looking evaluation of such cases, it might seem that it can.

According to Larry May, those who could have exercised leadership skills have a greater share of responsibility for failure to organize to prevent serious harm.[47] Recall *Beach rescue*. Let us assume for now that it would have been practically possible to organize in time to save the victim, but there was a general failure to bring this about. On May's reasoning, the multilingual, charismatic, and highly skilled motivator, who could have communicated with the various holidaymakers persuasively and quickly, and had also the organizational ability quickly to calculate the best way of acting, bears greater responsibility for this failure than the desperately shy, impractical man sitting near him.

Recalling the discussion of section (ii), a parallel point can be made about those holding positions of influence or authority in the collectivity or potential collectivity. In the climate change case, this would include those in positions of responsibility in existing institutional structures: leaders of national governments or international corporations, of international institutions, and even of religious groups. The reasoning for this is twofold: their position gives them more immediate say in any potential institutional change, and their influence over other individuals is much greater than most of us can command. They could, accordingly, have made more difference than the average individual.

However, others also have influence, even without the formal institutional role. These are those who happen (for some other reason) to hold sway. Were (say) Thierry Henry or Cheryl Cole to take up campaigning on green issues they would almost certainly have a great deal more impact than I would, because of the likely level of public support. (Compare Bono and Bob Geldof, campaigning on global poverty.)

There are two points to be made on this. Firstly, in general, it would be a mistake to conclude from such backwards-looking reasoning that more can be demanded of such individuals. It would be unfair that someone should incur burdens above the standard level of moral demandingness because of something she cannot help (her natural talents). However, more can be *expected* of such individuals within the limits of demandingness. Accordingly the claim is not that the rest of us lack a duty to work to promote collective action, or are required to put in less effort in so doing, but that it might be considered even worse—because of the difference they could have made with very little effort—for individuals in certain positions or with certain abilities to have achieved nothing. (Similarly, at the other end of the scale, whatever the limit of demandingness, less might be expected of those already comparatively badly off because they are likely to hit it sooner.)

Suppose you and I could each save a child from drowning but you could do so with much less personal cost, perhaps because you are an excellent swimmer, or because doing so would cause me to miss a job interview. Then, even assuming that each of us has a duty to save the child (the limit of demandingness is higher than the cost to either of us), you might be subject to even greater moral criticism than me if we both fail to do so.

The second point makes an exception to this. It hinges on my reference to 'something he cannot help', above, and concerns those who have taken on certain social or institutional roles. In so doing, they have (implicitly or explicitly) taken on additional responsibilities. For example, in *Beach rescue*, more might not only be expected but also be demanded of a lifeguard, because he has accepted specific duties as part of his job. In the climate change case, similarly, more could be demanded of the leaders of our current political institutions because they have implicitly accepted responsibility for fulfilling our weakly collective duties.

It might be objected that this is unfair, by appeal to a point I made myself in section (i): that our existing institutions were not designed to fulfil this weakly collective duty. It is, after all, a global-level duty, and the dominant political institutions are at state level. However, national governments, in acting on our behalf, also heavily influence how and whether we cooperate internationally. Accordingly, this objection looks disingenuous, especially—as Gardiner points out—given that state leaders have in no way denied that responding to climate change is a matter for governments to address, and have not called for new institutions to enable them to do so. On the contrary,

> existing leaders and institutions have not been slow to take up the issues and assume the mantel of responsibility—making many fine speeches, organising frequent meetings, promising progress, making the topic a campaign issue, and so on. In addition, we have the explicit commitment to act, and act ethically, registered in the UNFCCC and its ratification. Hence, even if this role was not originally envisioned, many political actors have acted as if it did belong to them, and that they were capable of discharging it.[48]

Denying that tackling climate change is exclusively the responsibility of our political institutions—rejecting the claim that this is the state's 'problem' and we have no more to do than suggest they solve it—does not mean demanding no more of those currently running such institutions than we do of each other.

CONCLUSIONS

Part Three has defended a primary individual duty to promote collective action to tackle climate change. This is supplemented by direct duties, when an individual has no promotional options or could promote change via direct duties.

Where, then, does this leave the standard 'green' lifestyle options currently open to me: getting the train rather than driving to the Lake District and rather than flying to London; forgoing that winter holiday in the sun; recycling; wearing an extra jumper and turning down the central heating; buying local rather than South American fruit and vegetables; and so on? I have not denied that, as an individual moral agent, I may have a duty to do many of these things.

Some of them at least can be defended as a part of promoting collective change. It could be counterproductive to campaign for general change without 'showing willing' to change my own lifestyle. More positively, in contributing to an existing collective effort by a subset (that is, fulfilling sub-collective direct duties), I might help to convince my own state or others that many individuals would be prepared to take on certain costs as part of a collective effort to tackle climate change. Going beyond this, character- and fairness-based cases can be made for fulfilling mimicking duties under certain circumstances. However, two things emerged clearly from Chapter Five. I cannot simply assume that such actions are all that are required of me, and I should not prioritize them over promotional or direct duties.

I have two points to press, in conclusion. Firstly, I must acknowledge the extent to which the arguments of this chapter are but a first stage in a longer process.[49] Section (i) outlined a number of possible promotional duties in the climate change case. Exactly how an individual should fulfil her promotional duties will depend to some extent on her particular situation: her position in society, her skills and resources, the other demands on her, and so on. Recalling the discussion of Zev Trachtenberg's work in Chapter Five, there is a limit to the extent to which we can determine what is appropriate in the abstract: the final details must be a matter for individual judgement.

However, before getting to that point, there is another stage in determining which promotional actions would be most effective. This stage requires us to answer a question not tackled here: that of what form of collective action is most promising. I have left it open whether the weakly collective duty should be fulfilled by pressing on with attempts at a global deal between states, the establishment of some new global-level institution, or even—at the other extreme—some kind of global citizens' movement. Such a movement might bring about mitigation through new 'green' behavioural norms. It might even (albeit less plausibly) secure adaptation and even compensation ends by cooperation through charities, green technology entrepreneurs, NGOs, or other non-state-dominated structures.

In referring to forms of collective action as more or less 'promising', I mean, in part, to make the obvious point that individuals should only promote schemes which meet appropriate fairness and legitimacy requirements. The more institutionalized the response at the global level, the greater the need for formal conditions of legitimacy of decision-making, and of accountability to those on whom collective decisions might ultimately be coercively enforced.[50]

Recalling sections (ii) and (v), 'fair' might be taken here as 'fair enough', in acknowledgement of the case for prioritizing effectiveness—and the fundamental interests of victims—over some considerations of fairness between duty-bearers. However, there is a distinction between fairness in terms of the distribution of non-significant costs, and fairness understood as not imposing a morally significant cost on individual duty-bearers. Recalling Chapter Three, there would be a strong case against imposing such costs even within Polluters and The Young, so long as there were some available alternative distribution. Within The Able, it is a requirement of the collectivized principle of beneficence.

However, what it would be most effective to do by way of promotion will also depend on which of these legitimate and reasonably fair collective schemes are 'promising' in another sense: that is, on which are actually most likely to happen. And *this*, in turn, will depend in part on where most pressure is exercised by those fulfilling promotional duties. Thus, there might be a collective action problem at this level, if many well-motivated individuals or groups all promoted different forms of collective response.

There are mitigating factors. To some extent, the decision could make itself. It would become clear to individuals where most effectively to direct their efforts if one clear front-runner emerged from these various endeavours. Moreover, crossover can be expected, as promotional efforts show (and can be couched so as more explicitly to show) a general commitment to action on climate change and a general view that it should be at the top of state and global agendas.

However, there is also scope for theorists to help. Between the general defence of promotion (undertaken here) and the point at which the details must be determined by individual judgement, further guidance could be provided by a combination of moral and political theory and empirical research. This would be designed to identify in general terms which fair collective solution could most easily be achieved, and to narrow down the defence of promotional duties to such duties as would promote that. This would build on a great deal of work already available, in sociology and law as well as in political theory.[51] However, it lies beyond this project.

My second point is this. Although I have rejected the compliance condition, I have not denied that there is a limit to the demandingness of the individual moral duties we acquire through our weakly collective predicament. Quite the reverse: it is only on the assumption that there is such a limit that we can assume the choice agonized over in Chapter Five to be one that individuals in general (and not just exceptional cases like Gore) will have to make. That is the choice between fulfilling promotional or direct duties, and performing those mimicking actions which do not also contribute to either.

However, the fact that there are limits to the demandingness of our moral duties does not leave us unaffected by the moral pull of our potential to make a difference even above that level. It is because of this, I suggest, that a fourth case for the weakly collective duty can be defended: that we need it in order to live fully at peace with ourselves as simultaneously moral agents and individuals with our own lives and relationships to maintain. Chapter Seven turns to this last, perhaps most controversial, possibility.

Part 4

Climate Change and Moral Baggage
*Collective failure, individual costs,
and marring choices*

7

Living With Ourselves

[T]his much he felt, that by whichever resolve he might abide, necessarily, and without possibility of escape, something of himself would surely die; that he was entering into a sepulchre on the right hand, as well as on the left; that he was suffering a death-agony, the death-agony of his happiness, or the death-agony of his virtue.[1]

Victor Hugo, *Les Misérables*

We might admire Sophie in certain respects, but no one would say that she lives the kind of life that is desirable for a human being to live. No one would want to be Sophie.[2]

Stephen Gardiner

Thus far, this book has offered three defences of what I call a weakly collective moral duty to organize as necessary to act on climate change mitigation, adaptation, and compensation. It has further argued that our primary individual duty in the absence of such collective action is to promote it.

However, this chapter goes beyond what can reasonably be demanded of the individual moral agent in fulfilment of such correlative moral duties. It considers more generally the plight in which she is left by continued collective failure to fulfil these weakly collective duties. In so doing, it makes the following four claims. These can be made with respect to individuals within each of the collectivities (The Young, The Able, and Polluters) assigned such a duty in the climate change case.

Costliness claim
Collective action on climate change could make it significantly less burdensome for us to fulfil our moral duties, in terms of the impact on our personal or interpersonal lives.

Irreconcilability claim
We need collective action on climate change in order to reconcile the three stand-points from which each of us faces the world: the personal, the interpersonal, and the impersonally moral.

Moderate marring claim
Because many individuals understandably experience their lives as marred by choices between central elements of the three standpoints, we (between us) owe it to each of these individuals to act collectively on climate change.

Universal marring claim
Because we are *all* marred, as moral agents, by choices between central elements of the three standpoints, we (between us) owe it to each of us to act collectively on climate change.

Given that these become progressively more reliant on intuitions—about what it means to be human—that others may not share, I would stress that the earlier claims do not stand or fall with the later ones, nor the rest of this monograph with any of them. It is also worth pointing out that to some extent this stands independent of earlier chapters: all but the first claim can be made regardless of whether promotional rather than direct duties are defended as primary, and at least the first two might be made independent of the view that there is a weakly *collective* duty to act on climate change, at all.

I begin (section (i)) by laying out what I mean by the three standpoints or perspectives from which each of us faces the world. Drawing on Chapter Six's rejection of the compliance condition, section (ii) then makes the costliness claim. However, I acknowledge that the findings of Chapter Four count against it, and suggest a modified version. Section (iii) clarifies what I am not doing, by considering and largely rejecting the claim that we are morally tainted by collective failure of this kind. Section (iv) makes the irreconcilability claim.

Going beyond this, I highlight a gap between what can morally, reason-ably be demanded of us in fulfilment of a duty, and what we can nonetheless be marred by not doing. Building on work by Stephen Gardiner, section (v) argues that these irreconcilable choices can understandably be experienced as marring or tragic.[3] It fills this out as meaning that, whatever they do, agents could experience fundamental regret. This makes the moderate marring claim. Finally, section (vii) explores the more controversial idea that we are all blighted or marred by such choices: that it is appropriate to experience them as marring even if we don't do so. This upholds the universal marring claim.

Let us begin, then, by thinking about what it means to be human.

(I) BEING HUMAN

I start with the following suggestion, inspired by Thomas Nagel. As individual human beings we each face the world from three different standpoints, or perspectives: the personal, the interpersonal, and the impersonally moral.[4] Each of the three gives us reason to act, and at least some of these are what might be called central reasons. They cannot be reduced to one another, within or across the perspectives, and they pick out actions required for full functioning within that perspective.

Let us begin, fairly obviously, with the personal. We are individuals with interests, desires, beliefs, and plans of our own. Each of us has her own life to lead and this life can go well or badly. At least for most of us, it is correspondingly impossible not to see and assess the world at least in part in terms of its impact on ourselves. As Nagel puts it: 'We see things *from here*.'[5] It is from the personal perspective that I would feel disappointment if bad weather prevented a planned holiday, or (more fundamentally) if I failed to secure my 'dream' job, or contracted a serious illness. I act from this standpoint when I eat banoffee pie, when I walk up mountains, read detective novels, or devote hours to writing philosophy.

As individuals, we have at least some broadly defined fundamental interests, which are prerequisites for full flourishing from the personal point of view. This much (which I think is uncontroversial) was laid out as a starting assumption in Chapter One. We need (at least) genuine, secure opportunities to enjoy continued life, bodily health, bodily integrity, affiliation, and practical reason, including being able to develop and pursue a meaningful plan of life.

Almost certainly, some fulfilment in the other two perspectives will be a necessary component of this individual flourishing. This, again, is obvious. Securing affiliation includes retaining the opportunity to forge and maintain close personal bonds with others.[6] Moreover, it is highly likely that an individual's conception of the good or plan of life will require her to show moral concern: to be motivated by the serious suffering of others.

However, this perspective cannot be reduced to either of the other two. On the one hand, some aspects of my own flourishing depend neither on my status as a moral agent nor on my enjoyment of satisfactory relations with others. (Examples are bodily integrity and health.) On the other, even those elements of my own flourishing which depend on my aiding the needy, or being a good sister, a good friend, and so on, are distinct in their contribution to the personal from that which they make to those other perspectives. There is more to my flourishing—to its *being* mine—than its contribution to overall welfare, or the maintenance of interpersonal loyalties. Nor, as will become clear below, are the other two standpoints reducible to this one. (Indeed it seems plausible that they would not contribute to the individual's flourishing in the same way if they were.)

The next perspective is interpersonal. As individuals, we form certain ties with other individuals: with them as individual persons, as co-members of certain groups to which we assign significance, and sometimes as both.[7] Not only can these relationships become integral to our own flourishing, but they might also be said to fall into the realm of the moral in two ways. Firstly, this may be a distinct moral framework, with the duties given rise to by such ties being appropriately considered *interpersonally moral*.[8] (With this in mind, it is worth noting explicitly that, although I may refer to the impersonally moral as the 'moral perspective', I do so for ease of expression.) Secondly, forming such relationships might prevent suffering in a general sense and so contribute to the impersonally moral standpoint.[9]

However, the significance of the special duties and ties—of the reasons for actions given by being in these relations—would be seriously misrepresented by any attempt to reduce them to either self-interest or impersonal moral duties. To make this point, we can borrow from Bernard Williams. Suppose I drop everything to rush across the country to care for a bereaved friend. If someone asks why, my answer is: 'Because he's my friend.' Were I to answer that he is my friend and so especially vulnerable to me, which gives me a special obligation to go to his aid grounded in my general duties to the vulnerable, I would be having, as Williams puts it, 'one thought too many'.[10] We would hope that my motivation would begin and end with his being my friend, and needing me. (To paraphrase Williams, this might be hoped *not least by my friend*.)

Alternatively, I might offer an explanation in terms of my own self-interest. I might say: 'He's my friend, I need friendships in order to live a full life, and I've come to rely on this friendship for that purpose, so it's in my interest to help him in order that our friendship be preserved.' But this is still further from capturing what friendship is about. Even though we are mutually dependent in this way (and even though, as I argued in Chapter Two, this dependence renders us a collectivity), our friendship cannot be reduced to some kind of spreadsheet: what I get out of what he does for me, as compared to the itemized costs to me, and vice versa.

Moreover, as I briefly highlighted above, it would considerably reduce the value that friendship could bring to my life if I evaluated it in these terms. This parallels a point brought out by Michael Stocker in his criticism of hedonistic egoism, which he deems 'schizophrenic'.

> Love, friendship, affection, fellow feeling and community are important sources of personal pleasure. But can egoists get these pleasures? ... [N]ot so long as they adhere to the motive of pleasure-for-self ... [Egoists can] get together and decide (as it were) to enter into a love relationship ... And they can do the various things calculated to bring about such pleasure: have absorbing talks, make love, eat delicious meals, see interesting films, and so on ... Nonetheless there is something necessarily lacking in such a life: love. For it is essential to the very concept of love that one care for the beloved, that one be prepared to act for the sake of the beloved. More strongly, one must ... act for that person's sake as a final goal ...[11]

The third standpoint is that of the impersonally moral agent. (To reiterate, it is 'impersonal' in that there may be—I think there are—special *moral* obligations acquired via interpersonal relationships.) It is from this standpoint that the severe suffering of any other moral subjects gives me reason to act: that I am motivated to act to prevent such suffering and not to cause it. This is so whether the range of moral subjects is delineated with conventional narrowness, to include only human beings, or extended to non-humans, as in Chapter Four. As with both the personal and the interpersonal standpoints, I am allowing for incommensurability—for genuine moral dilemmas—within this perspective: that is, for conflict between preventing and not directly causing harm.

Again, my moral performance (for lack of a better term) may contribute to my own flourishing. As section (v) will explore, it may even be a necessary part of it. However, the significance of the reason to act from the standpoint of the moral agent is not reducible to that. Suppose someone decides that the most rewarding life for her is one working to aid the victims of natural disasters. On a rather less impressive scale, suppose I give a few pounds to a homeless man and the warm glow from his grateful smile makes me feel better about myself all day. The individual's reason, from the moral standpoint, is not reducible to these contributions to individual flourishing.

If my companion asks me 'Why did you do that?', she might well recoil from the answer: 'Because it makes me feel good.' From the point of view of the impersonal moral agent, 'my religion requires me to give to charity', or 'my Mum likes it if I give to the homeless', or 'because he reminded me of my granddad, and I can't bear to think of my granddad begging on the street', all also miss the mark, however understandable from the other perspectives. From the impersonally moral standpoint, the reason is simply that the homeless man is a fellow human being—a moral subject—in serious need, and I can choose to alleviate that need.

It is important to be clear here. I am not claiming that we can only flourish in our own lives by being virtuous (although I will come closer to this Aristotelian view in the last section of this chapter). Rather, the claim for now is that we cannot function properly *from the impersonally moral standpoint* unless we are able to respond to the serious suffering of other moral subjects. (That is, to prevent it and, incommensurately, not to bring it about.) It is a central component of that standpoint that we are able to do so. Moreover, in parallel to the point from Stocker, above, it is likely that the moral perspective has to have this importance in itself to have its full significance *for us*: that is, in order to contribute as it might (for many, as it does) to our own flourishing. As with interpersonal relations, the person who attempts to do good to others as a means to improve her own welfare will have 'one thought too many'.

(II) THE COST OF DOING WHAT WE OUGHT

This section defends the costliness claim: that fulfilling our moral duties could be made less costly, in terms of their impact on our personal and interpersonal lives, by a collective framework for action on climate change mitigation, adaptation, and compensation.[12] However, as will become apparent, I have to distinguish here between conclusions following only from Parts One and Three, on which basis the costliness claim can be defended as it stands, or also from Part Two, on which basis only a modified costliness claim can be made.

Chapter Six rejected the compliance condition. This is the view, defended by Liam Murphy, that an individual's moral duties under less-than-total compliance are limited to what she would have to do in full compliance: that is, if everyone else did what she ought.[13] This condition is most plausibly read not as claiming that the individual need only do *exactly what she would* if everyone else were doing their share, but that she need not put in any more effort (incur greater cost) than under full compliance with some fair and effective collective or combined effort. Even thus read, however, I rejected it. I agreed that a situation of partial compliance is unfair, but pointed out that even a second-best situation can itself be more or less so. This will depend on how the costs of the moral default are allocated between the victims (who are hopelessly ill-equipped to bear it) and the other duty-bearers (who are not).

To reiterate, I am not claiming, with Peter Singer, that there are no limits at all to what the individual should sacrifice to fulfil her collectively incurred individual moral duties, right up to the point at which she is as badly off as those she is trying to aid. On the contrary, it was made clear in Chapter Six—and indeed was written into the very assumptions laid out in Chapter One—that there are limits to the costs that others can reasonably expect us to incur on their behalf. I suggested that the individual promotional duties of members of The Able should be curtailed by something like the condition in Singer's moderate principle of beneficence: that we should prevent 'very bad' things from happening unless, to do so, we had to sacrifice something morally significant.[14] That 'significance' might be filled out as involving serious, even if temporary, interference with the exercise of a central functioning. For The Young (or those not also in The Able) I suggested a minimal demandingness condition, in line with the weak principle of beneficence. I left it open whether somewhat heavier demands might be made of Polluters.

However, whichever of these limits is accepted, the cost to the individuals of fulfilling promotional duties up to that point is likely to be higher than would be required by a fair collective action. (At least, this is so insofar as we focus on our moral duties to humans.) Chapters Two and Three made clear that climate change mitigation and adaptation could be secured by the global affluent at less than significant cost to each. Considerations of fairness make it unlikely that those in The Young but not also in The Able would be assigned more than minimally costly duties. On this basis, then, the costliness claim can be defended: fair, effective collective action can be expected to decrease the cost to each individual of fulfilling her moral duties in respect to climate change.

Now, however, we must factor in Chapter Four, where I explored the natural next step of extending moral concern to non-human animals, species, and systems. By the end of that chapter we were faced with a set of conflicting, morally or incommensurately salient, reasons for collective action. Even collectively, we could not respond fully to each even if we went up to the limits of demandingness. So must we abandon the costliness claim? Not altogether. Rather, we can make only the following modified (but still significant) claim.

Modified costliness claim
Collective action on climate change could enable us to achieve considerably more from the impersonally moral perspective, at the same cost to each in terms of impact on our personal and interpersonal lives, than we would have been able to achieve individually.

Two points are worth stressing before moving on. Firstly, the defence of the costliness claim—in terms of our climate duties to humans—does depend on the rejection of the compliance condition. However, neither the modified costliness claim nor the rest of this chapter depends on it. Rather, they would still hold even if the limit of demandingness was set at the level that would be required by a fair collective scheme. Secondly, there is a sense in which, recalling Chapter Two, the costliness claim is an additional collective self-interest argument. It is better for each of us to be able to fulfil our moral duties at lower cost, so we have a prudential incentive to cooperate. However, this does not in itself imply a moral duty of all to each, since this book has not taken as read any moral principle on which we owe it to each other to make our moral duties easier to fulfil.

(III) MORAL TAINT

Having made the costliness claim, and modified it in the light of Chapter Four, the rest of the chapter goes beyond it. It asks whether the individual who has fulfilled her individual moral duties—that is, who has done what she could be blamed for not doing—could nonetheless be marred, or blighted, by collective failure to fulfil weakly collective duties.

Before embarking on this, however, I must distinguish mine from a related but different approach. On this rival view, an individual can be morally tainted as a direct result of collective failure to fulfil a weakly collective duty. Although neither guilt nor blame is necessarily appropriate, shame and some corresponding negative third-party judgement can be so.

Standardly, this kind of taint—taint as a direct result of what one's collectivity does or fails to do—is thought to attach to members of intentional, institutionalized collectivities, especially citizens of states. Thus, Germans, at the time, might all be considered tainted by the actions of the Nazi regime, or all UK citizens by the decision to go to war in Iraq. It might also be applied to members of smaller or less formally institutionalized (but still intentional) collectivities: to staff at a college funded by a corrupt regime, for example, or to Romeo as a result of the past acts of the Montague family. However, even if this notion of taint (as appropriate shame) does attach to members of actual collectivities (a claim I neither uphold nor deny here), it is more problematic when it comes to members of potential, or even *Should-be*, collectivities.

Larry May, who does consider taint appropriate in at least some cases of collective inaction, explains this as follows.

> In cases…in which the failure of many people to act is involved, shared responsibility normally does not entail guilt. Shame, though, is directly related to a person's conception of herself or himself, rather than to explicit behaviour (which is what guilt most commonly attaches to). Because shame concerns the self's identity, it is more appropriately felt than guilt when one's group fails to prevent a harm, since it is the association between the group's identity and one's own that generates the moral feelings, rather than what one has directly done. But since one's group associations are generally things one can do something about, they may generate responsibility and with it corresponding moral feelings. Shame seems to fit the bill here, and…so does moral taint.[15]

However, this seems too quickly to connect collective inaction—the failure of a potential collectivity to organize to act collectively—with the failure of some existing group to do something. In cases of collective inaction or weakly collective responsibility for harm there is no intentionally espoused group or even an actual, non-intentional collectivity. Rather, there is a scattered collection of individuals who could (and I have argued in the climate change case should) organize themselves to act together to prevent some serious harm. Accordingly, there is a danger of overlooking the distinction between taint as appropriate shame when there is some degree of individual control over the situation, and taint as moral pollution, independent of that control.

This second possibility is a dangerous and destructive one. It brings with it the possibility of being tainted-as-polluted completely independent of one's own decisions: taint from the unknowing and unintentional breaking of a taboo (Anthony Appiah uses the example of Oedipus) or that attached by some religious societies to women who have been raped. This can quickly be rejected: as Appiah notes, it is a relic of views long since discarded in the modern world.[16] The first notion keeps apart from this by introducing the component of individual control: something, at least, for which the individual can reasonably be held responsible. However, attempts to fill this out render it less obviously appropriate to the climate change case.

Let us consider two versions of the claim. On one option, an individual might be tainted by a shared attitude or culture—a sense of community affiliation or solidarity—which amounts to her upholding some informal, harm-causing institutional structure. On this understanding, staff and students in a university community might be tainted by a culture of racism which prompts some to discriminatory or abusive behaviour.[17] Metropolitan police officers in the early 1990s might all be tainted if it was indeed a racist culture in the Met that led to the long delays to the guilty verdict in the Stephen Lawrence case.[18]

In the climate change case, some theorists have attributed moral responsibility (and assigned moral duties) directly, on a parallel basis of participation in a harmful way of life.[19] However, the defence of the weakly collective duty, in Part One of this book, did not rely on shared attitudes or cultures. Rather, I defended an expanded understanding of collective responsibility for harm resulting predictably from aggregated, avoidable, individual actions. Similarly, in collective inaction cases, the duty depends on collective potential to cooperate in time to prevent harm. Recall *Beach rescue*. The potential collectivity of holidaymakers is responsible for collective inaction (failing to save the child) regardless of whether all are expressing some shared culture (perhaps the way of life of lazy holidays in the sun) or each is on the beach for some completely independent cultural, professional, or personal reason. Appeal to a shared culture or informal framework, or solidarity with shared attitudes, would not automatically render moral taint appropriate in these cases.

Alternatively, moral taint might be assigned in certain cases by appeal to what the individual can control: her membership of the relevant collectivity. May appeals to this later in the same book.

> Those individuals who can, but choose not to, distance themselves from groups that are contributing to harm are metaphysically guilty, and also morally responsible for, in the sense of being morally tainted by, the harms caused by their fellow group members or institutions.[20]

However, it is not clear that such reasoning transfers straightforwardly to cases of potential collectivities rather than established groups.

In cases of weakly collective responsibility for harm, the harms are the predictable result of aggregated individual actions, rather than directly caused by individual members or by strongly collective action. However, an individual could dissociate herself from the potential collectivity by ceasing the actions which in combination bring about harm. Thus, expanding on May's reasoning, we might appeal to the fact that the individual could control whether she is part of this potential collectivity to justify moral taint (appropriate shame) if she fails to dissociate herself in this way.

This would render negative moral evaluation (internal and external) appropriate even in situations where an individual neither causes a harm directly, nor contributes to it by upholding some shared culture or institution. Seeking to avoid such taint, by dissociation, is understandable. This is the mentality that declares, 'Let the lie come into the world but not through me', as Aleksandr Solzhenitsyn, quoted by Jonathan Glover, puts it.[21] It appeals to the desire to say: 'Well, at least *I* have nothing to be ashamed of', if, unable to change the overall outcome, you withhold from performing the action which is harmful in aggregate (perhaps at some significant personal cost).

This is intuitively compelling: so much so that Chapter Five left open the possibility that individuals have a character-based moral duty to opt out in collective harm cases where they have no other way of influencing the situation. Similarly, it is at least plausible to consider the individual tainted who has failed to exercise this option if it is the only thing that she could have changed. (I will come back to this shortly.) The intuitive force of this option lies in its being one thing the individual can control.

However, it is not clear in collective inaction cases, such as May's own *Beach rescue* example, that the individual does have this kind of control. One's associations with actual, intentional collectivities may, as May says, 'generally [be] things one can do something about'.[22] But they are not so here. How could one holidaymaker dissociate herself from the set of potential helpers, in any way that could be considered to *remove* moral taint? She could leave the beach, but she still would have been a potential helper, just one who had refused to help. Far from clearing her conscience, this would appear to make her worse.[23] Given this, to consider an individual morally tainted simply by being one of the set who could between them have made a difference would be to ignore whether she had any control over the situation.

Insofar as individuals in these situations have a choice, they have the option of trying to bring about group action to prevent the harm, or of aiding or protecting some victims themselves. Indeed, May himself points this out. 'For those who cannot distance themselves,' he says in the later chapter, 'their taint need not have any moral implications.'[24] Moreover, in discussing distributing responsibility for failure to act in collective inaction cases, he suggests that those best able to have influenced others to act should bear most negative accountability. (Consider, for example, the natural, charismatic leader in *Beach rescue*.) This sits oddly with the earlier direct connection of taint with responsibility for group membership in collective inaction cases.

To clarify matters, a further distinction is needed within moral taint as appropriate shame. This might be drawn as follows:

Association control taint
Taint because the individual failed to dissociate herself from the relevant collectivity or potential collectivity.

Outcome control taint
Taint because the individual had some potential, however small, to influence the overall result.

With this in mind, we can revisit cases of weakly collective responsibility for harm. In most such cases, individuals have outcome as well as association control taint. Not only could the set making up the potential collective have not brought about the harm and the individual not have been a part of that set had she so chosen, but the individual could also have done various things to try to influence what happened at the collective level. Recall *Weak bridge*, in which hundreds of people are pushing onto a bridge that can only safely hold fifty. As was discussed at length in Chapters Five and Six, individual options include not only opting out, but also shouting to the rest to stop, and publicly highlighting the situation and the danger.

In such situations, the aims of avoiding outcome control taint and avoiding association control taint could pull against each other. It might be that an individual could either remain in a harming set and try to bring about a different outcome (to stop or at least compensate for the harm), or get out of it altogether, but not both. Chapter Six argued that the individual's primary moral duty is to promote collective action. However, this leaves open the question of whether she might be tainted (shame-worthy) if she fulfils this duty but nonetheless the harm still happens.

There are two possible responses. One is to acknowledge the taint, because the individual has chosen to stay in the group, but to argue that she has an all-things-considered duty to bear it. (This is in parallel to what Appiah, citing Luther, refers to as 'an injunction to "sin bravely"'.[25]) In the absence of any considerations other than the prima facie moral pull on us of the serious suffering of other moral subjects—without any religious considerations, for example—it is not clear that such a distinction could go 'all the way down'. It is possible that negatively grounded weakly collective moral duties have a more stringent pull on the individual agent than do positively grounded ones, but the outright incommensurability of not helping and harming acknowledged in section (i) is blurred when it comes to the individual connection with weakly collective harms.[26] This is clear from Chapters One and Five. (In any case, if this were a genuine moral dilemma, between harming and not helping, it would seem inappropriate to say that the individual should feel shame. To consider shame apposite would be to consider her in some sense at fault.)

The alternative is that, if the individual has some other option available to her which could do more to prevent the victims from suffering, she is not automatically tainted by failure to dissociate herself from the harming set. It is, after all, those victims' interests that give the situation its moral significance in the first place. Often, if an individual is part of a harming set, she has more than one option. Why narrow the focus on responsibility for what one can influence or control to just this one: exit from the relevant collectivity or potential collectivity?

To reiterate, in parallel with Chapter Five's discussion of duties, I do not deny that an individual could be morally tainted by remaining in a harming set, if exit was her only means of exercising control over the situation. However, in general it is more helpful to focus on outcome responsibility than association control taint, in both weakly collective harm and collective inaction cases. On this, the avoidance of taint is a matter of choices which that individual could have made. If she has fulfilled these duties—if she has promoted collective action up to the limits of significant cost to herself—then it looks repugnant (in the same way as ascribing taint-as-pollution is so) either to criticize her moral behaviour, or to consider that she should be ashamed.[27]

However, by considering the choices faced by the individual in cases of weakly collective failure, it is possible to bring out another sense in which such situations can have a moral cost for her: a cost which does not carry overtones of moral criticism of the agent. Taint as shame is avoidable by doing all one reasonably could, but an individual can be marred—the notion to be used here—even if she has done everything she should. The focus shifts from whether she can be judged, to whether her life—her possibility of flourishing simultaneously in the three standpoints of human life—has been undercut. With this in mind, let us return to those three standpoints.

(IV) IRRECONCILABLE CHOICES

This section highlights certain choices as fundamental and, accordingly, as peculiarly difficult. These are choices between central components of one or other of the three standpoints from which, as human beings, we each face and assess the world: the personal, the interpersonal, and the impersonally moral. Anticipating section (v), such choices might be called marring or tragic, but for now I will refer to them simply as irreconcilable.[28] They can arise within or across standpoints. However, I will begin with the former. Within that, I will start where the archetypally searing examples belong: within the interpersonal standpoint.

Gardiner cites William Styron's *Sophie's Choice*: the woman forced by a Nazi doctor to choose between the lives of her two children.[29] Another familiar example is Sartre's student, deciding whether to care for his mother or fight for the Free French.[30] This time, the choice is between a direct personal relationship and interpersonal relations understood more broadly as loyalty to a particular group. In both cases, the individual has no alternative but to decide to give up something central to her interpersonal life.

Turning to the personal standpoint, it is a familiar observation from the capabilities approach that an individual is not fully flourishing if she has to choose between two basic needs or central capabilities. Consider Sen's example of Indian honey-gatherers who run the risk of being killed by Bengal tigers in order to make a living.[31] They, too, face an irreconcilable choice.

An individual might also face conflicting, incommensurate reasons in the moral realm. This possibility has been defended elsewhere by Nagel, as well as by Ruth Barcan Marcus.[32] Consider Williams' example: Jim, who is obliged to choose between shooting one man himself and seeing ten shot by another.[33] Williams uses this as a counterexample to act-utilitarianism: the point being that it is unreasonable to require Jim (as a moral duty) to kill the man. However, what matters here is that he, as an individual moral agent, has to choose between letting people die and intentionally causing death.

These are familiar examples. However, irreconcilable choices can also arise across the three standpoints. Consider the personal and interpersonal standpoints. With only one life jacket, an individual might face a choice between his own life and that of his dearest friend. A more complex example is Simon Yates, the climber who decided to cut the rope in the Andes in 1985. He believed that in doing so he was sending his friend and climbing partner to his death. Since he was himself by no means securely attached to the mountain face, both men could have been expected to die had he done otherwise. The choice was (or—as things by unlikely chance turned out—seemed to be) between taking active responsibility for the death of his friend and almost certainly dying himself as well.[34]

The demands of the personal and the moral perspective, or the interpersonal and the moral, can also clash fundamentally. On the former, imagine a person in the path of a runaway tram. The tram is hurtling towards six innocent people. If he moves out of the way, to save his own life, they will be killed. On the latter, a familiar example is the man who can save from a burning house either his elderly mother or a scientist whose research will save countless lives.[35]

Finally, the conflict might be three-way, so that only two of the standpoints can be reconciled. Will and Lyra, the protagonists of Philip Pullman's *His Dark Materials* trilogy, face just such a choice.[36] They are in love with each other but have to decide between living permanently in different worlds, living together at the cost of one or the other's health, or seeing each other regularly at the cost of failing to prevent the suffering of countless others.

I will come back shortly to the impact of these choices on the individuals concerned. For now, my aims are twofold. The first is to point out that situations may arise in which the three perspectives are irreconcilable. The second, to which I turn now, is to argue that such individual choices can arise in cases either where many individual duty-bearers have failed to act, or where there has been collective failure to fulfil a weakly collective duty.

This aspect is often overlooked in discussion of the kind of beneficence cases familiar from the debate on the compliance condition. Consider the following: a variant on the *Easy rescue* cases of Chapter Two.

Lonely Samaritan 1
Caroline and David are each (independently) on their way to the station when they pass a pond in which two children are drowning. By chance, they get there at the same time. Each of them can save one child at the cost only of wet clothes.

However, for either of them to save both would take longer. David would miss an important business meeting. Caroline would miss the train to visit her dying father, from whom she has long been estranged and who wants now to see her to be reconciled. David knows this but doesn't want to damage his new Armani suit, and so goes on his way without saving either child.

Unlike in *Easy rescue 1* (which was based on Singer's shallow pond example), it is not absolutely clear-cut that Caroline has a moral duty to save the second child.[37] At least, it goes beyond the relatively restrained principle of beneficence taken as read in Chapter One to say that she must. The cost to her of doing so is significantly higher. However, what matters here is that, because David has not fulfilled his (undoubted) duty to save one of the children, she faces irreconcilable conflict between the central elements of two of the three perspectives from which she faces the world: the moral and the interpersonal.

The same situation can result from collective failure to act. Consider:

Lonely Samaritan 2

There are more victims than Caroline can possibly save on her own. She can save one or two at only a minimal cost. If she takes the time to save three she will miss the train to see her father but could get a flight. She is terrified of flying, but it would get her there in time. If she saves five or more, she will miss the flight. At some point, well before saving all the children, she would make herself seriously ill.

David, Edwina, and Felix happen on the scene at the same time. Working independently, each could save some children, with costs increasing comparably with those of Caroline, but could not, even between them, save all. However, if all cooperated, they could use a boat to save all the children and still go on their way, with only a short delay and a cost to each equivalent to that to Caroline of having to get a more expensive train.

i) Most of the others go on their way.

ii) All stay but there is no cooperation, although each tries to save the children alone.

On either version, at some point Caroline will face an irreconcilable choice: a choice between the central demands of the moral and of either (or both) the personal and the interpersonal standpoints. The same is true of any of the other agents who remain on the scene. In both cases, this is the result of failure to act collectively: in version (i) because others, by leaving, have made such cooperation impossible; in (ii) because of combined failure to organize.

Thus far, this section has focused only on positive duties. However, as with Chapter Six's rejection of the compliance condition, the point can be made at least arguably more compelling by focusing instead on cases of weakly collective responsibility for harm.

Lonely Samaritan 3

As in *Lonely Samaritan 2* except that Caroline, David, Edwina, and Felix are landowners, whose failure to organize a rota to maintain their common fences has resulted in the children being able to get to the dangerous pond where they are now drowning.

Again, if Caroline continues to save the children, she will, again, face a choice between the central demands of the personal or interpersonal and the moral perspective. However, the impersonally moral reasons she has to act are given, at least arguably, still greater force by her being a member of the potential collectivity responsible for the plight of the children in the first place.

With this in mind, consider individuals faced with collective failure hitherto to organize ourselves to act on climate change mitigation, adaptation, and compensation. Part Three argued that the primary individual moral duties in these situations are promotional, supplemented by direct duties. However, the arguments of this chapter would apply whether promotional, direct, or even mimicking duties were defended as primary.

As moral duties—as something which can reasonably be demanded of us by others and that we can be blamed for not doing—their force is limited by their cost to us. (In other words, they include a demandingness condition.) However, these are duties we incur in our capacity as moral agents. From that impersonally moral perspective, we have central reasons to respond to the severe suffering of others, *and to go on responding to it*. This, as I will show, puts us in a similar plight to that of Caroline.

I will begin with direct duties, since the analogy with beneficence cases is most obvious there. So long as the weakly collective duty remains unfulfilled, there will always be more the individual moral agent could do: more victims of climate change she could be helping. However, if she continues to do so, there will come a point where she has to choose between responding to severe suffering in this way and maintaining some central personal interest or interpersonal tie of her own. She might have to emulate Charles Dickens' Mrs Jellyby: neglecting her own children to devote herself to the welfare of distant strangers.[38]

However, the same reasoning applies to promotional duties. Consider Caroline in *Lonely Samaritan 2(ii)*, but suppose for the sake of the example that the other, non-complying duty-bearers remain in the vicinity. Whether she focuses on saving individuals herself or on rushing around trying to persuade David, Edwina, and Felix to cooperate, the costs to her will mount up in a similar way. At some point, she will face an irreconcilable choice between putting in more effort and some central element of her own life or interpersonal relationships. The same is true of the individual promoting collective action on climate change. Until she exhausts herself and gives up all her projects and interpersonal ties, there will always be more that the serious suffering of others gives her a centrally important reason to do. (Even if she reached a point at which it would be impossible or futile for her to do more by way of promotion, she would still have the option of aiding victims directly. This takes us back to the paragraph above.)

To make this point in another way, we might consider the very high costs incurred by some who have, in practice, devoted themselves to climate change activism. Consider rainforest activist José Cláudio Ribeiro da Silva, killed only six months after acknowledging that his activism put him in constant danger of murder by vested interests.[39] Or climate activist Tim de Christopher, jailed for two years in July 2011 for using bogus bids to disrupt a Bush administration auction for the gas and oil industry.[40]

Moreover, such choices would arise even if the arguments of Chapter Five were mistaken, and an individual's primary duty were to cut her individual emissions.[41] Firstly, as was acknowledged there, it would be very demanding for some individuals to reduce emissions to a level equivalent to that within a fair collective scheme, where such cuts would have been eased by collective investment in technology, and structural improvements. (Recall, moreover, that if all three of the arguments of Part One are accepted, these are not simply emissions cuts to the point at which, if all emitted at that level, climate change would be made no worse. They are cuts to enable mitigation to past climate change as well.) Consider a low-paid worker in the UK with an ailing parent in Italy, who faces the choice of a budget flight to see her, not seeing her, or taking the train at a cost so exorbitant that he will not be able to feed his children or pay his rent that month.[42] His, like Caroline's, is an irreconcilable choice.

Moreover, once an individual had fulfilled her mimicking duties, she could still respond with promotion or direct aid to the serious suffering of the victims of climate change. From the impersonally moral perspective, this suffering would give her central reason to do so. This would be so even if mimicking duties had successfully been defended as exclusive, as the argument here concerns what an individual has central reason to do from one or other of the three standpoints, not what is her all-things-considered duty (what she can be blamed for not doing).

This completes the defence of the irreconcilability claim. If we are to reconcile the three standpoints from which each of us faces the world, we need some form of collective action on climate change.[43] The rest of this chapter will go beyond that hypothetical claim. It will argue that at least some of us need such reconciliation, because without it we face marring choices.

(V) IRRECONCILABILITY, MARRING, AND REGRET

Let us now focus on the plight of the individual agent faced with an irreconcilable choice. Such choices are properly considered 'marring' because, drawing on Gardiner's analysis of *Sophie's Choice*, they are situations in which, whichever way the individual decides, she may reasonably—or at least under-standably—find the decision hard, or in some extreme cases impossible, to live with. As I will fill out this notion here, they are situations in which, what-ever the individual does, it would be understandable for her to experience fundamental agent-regret.

The claim is not that it would be wrong to save oneself in the life jacket or tram cases, or one's mother from the burning house. I do not even have to conclude that Lyra and Will would have been wrong to maintain their rela-tionship rather than prevent the suffering of millions. Nor (as section (iii) made clear) do I even think that shame, or third-party moral condemnation, is necessarily appropriate. Rather, we can say of all these cases what Gardiner says of Sophie:

> Even though she makes a defensible (perhaps even 'the best') decision in that terrible situation, and even though she bears no responsibility for being in it, still she is right to think that her choice carries negative moral baggage. Although she is not to be blamed for the decision in the usual way, it is nevertheless true that her life is irredeemably marred by it.[44]

Within the personal standpoint, we can say straightforwardly that an indi-vidual is made worse off if she cannot secure one central interest or capability without losing another (or even putting it at risk).[45] Thus the language of mar-ring is unnecessary, although not irrelevant. However, turning to the imper-sonally moral perspective, it serves well to bring out the peculiar awfulness of the situation in which Williams' Jim finds himself. Whatever he does, he will have to live either with having, himself, killed another human being or with having failed to take the opportunity to save nine lives. As Gardiner says of Sophie, no one would want to be Jim.[46] (However, I think all of us would rather be him than Sophie: I am not claiming that all marring choices are on a par; simply that they *are* all marring.)

Nor would we want to be the man in the life-jacket case, dying or living with having let his friend die; or Yates, believing he must either actively end his friend's life, or lose his own life as well. The agent in the tram case, if he saves his own life, must live with having failed to save several others. The agent in the burning house must live either with having let his mother die, or hav-ing failed to do immeasurable impersonal good. We wouldn't want to be him, either, or Will or Lyra.

Such cases, I suggest, point to a gap between what an individual can be blamed for and what can, nonetheless, be bad for her in her capacity as a moral agent. This can be brought out by making a parallel point with respect to each perspective. The fact that you have fundamental interests of your own does not mean, all things considered, that you are entitled or required never to give any of them up, even though from that personal perspective you have central reason never to do so. The fact that you have friendships, parents, children, and other interpersonal loyalties does not render you all-things-considered entitled or required to sacrifice everyone and everything else for them, even though from *that* perspective you have central reason to do so. Equally, being a moral agent doesn't mean you are entitled or required to give up everything to prevent the alleviation of suffering, or to avoid causing it yourself, even though from the impersonally moral perspective you have central reason to do so.

The irreconcilability of the three perspectives is what renders it plausible to limit the demandingness of individual moral (or for that matter interpersonal) *duties*. But what these examples illustrate is that this irreconcilability will cost you, all the same. It is this cost that Gardiner refers to as 'baggage', and which I want to flesh out as fundamental agent-regret.

Regret is not the same as remorse. Nor is it the same as shame: it does not come with the same external entitlement to moral criticism. Nor, as I will elaborate below, need it come automatically with a wish to have done otherwise. However, it is both a real and an understandable (perhaps even an appropriate) reaction to certain situations: it captures a sense, not fully brought out by the account of flourishing in Chapter One, in which certain situations can impact seriously and centrally on individual lives over and above the demands of moral duties. This kind of regret is specifically attached to a particular agent or agents, who themselves are associated with particular outcomes (whether by having caused, or having failed to prevent them).

There are two key clarificatory points to be made. Firstly, there is a distinction between agent-regret, even in such cases, and spectator-regret. Recall the example of the runaway tram. The man who got off the track might understandably (perhaps appropriately) feel regret that, in saving his own life, he failed to prevent six deaths. He would feel this, moreover, in a way that a bystander powerless to do anything would not, although he too might regret the situation from his spectator perspective. The fact that the agent is in no way to blame for the outcome (assuming it is not his fault that he faces the marring choice in the first place) does not negate this regret.

To make this point, we might note, with Williams, that agent-regret extends even to involuntary actions:

> [E]ven at deeply accidental or non-voluntary levels of agency, sentiments of agent-regret are different from regret in general, such as might be felt by a spectator, and are acknowledged in our practice as being different. The lorry driver who, through no fault of his, runs over a child, will feel differently from any spectator, even a spectator next to him in a cab, except to perhaps the extent that the spectator takes on the thought that he himself might have prevented it, an agent's thought... We feel sorry for the driver, but that sentiment co-exists with, indeed, presupposes, that there is something special about his relation to this happening,

something which cannot merely be eliminated by the consideration that it was not his fault.[47]

In both cases, there is a core agent-connection with the bad outcome. On Carla Bagnoli's account, which goes beyond Williams', regret is a way for the agent of valuing the path that was not only not taken, but not taken *by her*.[48] In the context of this chapter, we can focus on cases where this 'valuing' includes recognition of the absolute centrality of these paths to one of the three central human standpoints. This has the advantage of separating fundamental regret from the kind of trivial regret-as-not-having-your-cake-and-eating-it associated with many day-to-day choices. (The regret at choosing between options on a menu, for example.[49])

Secondly, however, as Williams' own arguments indicate, there must be more to agent-regret in irreconcilable choices. The comparison with unintentional action is not meant to suggest that the situations are on a par. For the lorry driver, regret comes with a desire to go back and *do differently*, however impossible it would have been actually to act otherwise. After facing a marring choice, the individual might want the situation to have been different, but she cannot even wish to change what she did. Regret could just as well be associated with the other option, and perhaps more so.

Rather, if there is a spectrum from agent-regret in involuntary cases, through to the regret-as-remorse that is (or should be) felt in cases of voluntarily caused harms, then agent-regret in marring choices lies somewhere in between. This is in recognition of the fact that the individual made a choice: acted (or did not act) intentionally.[50]

The peculiar, all-permeating, nature of this regret captures the sense in which marring choices are hard (even impossible) to live with. Moreover, the individual is made worse off in an additional way *by having had to make the choice* (rather than having had the outcome she chooses just happen to her). Correspondingly, avoidably to put her in such a situation is to wrong her in a particular kind of way.

It would have been bad enough for Yates that his climbing partner fell to his death, but it is far worse to have had to choose between being the active means of that death and himself also dying. It would have been bad for Jim that ten men be shot in front of him, but it is much worse to know that he could have saved them. The Nazi guard does Sophie a terrible wrong in killing her child, but he does her an additional wrong—and one incommensurate to it—in requiring her to choose.

Against this background, recall Caroline in *Lonely Samaritan 1*, once she has saved one of the children. She faces two options, either of which she can understandably find very hard to live with: not to save a drowning child or to deny herself and her father this last meeting. Suppose she catches her train. Even if we assume she does not feel ashamed of what she has done, or wish she had done otherwise, still she might fundamentally regret not only the situation but her own connection with it. This, on Bagnoli's account, is because she recognizes the central value of the outcome not chosen: the outcome on which the life of another moral subject was saved, and saved *by her*. Even if we assume that she is not to be criticized for what she did, there remains a distinction between this situation and that in which a comforting friend could say to her: 'You couldn't have done more. You were physically incapable of saving another child.' Here, they can say only: 'You couldn't have done more. It would have cost you your last chance of rebuilding a relationship with your father.' To this, she could always respond: 'But I still could have done it. It was still *my* choice.'

The same applies if she saves the second child. She has lost something central to the interpersonal standpoint, and has, again, lost it through her own decision. Even if she does not wish that she had done otherwise, she can regret in a fundamental way the path that she did not take. Moreover, David put her in this situation by failing to save even one of the children. Accordingly, over and above the duties he has violated to the victim, he has done her a special kind of wrong.[51]

In *Lonely Samaritan 2* or *3*, Caroline again faces a marring choice. At some point, she must either sacrifice something central to her personal or interpersonal life or fail to save additional victims. Whatever she does, her decision comes with 'baggage' (personal, interpersonal, or moral), because it would be understandable for her to feel fundamental agent-regret. However, she is now in this predicament because—and so long as—there is no collective action. In *2(i)*, the defaulters, between them, have rendered impossible collective action to fulfil the weakly collective duty. It is they who have wronged her. In *2(ii)*, it is the failure of all four to organize which has imposed marring costs on each of them. In *3*, in addition, the plight of the children is itself the result of weakly collective responsibility for harm.

Let us now consider the plight of the individual moral agent faced with failure to act collectively on climate change. Section (iv) spelled out the irreconcilable choices that would arise between continued promotion, direct aid, or even sometimes mimicking, and central elements of the personal or interpersonal standpoint. There will always be more the individual could do—has, from the moral standpoint, reason to do—but at some point this would require giving up something also of central importance. Does the moral agent try a little harder to save the world, if it means abandoning her own family, or her own ambitions? Whatever she decides, she will have to live with having done less than she could have done: less to maintain her own life and relations, or less in responding to the desperate needs of the indefinitely many victims of climate change.

If mitigation, adaptation, and compensation are collectively achievable but we fail to achieve them, then we (as a collectivity or potential collectivity) leave individuals facing marring choices: choices where, whatever they do, they can experience fundamental agent-regret. This is most clear-cut if we focus on the broadly mutually fulfillable weakly collective climate duties we owe to our fellow human beings. However, it is so even if, following Chapter Four, not all the adaptation and compensation ends we have central reason to secure could be so secured even through collective action. In acting collectively, we could do a great deal more towards securing them. (I will come back to this in section (vii).)

However, it is important to distinguish between the two levels of the marring claim. This is because of concerns about paternalism. An objector to the reasoning above might point out that not everyone experiences these kinds of choices as giving rise to fundamental regret. How, then, can I say that we are 'wronging' each of us by collective failure? Perhaps it simply doesn't matter to everyone that they be able to reconcile these standpoints, in which case who are we to say that they are marred by inability to do so? Another way of putting this is: surely it only matters *for me*, if I am marred in the impersonally moral or interpersonal perspective if—and insofar as—that standpoint plays into the personal one.[52] Perhaps the reason Sophie's choice is such a searingly terrible example is because of the cost to her in personal terms: the destruction of her potential for a flourishing life.

To accommodate this divergence in intuitions, I offer two levels of the argument. On the moderate marring claim, these choices can be understandably experienced as marring by those for whom the interpersonal and impersonally moral perspectives are central and motivating. They are bad *for them*—from the personal perspective—in a fundamental sense. Accordingly, we owe it to these individuals that we not impose such choices on them.

There is a possible objection to this: that in curtailing the scope of the claim I have also weakened it, because it becomes a question simply of how much space an individual is 'owed' to be able to pursue her own conception of the good. However, I have two responses. Firstly, we would standardly consider an individual wronged if she were avoidably rendered incapable of pursuing her conception of the good. (Always assuming, of course, that that pursuit did not seriously harm others.) Moreover, this is not just *any* conception of the good. It is committed only to recognizing fully the impersonally moral standpoint, which in turn is grounded only in the significance (the moral 'badness') of the avoidable severe suffering of moral subjects. This is the same standpoint that underlines those key moral principles—the no-harm principle and the principle of beneficence—which were taken as a relatively uncontroversial starting point in Chapter One.

To make the universal marring claim, we must go further, to suggest that we are *all* marred by inability to reconcile the three standpoints, whether we consider ourselves so or not.

(VI) ARE WE ALL MARRED BY TRAGIC CHOICES?

Given that it relies on very controversial intuitions, this section should be treated as detached from the rest of this book, and indeed the rest of this chapter, both of which stand independent of it.

I claimed in section (v) that a moral agent who stops promoting collective (or taking direct) action on climate change is marred *from the impersonally moral perspective*. The question, then, is whether reconciling all three perspectives is in fact an essential part of being human, in which case fundamental regret would be not only understandable but appropriate in these situations. I believe there is at least some plausibility, grounded in strong shared intuitions, to the idea that it is.

Again, we can start with cases of involuntary actions. As Williams says of his lorry driver:

> Doubtless, and rightly, people will try, in comforting him, to move [him] from this state of feeling, move him indeed from where he is to something more like the place of a spectator, but it is important that this is seen as something that should need to be done, and indeed some doubt would be felt about a driver who too blandly or readily moved to that position.[53]

Even more might such doubt be felt about those who could make marring choices and consider themselves unmarred, even while (again, perhaps even more so) others would seek to help those who did experience them as marring to 'learn to live with it'. It seems to me that something would be not quite right about Sophie if she had not suffered from her choice: if she could have carried on, grieving (of course) for her daughter, but with no additional pain from having herself spoken the words that condemned her. Many of us would, I think, look askance on Yates if he could have moved on from his choice without agonizing about it, even while acknowledging that he did the least bad thing he could (perhaps the right thing) under the circumstances. The same would be true of Jim if he had shot the man himself and suffered nothing through having done so, or Caroline if she had left the second child to drown (or, indeed, abandoned her last meeting with her father) without any associated regret. The idea underlying this is that there is something not fully *human* about anybody who doesn't experience the central pull of each of the three standpoints.

This brings us to a final twist in the argument. Section (iii) rejected the idea of moral taint as resulting directly from negative collective outcomes, even if the individual either could not change those outcomes or had tried, up to the limits of demandingness, to do so. Taint was understood as rendering it appropriate that an individual agent feel shame, and that she be negatively morally evaluated by a third party. But if the arguments of this section are correct, then while a person faced with these irreconcilable choices would be very greatly pitied so long as she *did* experience such regret—while she might be entitled to assistance to 'learn to live with it'—she could appropriately be negatively evaluated if she did not. While no criticism need attach to her for being in the situation or for the choice she makes in it, it might nonetheless be felt that there is something lacking in her if she could make that choice lightly.

Amending section (iii), an agent needn't be tainted by failure to fulfil a weakly collective duty, but she might be so. She might be tainted not only (as was allowed there) because she had failed to exercise what control she could over the situation, but also because, when faced with marring choices as a result of such collective failure, she had experienced no fundamental regret.

If this further point is accepted, then the universal marring claim follows. To live fully at peace with ourselves as human beings, we need the three standpoints to be reconcilable. Accordingly, building on the previous sections, the three weakly collective duties to act on climate change are duties not only to its victims, and not only to those among us who do experience such irreconcilability as marring, but to all the rest of us as well.

I have one final point to make before turning to some probable objections. Although there are parallels, the model of a full human life underlying the universal marring claim need not reduce to a virtue ethics approach (such as those discussed in Chapter Five) on which an individual can flourish only if she lives in accordance with certain character traits. The idea is that being fully human involves seeing and responding to the world at least in part from the impersonally moral standpoint: a standpoint grounded, as was stressed in section (v), in the central significance of the serious suffering of our fellow moral subjects.[54]

(VII) OBJECTIONS

This section will anticipate a number of objections. The first is this. If collective action on climate change presents us with all these marring choices, why don't more of us experience them as such? ('If we're all marred, how come we're so unbothered?') This differs from the earlier objection that some don't experience any choices between the central standpoints as marring. It acknowledges some such choices to be so (Sophie's or Jim's, for example), but points out that most of us don't feel this way about the climate change case. Indeed, for many of us, not only do we not experience fundamental agent-regret when we choose our own most central personal or interpersonal ends over promoting effective action on climate change: we don't even get to that point. Most of us fail even to fulfil our individual duties as identified in Chapter Six.

There are two levels of response to this. The first, in parallel to the distinction between the two marring claims, notes simply that so long as there are some who do experience them as marring, then they, at least, are owed collective action to fulfil weakly collective duties. (To reinforce this, when we don't know exactly who will be harmed by our actions but know it will be harmful to some, this is often taken as a case for precaution. If you have reason to believe one of your child's party guests has a serious nut allergy, but don't know which, you ought not feed any one of them your delicious peanut butter cookies. If by some unlikely fluke Sophie had been utterly unmoved by her choice, it would still have been wrong of the guard to have imposed it on her, because he couldn't possibly have known that in advance.)

The second response recalls the previous chapter. Perhaps we do not experience these choices as marring not because they are not so, but because we have developed elaborate social and psychological mechanisms of denial. If—as Chapter Six argued—we are so adept at denying or blocking reality to deal with situations where we are not even doing our moral duty, how much more can we be expected to do so in marring situations?[55] After all, if reconciling the three standpoints is consistently impossible for the individual, perhaps the nearest she can get to 'living with herself' is by blocking off central elements of one or more of them. In the same way, presumably, devoting oneself entirely to tackling climate change would require cutting oneself off psychologically from many of the demands of the personal or interpersonal. We must do so if we are not—as Simon Hailwood puts it—to be driven mad.[56]

However, this gives rise to a further objection. If individuals have such effective ways of dealing with what could be marring situations, why should we owe collective action to them? Why—if we owe them anything—isn't it merely the help to develop these psychological masking techniques (many of which, drawing on Kari Marie Norgaard, are socially constructed)?[57] My response is threefold.

Firstly, if we think (with section (vi)) that there is something centrally human about these standpoints—and about being able to reconcile them— then this looks very much like treating a symptom rather than a disease. There is a distinction (to which I will return below) between cases where there is no alternative but to develop psychological masking techniques— where, in other words, the marring choice is collectively as well as individually unavoidable, so the only thing to do is develop ways to avoid perceiving it as such—and cases where there is the option of preventing the marring in the first place, through collective action to reconcile the three standpoints.

Secondly, if Part One convinced, then we, weakly collectively, are playing the part of the moral defaulter (of David, in *Lonely Samaritan*). This is not a case of failing to save someone from a marring choice, but of putting them into it by failing to do as we ought. Given this, the offer of psychological or socio-psychological adaptation—as an alternative to not imposing the choice in the first place—looks not only inadequate but insulting. Imagine the Nazi guard saying to Sophie: 'It's okay, I'll make you make this choice, but I'll pay for therapy in advance so you won't suffer anything extra from having made it.'

This reasoning applies on either the moderate or the universal marring claim: whether we are making a moral general claim about what each of us needs fully to be human, or concerned with avoiding marring only as a part of the individual's own conception of the good. Imagine offering therapy to a Muslim (or a vegetarian) whom you had just forced at gunpoint to eat pork. You might very well owe him that, at the very least, but it in no way negates the wrong done in inflicting the marring choice in the first place. More generally, there is something deeply disturbing about teaching people to resist the pull of the impersonally moral, if there is any alternative. One can imagine a Roman saying to a child upset by gladiators dying in the Colosseum: 'You'll toughen up and get used to it.' This may be true, but it is hardly the best outcome.

Thirdly, these psychological and socially organized barriers are not a cost-free way of dealing with irreconcilable choices. If they are tricks we have to play on ourselves every day, every time we buy clothes for our children or decide what to cook for supper, then there is a danger that they will detach us from the impersonally moral perspective altogether: enable us to deny the situation even below the point at which we would have fulfilled our moral duties.

In the climate change case, this was precisely the point borrowed, above, from Chapter Six. Too many of us have adapted not only not to experience irreconcilable choices as marring, but to live quite easily without remedying the serious suffering of others when we could do so between us at comparatively low cost to ourselves. In the Swiss focus groups carried out by S. Stoll-Kleemann and her colleagues, or among the residents of Bygdaby studied by Norgaard, socio-psychological techniques had proved so effective as to enable individuals to live without fulfilling promotional, direct, or even mimicking duties.[58]

Another way of putting this is as a positive choice: collectively, we have to decide what kind of people we want to be and the kind of world we want to live in. Is this to be the current world, in which we have become so increasingly detached from the impersonally moral perspective that we are in danger of forgetting how to react as moral agents altogether? Or one in which individuals are enabled, as far as possible, still to see and respond to the world from all three standpoints: personal, interpersonal, and impersonally moral?

Against an increasingly depressing global political reality, this may sound utopian to the point of naïveté. However, it is a challenge that at least some collectivities have met once, via the creation of the welfare state. In terms of untold individual suffering, which could be but is not prevented at the collective level, the current world rather resembles Victorian Britain. But there, at least, things did get better: the three standpoints became, at least for a few generations, closer to being reconciled. They ceased to be so when our collective potential to aid (or to harm) ceased to be manageable at the level of the individual state.[59] Faced with a globalized and warming world, we can either try to suppress the impersonally moral standpoint through these psychological barriers, or we can respond collectively, and retain all three.[60]

This discussion also allows us to respond to a flipside to the first objection. If all these are marring choices, how do I avoid claiming that I face particularly unpleasant marring choices all the time: at the extreme, to kill myself and have my organs donated to save the lives of others.

The response is that, in a sense, I do, but here we see the positive and necessary role of some of these mechanisms of denial. We don't experience these as marring choices because (appropriately in these cases) we have evolved not to. Such cases are importantly distinct from the climate change one, because there is not even a collective way out. We can invest in medical research and endeavour to encourage as much donation as possible of organs of those who have died by accident, but we cannot, even between us, entirely prevent the suffering. Thus, we have to find another way to see these cases differently.

Living within the three standpoints, the idea is collectively to make them *as compatible as possible*: by collective avoidance of marring choices if we can, and by developing ways to see cases differently where we lack that collective option. To return to the analogy above, acting collectively on climate change, rather than leaving individuals to find psychological techniques to live with it, is like curing an epidemic, rather than each finding ways of putting up with it. However, once we reach the limits of what can be cured, then there is nothing else to do but foster such palliative tools.[61]

In the climate change case, this becomes important when we factor in the conclusions of Chapter Four. Once we take seriously the moral status of non-human animals, species, and systems, we face salient and incompatible reasons to act. Once we have reached the limits of demandingness—that is, once collective action itself can no longer prevent irreconcilable choices— then, again, we might appropriately resort to developing techniques that will enable us to live with the situation.

The third objection claims that experiencing some marring choices may be a necessary—or at least an important—part of developing as a person. I have two replies. Firstly, I struggle to see how this could apply to choices that are marring at the fundamental, irreconcilable level discussed here. (It might be said that some people—some great heroes, say—would not have become who they are if they had not faced marring choices, but that is a rather different claim: it does not tie full flourishing to such choices.) Rather, it is tough-but-not-marring choices that might plausibly be 'necessary', in that they provide a means for us to learn to reconcile the three standpoints. Examples would be the choices between incompatible career paths with which Bagnoli associates genuine agent-regret, or the choice to fulfil a clear-cut moral duty which nonetheless comes with a perceptible cost.[62] In such cases, the three perspectives can be reconciled, at least in their fundamentals, but each cannot always be maximized.

However, it can also be pointed out that the proposed collective action would not rule out all marring choices. Even if we would, we could not collectively legislate against all small-scale or emergency dilemmas: against Yates' choice, or *Easy rescue 1*. If such predicaments are really supposed to be character-building, opportunities for such formative experiences would remain.

The fourth objection is that collective action is unnecessary because each individual could reconcile the standpoints by subsuming the personal into the impersonally moral: by genuinely adopting as her own plan of life one of constant activism on climate change, and developing all her personal relationships with others committed to the same goal.

Again, there are two responses. Firstly, even assuming (which is unlikely) that all of an individual's central personal relationships, including those into which she is born, could be fitted into such a plan of life, there remain incommensurate elements within the personal perspective. If an individual's plan of life required taking all the promotional action on climate change physically and mentally possible, she would be unable to secure one central capability (practical reason) without in the process undermining others. This, too, is an irreconcilable choice. (Recall the activists considered in section (iv), facing imprisonment or death as the price of their commitment to campaigning for a collective-level response to climate change.)

Secondly, even if this were true of some persons, it would not be possible for all. Nor would we wish it to be so, any more than we would want to detach ourselves from the impersonally moral standpoint altogether. As Susan Wolf argues, if ours were a world of moral saints, we would have lost a great deal that we have reason to value: the comedy of Groucho Marx; the mouth-watering expertise of the head chef at the Lutèce.[63] Or, for that matter, the poetry of T. S. Eliot, Kiri Te Kanawa's voice, or Rafael Nadal's serve.

Nor are the characteristics of someone single-mindedly devoted to just one goal those we would necessarily want in ourselves or our friends and family. (Imagine, as Carol Ann Duffy so wittily does, being married to Sisyphus.[64]) As Wolf puts it: 'I don't know whether there are any moral saints. But if there are I am glad that neither I nor those about whom I care most are among them.'[65] We admire and aspire to other things besides moral superiority: to the grace of Katharine Hepburn, the 'cool' of Paul Newman, to use Wolf's examples. Without space to develop our personal relationships, including with our children, we would all be Mrs Jellybys, and that, as Stocker points out, could in the end be worse for everyone.[66]

CONCLUSIONS

This chapter has outlined the plight of individual moral agents in cases of collective failure to act on climate change. It has analysed this not in terms of moral taint, as passing directly to an individual from collective moral failure, but in terms of the choices facing individual agents. It has been claimed that collective action on climate change can make it significantly less costly for us to fulfil our moral duties (or at least can enable us to do more from the moral perspective at the same cost); that a collective response is necessary for individuals fully to reconcile the personal, interpersonal, and impersonally moral standpoints from which each of us faces the world; and, finally, that there is a sense in which 'we' owe this collective action to some (or all) of us. This is because choices between central elements of the three standpoints can be (or are) marring. In making this last claim, the chapter has added a fourth to the three cases made in Part One for a weakly collective moral duty to act on climate change.

In building on this view of what it means to be human, I have gone beyond the relatively uncontroversial assumptions with which I began this monograph. I acknowledge this, and reiterate that my earlier arguments do not stand or fall with the claims defended here. (Alternatively, as I have also stressed, the reader unconvinced by some of my earlier arguments might nonetheless find grounds for agreement here.) However, for all its reliance on intuitions that some at least find problematic, I consider this an important part of a full discussion of climate change as a moral problem. Inspired by recent work by Gardiner, I have endeavoured to consider climate change not only in terms of what we are doing to others, or even in terms of its practical impact on some of us, but also in terms of what it does to us as moral agents. We need to think about the kinds of people (or 'scum') we will have to make ourselves, if we are to live in a world of collective failure to meet such an urgent, and so-much-encompassing, collective challenge.[67]

Conclusion

Climate change is a challenge to our standard moral thinking. It is a global-scale problem, but one that does not result from intentional collective action and to which we are not yet set up to respond collectively. How, then, do we explain the widely shared intuition that we should be doing something about it? And what does that mean for me, as an individual moral agent?

This book has attempted to answer these questions. I have defended a weakly collective duty to organize as necessary to act on mitigation, adaptation, and compensation, with a primary individual correlative duty to promote fair, effective collective action. In the climate change case, I have identified three global-level collectivities or potential collectivities with such duties.

The Young have a weakly collective duty to mitigate climate change grounded in the principle of moralized collective self-interest. This itself is based on an expanded, non-intentionalist model of collectivities, combined with a collectivized version of the weak principle of beneficence. The Able have a duty to organize to act collectively on mitigation and adaptation, defended by appeal to a moderate version of the collectivized principle of beneficence. Polluters, who are required to act together on mitigation, adaptation, and compensation, must do so in compliance with the collectivized no-harm principle. This itself can be defended by appeal to an expanded understanding of collective responsibility for harm: weakly collective responsibility for harm resulting predictably from aggregated, avoidable individual acts.

The idea behind this threefold approach is to reinforce the case for the correlative individual duties with complementary but largely independent foundations. The reader who rejects one of these arguments—who perhaps rejects all but the weakest principle of beneficence, or who maintains despite the arguments of Chapter Three that any assignment of collective responsibility for harm requires intentionally collective action—could still be convinced by the others. If all are accepted, then, as outlined in Chapter Three, three collectivities or potential collectivities have been identified whose weakly collective duties could, in practice, fairly be fulfilled by collective action at the level of the global affluent.

In Part One, these were defended as duties to our fellow humans: future generations as well as those already suffering central deprivations as a result of climate change. However, given that we started from the moral significance of securing the fundamental interests (or capabilities) of individual humans, it is natural to extend the sphere of moral concern to at least sentient non-human animals. Having done so, as was found in Part Four, it becomes necessary either to face some highly counterintuitive implications or to go further still, and accept that we may have moral duties to species and systems, or at least duties of incommensurate importance to protect or not to destroy them. In the climate change case, this yields further challenges. While the case for mitigation is mostly reinforced, the picture is greatly complicated with regard to compensation and adaptation. The three weakly collective duties, broadly mutually fulfillable in the human case, become a medley of morally salient but incompatible ends.

Armed with the framework of weakly collective duties, we are better equipped to answer the individual-level question. So long as there is no fair, effective scheme to fulfil the weakly collective duty, within which she can simply do her share, what should the individual moral agent do instead? Mimicking duties, which require the individual to imitate what would be asked of her by a fair collective scheme to fulfil the duty, have widespread appeal. However, attempts to fill this out philosophically fail to defend such duties as either primary or exclusive. Instead, it was argued in Part Three on the basis of effectiveness, fairness, and efficiency that the individual's primary duty is promotional: to do what she can towards bringing about the necessary collective action. Duties to protect the interests at stake or mitigate the harm directly, oneself, or as part of a like-minded subset, are supplementary.

That is not to say that individuals should not cut their own emissions (the central mimicking action in the climate change case). Where it is impossible to fulfil either promotional or direct duties, there may be a 'clean hands' case for mimicking among Polluters. Moreover, considerations of fairness to future cooperators could dictate mimicking so long as it does not conflict with promotional or direct duties. Finally, mimicking actions can be a necessary or the most effective means of fulfilling promotional or direct duties. However, individuals cannot assume that mimicking is all that is required of them, and it should not take priority in cases of conflict with promoting collective action.

There are, of course, limits to the demandingness of these individual moral duties. This was discussed in Chapter Six. But even beyond the question of what they can be blamed or criticized for not doing, collective failure to act on climate change can have a central impact on individuals as moral agents. It was argued in Part Four that unfulfilled weakly collective duties can leave individuals facing marring choices: choices where, whatever the agent does, she can understandably or appropriately experience fundamental regret. This, then, makes the fourth and final case for the weakly collective duty. Collective action on climate change is something we owe to ourselves, to enable us to live fully at peace with ourselves as simultaneously moral agents and individuals with our own lives and relationships to maintain.

Having summarized the argument, I wish to conclude with five comments on the challenges it, in turn, has raised. Firstly, Chapter Four greatly complicated the picture of our moral duties in relation to climate change. As things stood at the end of that chapter, it would be impossible simultaneously to fulfil all three weakly collective duties to humans, non-humans, and species and ecosystems. This leaves us with a choice. On one option, as moral philosophers, we must come up with some overall metric within which to justify prioritizing certain morally significant interests or duties over others (say, human over non-human interests, and/or weakly collective duties not to harm over duties to aid). If this turns out to be impossible—as we have good reason to think that it will—then we have yet another weakly collective duty. This is a duty to organize ourselves so as to pick out the best (or least bad) way of trading off these incommensurably salient ends against one another.

Secondly, recall what was said in closing Chapter Six. In defending promotional duties as primary, I have deliberately left open exactly what form this collective action should take: a more effective global-level deal between states, action led by a smaller set of states, a new global institution, or even cooperation across individuals on a global scale, bypassing governmental institutions. However, where an individual could optimally direct her promotional efforts will depend not only on her individual talents and circumstances (to which extent she must, inevitably, exercise her own judgement), but also on what forms of collective action can be defended as legitimate and fair (or, recalling Chapter Six, as fair enough). It will also, importantly, depend on which among these actually has most chance of happening.

To some degree, this in its turn will depend on what is most vigorously promoted: if one such form of action were to emerge as a clear favourite, this would be a reason for promoting it. Moreover, promotional efforts in the meantime can and should demonstrate a more general commitment to action on climate change, over and above pushing particular schemes or policies. Bringing these two together, it might even be claimed that this is the only way to reach an outcome: for various potential effective and at least reasonably fair solutions to be promoted until one emerges as salient by virtue of its more widespread appeal.

However, this would leave the individual unnecessarily unguided in making her decision. There is a further role for researchers in this process of determining what best to do: for political philosophers, of course, but in combination with those very many already undertaking empirical studies of the situation from a political, legal, or sociological point of view.[1] The task, which goes beyond the exercise in moral philosophy undertaken here, would be to draw some conclusions from across this broad, interdisciplinary body of work: to identify some acceptable collective outcomes as more promising than others, and enable individuals to narrow their range of possible promotional actions accordingly.

Thirdly, beyond the brief discussion at the end of Chapter Three, I have not focused here on what exactly a fair distribution of burdens would look like, within whatever scheme was ultimately adopted. This was deliberate: the distribution of the burdens of climate change mitigation, adaptation, and compensation is the subject of ongoing debate elsewhere.[2] However, that debate has generally operated in terms of states, whereas on the weakly collective model defended here, even if a global scheme were in practice organized via states, it would have to approximate a fair distribution across individuals. In particular, it would have to allow for members of all three collectivities or potential collectivities from less developed countries, and for some members of developed world states who are not in The Able. This is not impossible.[3] But it does mean that a truly (or even approximately) fair global system, organized via states, would need to be conducted at two levels. Burdens could, in practice, be allocated across states, but they would then have to be distributed within each state so that those on whose behalf that state had (as it were) acquired them would be those who ultimately bore the costs.

Fourthly, this book has focused, with unapologetic narrowness, on climate change. It has done so because this is a special case. As well as being so peculiarly urgent and undeniably global, climate change combines all three of the arguments for the weakly collective duty defended in Part One. However, each of those individual arguments could transfer into other spheres, bringing with them parallel conclusions regarding individual duties, and the danger of widespread irreconcilable or marring individual choices where weakly collective duties remain unfulfilled. It is worth briefly acknowledging some of these here.

The non-intentionalist account of when we constitute a collectivity and the principle of moralized collective self-interest have widespread implications: not only in terms of other possible global collectivities and associated moral duties (for example, mutual dependence through the fundamental interests at stake in avoiding nuclear war), but also for the weakly collective and correlative individual duties that we might acquire through mutual dependence on a smaller scale. These implications are perhaps particularly interesting if the arguments of Chapter Four convinced, and we accept that we are co-members of many of these collectivities with non-human animals. For example, even if the general principle of beneficence were rejected for non-humans, this expanded understanding of collectivities could provide the basis for an account of our positive duties to at least some non-human animals.

The arguments from collective ability to aid and collective harm also extend beyond the climate change case. It would be a natural move to expand the former to the field of global poverty, although by the same token almost an unnecessary one. Several of those theorists on whom I based my defence of a collectivized principle of beneficence made their parallel arguments in that sphere.[4] However, the argument from weakly collective harm might, at least arguably, also be extended in this way. This would go beyond the idea, explored intensively in recent cosmopolitan literature, of duties grounded in membership of harmful global economic, political, or legal institutions, or as playing a part in harmful structures or patterns of behaviour.[5]

Key points also transfer to other environmental problems. Some or all of the arguments in Part One might plausibly be applied to the related question of the ethics of natural resource depletion (the other side, as it were, of the climate change coin). They might also transfer to cases of more localized pollution, where the duty-bearing collectivities or potential collectivities would be smaller but where, once again, there would be significant implications for individual duties. Following Chapter Four, the arguments from collective harm and collective ability to aid might also extend to biodiversity loss in general. However, recalling Chapter Two, further argument would be needed to show that this was a fundamental interest loss to all—or even many—human beings.

Finally, I have not touched here on the question of human population growth. However, its significance can at least partially be brought out within this model. The total number of people will affect both the level to which all could emit without climate change getting worse (that is, the cut-off point for membership of Polluters), and the size of individual sacrifice required in fair fulfilment of the weakly collective duty. Given this, two points can be made. Firstly, if the size of a collectivity or potential collectivity alters as a result of the combined actions of only some of its members, and this in turn influences how burdensome fulfilling weakly collective duties will be, then further questions are raised about the appropriate distribution of burdens. Secondly, more generally, a weakly collective duty might be defended to stabilize or reduce world population as part of fair mitigation of climate change. Both possibilities raise innumerable challenges of their own: questions difficult enough in themselves, and made more so by how emotively they are generally received. However, they should not for that reason be ignored. We need to talk about population. We need to do so, moreover, as an issue inseparable from considerations of both climate and global justice. However, this lies beyond the scope of this project.

I hope, then, that the arguments I have offered will have implications well beyond my current focus. But I also hope that the book as it stands has left us better able to make sense of the situation with which, as individual moral agents, climate change has presented us: that it has given us a better grasp of the duties each of us acquires as one of the many individuals who could, *between us*, make a difference. If this is so, then it has fulfilled its aim.

In some ways, the message may seem a tough one. I have argued that the individual cannot consider herself 'apart' from the problem of climate change. Rather, she must regard herself as one of two or three collectivities or potential collectivities morally required to act on it. As individuals, we cannot be complacent. We cannot step back, tell ourselves, 'This is the government's problem', and ignore it until told by the government what we need to do. But seen in another way, this is a positive message: this is *our* problem, so its solution is in our hands. We should not despair at the failure of our governments to come up with an effective response, because that is not the end of the story. It is up to us to find ways of acting together, by influencing, amending, supplementing, or if necessary bypassing those institutions. As morally motivated individuals—as those individuals who want, at least, to do the right thing—we may still be depressed by the size of the problem and by the number of others who are apparently unmotivated by it. But we need no longer feel quite so lost.

Key claims and definitions

(i) Interests and collectivities

Fundamental interests
An individual human being has a fundamental interest in retaining the capability (genuine, secure opportunity) for continued life, bodily health, bodily integrity, affiliation, and practical reason.

Secure functionings claim
Significant, ongoing risks to central functionings, from which an individual cannot opt out, render those functionings insecure and so deprive the individual of the associated capability.

Non-intentionalist model
A set of individuals constitutes a collectivity if and only if those individuals are mutually dependent for the achievement or satisfaction of some common or shared purpose, goal or fundamental interest, whether or not they acknowledge it themselves.

Potential collectivity
A set of individuals who would, were they to espouse some goal, be mutually dependent for its achievement and so constitute a collectivity.

Should-be collectivity
A set of individuals who:

- would, were they to espouse some goal or goals, constitute a collectivity; and
- have a moral duty to espouse that goal.

The Able
The potential collectivity composed of those (the global affluent) who could contribute to action on climate change mitigation and adaptation at less than significant cost to themselves.

The Young
The collectivity made up of those with fundamental interests at stake in mitigating climate change.

Polluters
The potential collectivity made up of those emitting greenhouse gases above the level at which, were all emitting at that level, climate change would not be worsened, and whose individual emissions over that level are avoidable without the loss to them of some fundamental interest.

(ii) Principles and duties

Weakly collective duty
A duty requiring some collectivity or potential collectivity, which is not yet set up for collective action, to organize as necessary to secure some particular end.

Weak principle of beneficence
An individual (moral agent) has a moral duty to prevent the serious suffering (deprivation of a fundamental interest) of some other human being or human beings (moral subject(s)) if she can do so at minimal cost to herself.

Moderate principle of beneficence
An individual (moral agent) has a moral duty to prevent serious suffering (deprivation of a fundamental interest) by some other human being or human beings (moral subject(s)) if she can do so at less than significant cost to herself.

Collectivized weak principle of beneficence
A set of human beings (moral agents) have a duty to cooperate to prevent the serious suffering (deprivation of a fundamental interest) of another human being or human beings (moral subject(s)) if they can do so at minimal cost to each.

Collectivized moderate principle of beneficence
A set of human beings (moral agents) have a duty to cooperate to prevent the serious suffering (deprivation of a fundamental interest) of another human being or human beings (moral subject(s)) if they can do so at less than significant cost to each.

Principle of moralized collective self-interest
A set of human beings (moral agents) who are mutually dependent through a common fundamental interest have a weakly collective duty to cooperate to secure that interest, so long as this is possible without those individuals having to sacrifice some other fundamental human interest.

No-harm principle
An individual (moral agent) has a moral duty to avoid inflicting serious harm (deprivation of a fundamental interest) on another human being or human beings (moral subject(s)) *at least* if she can avoid so doing without suffering comparable harm herself.

Weakly collective responsibility claim
A number of individuals who do not yet constitute a collectivity (either formally, with an acknowledged decision-making structure, or informally, with some vaguely defined common interest or goal) can be held collectively morally responsible for serious harm (fundamental interest deprivation) which has been caused by the predictable aggregation of avoidable individual actions.

Collectivized no-harm principle
A set of human beings (moral agents) have a moral duty to organize themselves as necessary to prevent serious harm (deprivation of fundamental interests) to another

human being or human beings (moral subject(s)) resulting from the predictable aggregation of their avoidable individual acts, where:

- a result is 'predictable' if it is reasonably foreseeable to the individuals both that the actions in combination will cause the harm, and that others are relevantly similarly motivated to act; and
- an action is 'avoidable' if the agent has alternative actions available to her which would not deprive her of fundamental interests.

(iii) Correlative individual duties

Mimicking duties
Duties to do what would be required of one as part of a fair collective scheme to fulfil the duty.

Promotional duties
Duties to attempt to bring about the necessary collective action.

Direct duties
Either:

> *Protecting duties*: duties to protect the interests at stake
> *Mitigating duties*: duties to mitigate the harm directly

And, within each:

> *Individual version*: fulfil the duty acting on one's own
> *Sub-collective version*: fulfil the duty acting in combination with a like-minded subset.

(iv) Marring and costliness

Personal standpoint
Perspective on which events, actions, and situations are assessed from the point of view of their impact on the individual's own desires, goals, interests, or capabilities.

Interpersonal standpoint
Perspective on which events, actions, and situations are assessed from the point of view of their impact on the individual's relations with specific others.

Impersonally moral standpoint
Perspective on which events, actions, and situations are assessed according to what the individual owes to others, or what it would be good or bad (better or worse) for her to do in terms of its impact on them, simply because they are moral subjects.

Marring choices
Choices where, whichever way the individual decides, she can fundamentally regret not having taken the other option.

Costliness claim
Collective action on climate change could make it significantly less burdensome for us to fulfil our moral duties, in terms of the impact on our personal or interpersonal lives.

Modified costliness claim
Collective action on climate change could enable us to achieve considerably more from the impersonally moral perspective, at the same cost to each in terms of impact on our personal and interpersonal lives, than we would have been able to achieve individually.

Irreconcilability claim
We need collective action on climate change in order to reconcile the three standpoints from which each of us faces the world: the personal, the interpersonal, and the impersonally moral.

Moderate marring claim
Because many individuals understandably experience their lives as marred by choices between central elements of the three standpoints, we (between us) owe it to each of these individuals to act collectively on climate change.

Universal marring claim
Because we are *all* marred, as moral agents, by choices between central elements of the three standpoints, we (between us) owe it to each of us to act collectively on climate change.

Glossary of philosophical terms

Ability to Pay Principle
A principle prominent in the debate on distributing the burdens of dealing with climate change, according to which the burdens should be borne by those with the greatest ability to pay.

Adaptive preferences
Preferences which adjust in response to circumstances. This can be a problem for theories of distributive justice based on preference satisfaction: the very deprived can adapt to be satisfied with an objectively very low quality of life; at the other extreme, the affluent may develop expensive tastes and require extra resources to secure the same preference satisfaction.

Autonomy
Being able to plan one's own life in a meaningful sense. On Joseph Raz's account (adopted here), this requires freedom from coercion and manipulation, appropriate mental faculties, and an adequate range of both long- and short-term options.

Basic needs
The means to secure a minimally decent life, including health, nutrition, and some basic education.

Beneficiary Pays Principle
Another principle prominent in the debate on distributing the burdens of dealing with climate change, on which those burdens should be borne by those who have benefited most from the actions and processes which brought about climate change.

Categorical imperative
Immanuel Kant's unconditional moral imperative, taken here on its first formulation. This requires the individual moral agent to act only in line with maxims (rules for conduct) which she can consistently will that everyone else should live by as well.

Capabilities approach
Political philosophy pioneered by Amartya Sen and Martha Nussbaum, on which capabilities to exercise central functionings are the appropriate metric for distributive justice, and for targeting aid (nationally or globally) to the least advantaged.

Collectivity
A set of individuals taken as a group. On Keith Graham's conditions, a collectivity does something distinct from what its individual members do, it survives changes in those members, and it plays a necessary part in adequately capturing the significance of some of their individual acts.

Compliance condition
Liam Murphy's condition on the principle of beneficence, on which an individual cannot be expected to do more under partial than she would have to do under full compliance with the principle.

Consequentialism
A moral theory on which the rightness or wrongness of individual conduct is ultimately determined by consequences. For this project, the focus is on the alleviation of severe suffering.

Act-consequentialism
The individual moral agent should perform the act with the best consequences.

Rule-consequentialism
The individual moral agent should act in accordance with the moral rules that would have the best consequences if the majority of people followed them.

Cooperative consequentialism
The individual moral agent should do what would bring about the best results in combination with those others similarly motivated.

De re/de dicto
In this context, the distinction between two ways of picking out an object or person: as that particular object or person, or as the object or person occupying some position or role. (For example, 'I want to meet the president of the United States' could mean 'I want to meet Barack Obama' (*de re*) or 'I want to meet whoever happens to occupy the role of President of the United States' (*de dicto*).)

Ethics
Moral philosophy. The focus here is on *normative ethics* which investigates methods of determining whether an action or course of behaviour is moral (good or bad, right or wrong), and *applied ethics*, which attempts to determine moral responses to particular situations.

Intentionalism
An influential view in the philosophy of social science, on which sets of individuals constitute collectivities when those individuals think of themselves as doing so: either because each considers herself to be a member of some group with the others, or because of joint commitment to some purpose or goal.

Moral agents
Moral duty-bearers; those who can be held morally responsible for their actions.

Moral subjects
Those to whom we have moral duties.

Negative vs. positive duty
The distinction between duties not to harm moral subjects (*negative duties*) and duties to aid them (*positive duties*).

Non-identity problem
In this context, the problem of how duties to tackle climate change can be grounded in duties not to harm members of future generations, when the combined actions that cause climate change also change who future individuals are (e.g. by changing the times at which children are conceived). Assuming their lives are at least worth living, future individuals have not been made *worse off* by the combined actions that result in climate change, because without it they would not have existed at all. So how can we be said to have harmed them?

Normative
Concerns questions of value (how things ought to be) rather than descriptive fact.

Overdetermination
An effect is overdetermined if there are more causes present than would be necessary to bring it about.

Polluter Pays Principle
Prominent principle in the debate on distributing the burdens of dealing with climate change, on which the burdens should be borne by those who caused the problem.

Rational altruist's dilemma
The dilemma facing an individual in the following situation. She is motivated to do good and is one of many similarly motivated agents, each of whom has the option of performing action X or action Y. If she performs action X, this will make no perceptible difference to the overall outcome. She knows she could do good directly by performing action Y instead. However, she also knows that if all the agents were to perform action X, it would do much more good than if they all performed action Y.

Reflective equilibrium
A process of working backwards and forwards between our strong intuitions about particular cases, the moral principles we think apply to such cases, and underlying theoretical considerations. The idea is to revise each as necessary, until they can be made consistent with one another. (In political philosophy this is particularly associated with John Rawls.)

Strong principle of beneficence
Principle defended by Peter Singer, on which an individual (moral agent) has a moral duty to prevent serious harm to another human being or human beings (moral subject(s)) if she can do so at less than comparable cost to herself.

Utilitarianism

A version of consequentialism, on which actions or moral rules are assessed by their impact on overall (or average) welfare.

Virtue ethics

A moral theory which emphasizes moral character rather than duties, rules or consequences. The idea is that the moral agent should act in accordance with certain character traits, or virtues (for example, benevolence, or fortitude).

Notes

NOTES ON CHAPTER ONE

1. Stern 2006: i.
2. Lichtenberg 2010: 558.
3. Examples adapted from Dostoyevsky 1866: 1–83; Singer 1972.
4. This challenge has now repeatedly been raised. See e.g. Jamieson 2007a, 2010; Lichtenberg 2010; Scheffler 1995.
5. Jamieson 2007a: 475.
6. Lichtenberg 2010: 557–9. Her last evocative phrase is borrowed from Petersen 2008.
7. In Stephen Gardiner's terminology, I make a start on tackling the 'theoretical storm': the 'current theoretical ineptitude', which is one of three simultaneous challenges making climate change such a peculiarly intractable problem. His other 'storms' are the global and intergenerational asymmetries of power which make it so difficult to achieve an ethical response. (Gardiner 2006, 2011b.)
8. See e.g. Arnold 2011: 7–10; Gardiner 2004: 559–69; Garvey 2008: 7–31; Page 2006: 22–49; Vanderheiden 2008: 3–9.
9. Bernstein et al. 2007: 30.
10. Bernstein et al. 2007: 37–9. *Very high confidence* represents an approximately 9 out of 10 assessed chance that a finding is correct; with *high confidence* 8 out of 10; *medium confidence* 5 out of 10; *low confidence* 2 out of 10; and *very low confidence* less than 1 out of 10. *Very likely* here means a more than 90 per cent probability. (2007: 27.)
11. Bernstein et al. 2007: 32–3.
12. Peterson et al. 2012.
13. For an account of this consensus, including its recognition by leading global corporations, see Arnold 2011: 2–7. Even the American Association of Petroleum Geologists acknowledges this wealth of evidence, although it stops short of unequivocal support. (American Association of Petroleum Geologists 2007.) Former sceptic physicist Richard Muller changed his position in July 2012 after his own Berkeley Earth Surface Temperature project found average land temperatures to have increased by 1.5°C over the previous 250 years. (Berkeley Earth Surface Temperature 2012. See also Muller 2012.)
14. American Geophysical Union 2003; American Meteorological Society 2007; Omenn et al. 2006.
15. Omenn et al. 2006. This has been reinforced by a letter to the US senate from the AAAS and 17 other scientific bodies. (American Association for the Advancement of Science et al. 2009.)
16. Karl et al. 2009: 9.
17. Australian Academy of Sciences et al. 2001.
18. Academia Brasiliera de Ciências Brazil et al. 2005.

19. African Academy of Sciences et al. 2007; European Academy of Sciences and Arts 2007; European Geosciences Union 2005; International Council of Academies of Engineering and Technological Sciences 2007. See also e.g. InterAcademy Council 2007.

20. Oreskes 2004: 1686. Oreskes surveyed the abstracts for 928 peer-reviewed articles listed on the ISI database with keywords 'climate change'. Of these, 75 per cent 'explicitly or implicitly accept[ed] the consensus view'. The remainder '[took] no position on current anthropogenic climate change'.

21. Doran and Zimmerman 2009: 22–3.

22. Wherever it comes from, it is alarmingly pervasive: Zimmerman and Doran estimate from Gallop survey data that only 58 per cent of the US general public think that human activity contributes significantly to changes in average global temperatures. (2009: 22.)

23. Arnold 2011: 2–3.

24. For an account of this influence—channelled via a small cohort of highly vocal scientists—see Oreskes and Conway 2010. See also Arnold 2011: 3.

25. Bernstein et al. 2007: 44–5. See also Karl et al. 2009: 9. The IPCC also warns that 'anthropogenic warming could lead to some impacts that are abrupt or irreversible'. (Bernstein et al. 2007: 53–4.) See also e.g. Committee on Abrupt Climate Change et al. 2002: 108; Gardiner 2009; Hansen 2008; McKinnon 2009; Pearce 2007. However, the arguments for the weakly collective duties do not require me to focus on the risk of abrupt or runaway climate change.

26. Stern 2006: iv.

27. As such, it incorporates elements of Nussbaum's 'Senses, Imagination, and Thought' as well as her category of 'Practical Reason'. (Nussbaum 2000b: 78–9.)

28. Sen 1999: 74. See also e.g. Sen 1980; Wolff and de-Shalit 2007. In taking the capabilities to identify the prerequisites for a fully flourishing human life (rather than simply what can be taken as such for political or practical purposes) I am more in line with earlier than later versions of Nussbaum's account. See e.g. Nussbaum 1992, 1998, 2000a, 2000b: 34–110.

29. On adaptive preferences, see e.g. Elster 1983: 109–40; Mill 1869: 484–7; Nussbaum 2000b: 111–66; Sen 1987: 45–7. On 'equality of what?', see e.g. G. A. Cohen 1989; Dworkin 1981a, 1981b; Sen 1980.

30. Sen 1980: 215–16.

31. Nussbaum 2000b: 78–80.

32. See e.g. Wolff and de-Shalit 2007: 51–7.

33. Raz 1986: 369; Stewart 1996: 64.

34. Stewart 1996: 49. See also e.g. Streeten et al. 1981; Wiggins 1987: 1–57. Sen also highlights a subset of capabilities—basic capabilities—as identifying a level 'below which people count as being scandalously "deprived"'. (1993: 41.)

35. Raz 1986: 370, 72–7. (Italics added.)

36. Cocker et al. 1995. Those who prefer their examples literary can substitute Wolff and de-Shalit's example of George Orwell, 'down and out in London and Paris, but a telegram away from sanctuary at the Ritz'. (Wolff and de-Shalit 2007: 65, citing Orwell 1933.)

37. Wolff and de-Shalit 2007: 64–84.

38. Stern 2006: vi. (Italics in original.) Climate change also has implications every bit as serious for the non-human world. See e.g. Bernstein et al. 2007: 48. I will return to these in Chapter Four. However, the moral case for collective action can be made even if we restrict our attention—as so many do—to human beings.
39. Caney (2006; 2009a) and Holland (2012: 151–7) make parallel points, the former arguing that climate change violates human rights, the latter drawing on Nussbaum's list of capabilities.
40. Bernstein et al. 2007: 48.
41. Bernstein et al. 2007: 48.
42. On increased risks of conflict, see e.g. Karl et al. 2009: 47–8, 89; Stern 2006: vii–viii.
43. Holland 2008: 323.
44. Verbruggen 2007: 818, 809.
45. I will not comment on geoengineering solutions, or such alternatives as emigration to other planets. See e.g. Gardiner 2010, 2012; Karlsson 2006: 244–8. If such options were defensible, which I am far from allowing, the main arguments of this book would not be undermined. We would be required to organize to secure immediate and effective development of the necessary technology, with a fair distribution of costs.
46. Bernstein et al. 2007: 65.
47. Academia Brasiliera de Ciências Brazil et al. 2005.
48. Omenn et al. 2006.
49. See e.g. Lomborg 2001: 300–24; Nordhaus 1997.
50. Caney 2008, 2009c; Parfit 1984: 356; Stern 2008: 12–15.
51. Mill 1859: 14.
52. Ross 1930: 21; Shue 1981: 587. (Italics added.) Both Mill and Shue go further than is required here, where the focus is on moral duties rather than the legitimacy of coercive interference to prevent harms.
53. Lichtenberg 2010: 573.
54. By a bystander, I mean, for ease of example, someone who isn't themselves even innocently the cause of the threat to my life, and who isn't themselves exposed to the same threat.
55. Caney 2009a: 88.
56. Caney 2009a: 88.
57. Moreover, as Caney also stresses, the possibility of providing compensation in no way justifies doing the harm in the first place. (2009a: 88.)
58. Singer 1972: 231.
59. Murphy makes this point. (1993: 268.)
60. Ross 1930: 19–27.
61. As lovers of Evelyn Waugh will no doubt point out, in the hauntingly sinister conclusion to *A Handful of Dust*, from which I have adapted my example, there is no suggestion that constantly reading Dickens is required to save the listener's life. Nor does the unfortunate hero have any choice about undertaking the task. (Waugh 1934: 321–40.)
62. Of course, this distinction between temporary and permanent deprivation does not apply to the capability for continued life.

63. I will come back to this in Chapter Seven, but it is arguable that our personal ties have a significance in themselves which reduces neither to their contribution to the exercise of affiliation, nor to the performance of impersonal moral duties. In this case, an independent condition could be drawn up in terms of significantly affecting the functioning of a key relationship. Equally, note that I focus here on victims who are strangers to the duty-bearer, because we are concerned with duties to other human beings only insofar as they are human beings. Much more might be demanded of me in aiding those with whom I have a personal relationship.

64. Murphy 1993, 2000.

65. In fact, Murphy himself is considerably more demanding, in such cases, than the model defended here. (2000: 97–101.)

66. Lichtenberg 2010: 563–75.

67. Parfit 1984: 352–79, 1986.

68. Vine 2002. (Apologies to crime fiction fans for the spoiler.)

69. Two further possibilities, which I will not draw on here, are defended by Alan Carter and Edward Page, respectively. Carter 2001 appeals to the fact that a given individual does not cause all members of future generations to be different. So long as there are some future persons who are made significantly badly off as a result of *my* action, and would have existed independently of it, I shouldn't have acted as I did. However, this cannot help here: the weakly collective harm argument in Chapter Three appeals to the impact of our combined actions. Page (2006: 150–8) appeals to the rights of future generations taken as groups. However, it is beyond the current project to defend the fundamental interests of human communities as morally significant in themselves.

70. Parfit 1984: 369.

71. C. Hare 2007.

72. Parfit 1984: 357–9.

73. Weinberg 2008.

74. Woodward 1986: 810–11. See also Parfit 1986; Woodward 1987.

75. Caney 2006: 266–8. John Nolt argues that we are unjustly dominating future generations, despite giving them the benefit of existence. (2011c: 71–2.)

76. Harman 2009: 139. See also Harman 2004.

77. Shiffrin 1999.

78. See e.g. Page 2006: 145; Woollard 2012.

79. McDermott 2008: 13.

80. McDermott 2008: 20.

81. See e.g. Brighouse 2010.

82. Lichtenberg and Scheffler, pointing out the shortcomings of standard theories of individual responsibility, are concerned with globalization in general. (Lichtenberg 2010; Scheffler 1995.)

83. Goodin 1985: 134–41; Shue 1980: 35–64.

84. That is, even our weakly collective duties to our fellow humans would become mutually unfulfillable.

85. Jamieson 2011: 36.

86. Goodin 1985: 134–41; Held 1970; May 1992: 105–24; Shue 1980: 35–64.

87. Maltais Forthcoming; Murphy 1998, 2000.

88. Sinnott-Armstrong 2005.
89. Gardiner 2010, 2011b: 385–96, 2012; Nagel 1991: 10–20, 53–62.

NOTES ON CHAPTER TWO

1. Dickens 1837: 316–17.
2. Speech to the UK Parliament (Obama 2011).
3. Sections (i) and (ii) of this chapter draw extensively from my earlier defence of the non-intentionalist model: Cripps 2011b: 2–9, 13–18.
4. See Gilbert 1989: 93–214, 2006: 93–184. Note, however: firstly, that I have used more general terminology than Gilbert; and secondly, that in arguing that we do form collectivities under these circumstances, she is not necessarily committed to the view that we could never do so otherwise. Indeed, she has stressed in personal correspondence (4 March 2011) that she is open to discussions of alternative interpretations of 'collectivity'. Other intentionalist accounts include: Caws 2005; Gould 1988: 71–80, 109–13; Kutz 2000: 66–112; Tuomela 2002: esp. 131.
5. To clarify, this model does not require that goals be taken as subsets of interests, let alone of fundamental interests: individuals can have goals which correspond to trivial interests, or are even contrary to their fundamental interests. However, the special-case ascription of moral duties, in sections (v) and (vi), concerns only those collectivities where fundamental interests are at stake.
6. Intentionalists need not adhere to the still more controversial idea that membership must be voluntary, although that might seem implicit in Gilbert's account.
7. Thanks to David-Hillel Ruben for the example. For a parallel argument at state level, see Cripps 2011b: 9–10.
8. Gilbert 1989: 233.
9. Gilbert 2006: 239.
10. A further difficulty with such 'add-on' rules is that they leave the intentionalist vulnerable to accusations of circularity. See Cripps 2011b: 6–13.
11. In making the first option explicit, I have modified my argument from Cripps 2011b.
12. Sheehy 2002: 384–5.
13. These are adapted from Graham's sufficient conditions for constitution of a collectivity. (2002: 68–9.)
14. To put this more formally, the collectivity has expressive or descriptive autonomy. See e.g. Graham 2002: 83; Macdonald and Pettit 1981: 115.
15. Macdonald and Pettit use this in the context of institutions. (1981: 119.)
16. Cripps 2011b: 9–10.
17. Nozick 1974: 93–5.
18. Nussbaum 2000b: 78–80.
19. Bernstein et al. 2007: 53.
20. Nussbaum 2000b: 80.
21. Bernstein et al. 2007: 48. See also e.g. Thomas et al. 2004.
22. Raz 1986: 369–78.
23. Wolff and de-Shalit 2007: 56.

24. Page 2007: 464.
25. Holland 2008: 324. (Italics in original.) See also Holland 2012; Jamieson 2011: 34–5. Holland's meta-capability involves 'being able *to live one's life in the context of ecological conditions that can provide environmental resources and services that enable the current generation's range of capabilities; to have these conditions now and in the future*' (2008: 324; italics in original). However, it is unclear to what extent this is a meta-capability rather than simply a necessary condition for the exercise of any of the other capabilities.
26. Wolff and de-Shalit 2007: 63–84. An opportunity is genuine, rather than merely formal, if the individual can take it up without an unreasonable cost in terms of other functionings.
27. Examples taken from Wolff and de-Shalit 2007: 65, 67. They borrow the first from Sen 1999: 8.
28. Wolff and de-Shalit 2007: 68.
29. See e.g. Finkelstein 2003; Perry 2007.
30. Wolff and de-Shalit 2007: 67–8.
31. Shue 2010: 152. This does not mean that, given such a risk and given that I cannot reduce it, I would be better off knowing about it than otherwise.
32. Nozick 1974: 42–5.
33. Weir 1998.
34. Wolff and de-Shalit 2007: 68–9.
35. Example adapted from Wolff and de-Shalit 2007: 69.
36. Parallel examples are in Wolff and de-Shalit 2007: 65. See also Chapter One.
37. As Wolff has pointed out, it is also essential that my model can distinguish between the risk imposed by climate change and that of some other (possible but improbable) global-level disaster such as a meteor strike. The requirement that the risk be 'significant' is one way of doing this. For a further, policy-orientated normative account of risk and climate change, see Moellendorf 2011. Moellendorf argues that both procedural and substantive considerations are relevant in determining what counts as 'too risky', and incorporates a further element of uncertainty in identifying dangerous climate change for the purposes of guiding international (in particular UNFCCC) policy.
38. Shue 2010: 148.
39. Note that nothing I have said excludes the possibility that I might permissibly choose to give away or destroy a kidney.
40. Karl et al. 2009: 47–8, 89. See also Bernstein et al. 2007: 52.
41. Stern 2006: viii. See also Bernstein et al. 2007: 50.
42. Bernstein et al. 2007: 50.
43. For recent research linking extreme weather events in 2011 to climate change, see e.g. Peterson et al. 2012.
44. See e.g. IPCC 2007: 9, 15.
45. Stern 2006: xxvii.
46. Lomborg 2001: 323, cited in Gardiner 2011b: 257–8. See also Schelling 1997: 10; Stern 2006: xii.
47. For an analysis of the latest UNFCCC Conferences of Parties, see Rajamani 2011, 2012. See also e.g. Gardiner 2011b: 128–40; Jamieson 2008.

48. Jamieson 2011: 36. See also Maltais Forthcoming.
49. Hobbes 1651: 86–129. See also e.g. Hampton 1986: 74–9.
50. Jamieson 2011: 36.
51. To reiterate Chapter One, I am assuming a way round the non-identity problem.
52. Future generations are not the only passive members: consider the current generation of infants, and those with severe intellectual disabilities.
53. Because of the likelihood that there is only a limited window of opportunity within which to secure action on mitigation, it might be objected that most future generations are powerless with respect to the overall end. This does not undermine the claim that there is a collectivity, as things currently stand. Almost any potentially ongoing collectivity could cease to be such if one generation of members undermined all possibility of securing the shared goal or interests.
54. E.g. Gilbert argues that obligation follows from joint commitment, and so from membership of intentionalist collectivities. (2006: esp. 147–64.)
55. See also e.g. Gilbert 2006; Nagel 2005.
56. It is arguable, in analogy with Goodin, that we could defend the special duties to members of our own family in this way. (1985: 70–91.) However, as Chapter Seven will explore, there is a sense in which interpersonal ties also generate reasons to act incommensurate with general or impersonal moral duties.
57. Goodin 1985: 134–41; Held 1970; May 1992: 105–24; Shue 1980: 35–64.
58. Singer 1972: 231.
59. '[T]he action specified in the circumstances may have been said to have been obvious to the reasonable person.' (Held 1970: 477.)
60. May 1992: 37–40.
61. May 1992: 109.
62. Gansberg 1964.
63. May 1992: 112–13. On Held's account, while the collection of individuals in such cases cannot be held responsible for the actual failure to prevent the harm, they can be held so for failure to establish a decision-making procedure. (1970: 471.)
64. Shue defends a duty to create or amend institutions where necessary to protect basic rights. (1980: 51–60.)
65. It is, of course, crucial that such consent is free and informed. (See e.g. Shrader-Frechette 2002: 77–8.)
66. Of course, this disruption could be a more-than-minimal cost in itself. In some cases, it could interfere so much with pursuit of the individual's plan of life as to count as 'significant' and so count against even the moderate principle of beneficence. However, it would not do so if it came as part of preserving some other fundamental interest. A broken leg is a morally significant cost to me, but not if it is a necessary part of saving me from being permanently disabled.
67. This is to stabilize greenhouse gases at 500–550ppm CO2e (equivalent carbon dioxide) by 2050. (Stern 2006: xiii.)
68. Nor, although I do not discuss it here, would it seem unfair for Peter to take on greater burdens in fulfilling the duty.
69. See e.g. Shue 1993.

70. Nussbaum 2000b: 80. This has to be taken into consideration. When it comes to bringing the principle of beneficence into force, I could strengthen my argument by relying on the least controversial fundamental human interests. When it comes to rejecting appeal to other such interests as grounds for denying the duty, the reverse is true.
71. Nussbaum 2000b: 80.
72. See May 1992: 120–2.
73. For a discussion of consent and future generations, see Shrader-Frechette 2002: 105–13.

NOTES ON CHAPTER THREE

1. Priestley 1950: 217.
2. Jamieson 1992: 323.
3. This raises the possibility, put to me by Lynn Dobson, that parents could constitute a potential collectivity with a weakly collective duty to mitigate climate change, because they each have moral duties to secure a safe environment for their children and this could only be achieved through cooperation. (This is distinct from the possibility noted in Chapter Two: that parents form an actual collectivity through the shared goal or interest of avoiding suffering for their children.) This is a potentially interesting line of argument, but I do not pursue it here.
4. This example is borrowed from May 1992: 110–11. He uses the term 'putative group' rather than potential collectivity.
5. The argument there drew on: Goodin 1985: 134–41; Shue 1980: 35–64; Held 1970; May 1992: 109–22.
6. Singer 1972: 231.
7. Based on Unger 1996: 25. This assumes, of course, that an individual Westerner can benefit a member of the global poor: a view which has been questioned by Wenar 2003. See also Lichtenberg 2010: 564.
8. See e.g. Arneson 2004; Kamm 2004; Miller 2004; Murphy 1993; Singer 2004; Unger 1996.
9. If successful, this objection might also have implications for the argument from moralized collective self-interest. However, it need not necessarily do so, because on some versions the objector would allow that we have minimal duties of beneficence to those far from us, but maintain that the burdens we can be expected to bear are much lower than in local cases.
10. Lichtenberg 2004: 87; Unger 1996: 33–6. As Frances Kamm points out, there is even ambiguity about the notion of 'distance'. Is this distance from the victim, from the threat, or from the means of preventing harm? (Kamm 2004: 59–61.)
11. That is, we need not accept moral internalism, or the view that the reasons that justify moral action must also motivate an agent to take that action: that once I appreciate what I ought to do, I must be motivated to do it. This is a point made by Gardiner (2011a: 41–2) against Jamieson (2010: 435–8) to which I will return in section (iv).
12. Lichtenberg 2004: 83.

13. See e.g. S. Cohen 2001: esp. 293. Kari Marie Norgaard, to whose work I will return in Chapter Six, reaches parallel conclusions in the climate change case. (2011: 211–22.)

14. See e.g. Nussbaum 1990, 2000b; Sen 1992, 1999; Wolff and de-Shalit 2007.

15. Recalling Chapter Two, the individual might of course also secure a sufficiently fundamental benefit (preserve another central capability) to prevent this counting as a significant overall cost. However, for now, we can assume that this is not the case.

16. This is applied *ex ante*, to allow for the possibility that a cooperative scheme comes with a moderate risk of serious costs to some. On the capabilities account outlined in Chapter One, high risks to central functionings would undermine the corresponding capabilities and so count as significant costs in themselves.

17. Stern 2006: xiii.

18. Stern 2006: xxi.

19. See e.g. Shue 1993.

20. For a parallel point see e.g. Shue 1988: 696.

21. In parallel with the motivation problem in the Hobbesian state of nature. See e.g. Hampton 1986: 74–9.

22. That is not to say that those with the relevant organizational or motivational skills might not be liable for greater backwards-looking criticism. Nor, to pre-empt Chapter Six, is it to deny that some individuals might have direct rather than promotional duties in the absence of collective action.

23. See e.g. Victor 2006. However, Gardiner is sceptical as to the possibility of effective progress through less than global-level action. (Gardiner 2011b: 95–6.) I will come back to this in Chapter Six.

24. Jamieson 2011: 36.

25. Section (iii) is an updated version of an argument originally put forward in Cripps 2011a: 174–82.

26. This goes beyond not only the standard, corporate understanding of collective responsibility, but also May's expansion of the notion to include informal groups such as mobs. (May 1987.)

27. I have elsewhere distinguished this model from May's shared responsibility and Kutz's account of environmental damage as an unstructured harm. (Cripps 2011a; Kutz 2000: 171–91; May 1992: 37–42.) Steve Vanderheiden appeals to collective responsibility as 'a useful construct for identifying a responsible party when all individual acts appear faultless'. However, he focuses on the state level, arguing that '[b]y viewing aggregate national luxury emissions as a faulty contribution to global climate change, we can more easily see how the individual acts that comprise that aggregate set of acts might plausibly confer fault among all group members and, when combined with the allocation of responsibility to citizens in democracy for the consequences of national policies, thus why all might defensibly be held liable for the expected harmful consequences of global climate change'. (Vanderheiden 2008: 180.) The closest parallel to weakly collective responsibility is Elizabeth Ashford's discussion, recently brought to my attention, of multiplicative harms. She suggests that such cases count as large-scale human rights violations, and that the claim of victims is 'against the whole group of agents'. (2006: 228.)

28. It is worth stressing again that I err—if I do—on the side of generosity to potential duty-bearers. Anticipating Chapter Six, it is also worth distinguishing this condition for membership of the potential collectivity from the limits of demandingness of correlative individual duties where there is no weakly collective action.

29. I take this to be the standard view, although it is not uncontroversial. (See e.g. Thomson 1990.) However, the relevant question for this project is whether the individual or potential collectivity can be held morally responsible where there is reasonable foreseeability, not whether there is a claim against them even without it.

30. Again, this is not uncontroversial. It might appear to run contrary to the doctrine of double effect: '[T]he thesis that it is sometimes permissible to bring about by oblique intention what one may not directly intend.' (Foot 1978: 20.) However, this doctrine has been widely called into doubt, and does not exclude the possibility that it is sometimes impermissible to bring about an effect even obliquely.

31. Murphy 1993: 278. However, I reject the compliance condition in Chapter Six.

32. Recall the distinction, in Chapter Two, between active and passive subsets of actual collectivities.

33. That is not to deny that the bystander would have a positive moral duty to save the child, if he could do so alone, or that he would be part of the larger potential collectivity with a weakly collective duty to do so if it would require cooperation. This would be to deny the principles of beneficence. However, responsibility falls in the first instance on the teenagers.

34. As Singer points out, residents of the US, Japan, and Western nations were already several times above this level by the start of this century. (2002: 35.) For evidence of growing national carbon footprints, see Global Footprint Network.

35. Feinberg 1970: 202–3.

36. Feinberg 1987: 179.

37. For a defence of a still broader accumulative harm principle, see Kernohan 1998.

38. In Jamieson's *Jack 6*: 'Acting independently, Jack and a large number of unacquainted people set in motion a chain of events that prevents a large number of future people who will live in another part of the world from ever having bicycles.' (2010: 436.) As Gardiner points out, this is a problematic analogy because the loss of a bicycle is much less serious than the deprivations caused by climate change. (Gardiner 2011a: 43–4.) In assigning weakly collective responsibility to all cases of twofold predictability, rather than appealing to the individual's being part of a pattern of action, I go beyond Gardiner's own response to Jamieson. (For his example, *George and his buddies*, see Gardiner 2011a: 47.)

39. Jamieson 2010: 435–8.

40. In other words, Jamieson is an internalist about moral reason. (Gardiner 2011a: 41–2.)

41. Shue 1999a.

42. Shue 1999a: 39.

43. See e.g. Doran and Zimmerman 2009: 22.

44. For example, the most cursory perusal of Wikipedia yields the statement that 'scientific opinion on climate change is that the Earth's climate system is unequivocally warming, and it is more than 90% certain that humans are causing it through activities that increase concentrations of greenhouse gases in the atmosphere', as well as the information that 'no scientific body of national or international standing has maintained a dissenting opinion'. (Wikipedia 2012.)

45. See e.g. 'The Ultimate Climate Change FAQ'. (*The Guardian.*)

46. Although I do not use this terminology, each weakly collective duty could be said to be *perfect*, in the sense that it clearly identifies both the duty-bearers (the collectivity or the potential collectivity) and the victims. Individual correlative duties when no collective scheme is in place are imperfect, but are moral duties nonetheless. They are then made perfect by collective action, which assigns specific duties to each individual. See e.g. Ashford 2006: 234–6; Shue 1988: esp. 688, 703–4.

47. For an ideal preference model, see e.g. Richard B. Brandt 1979.

48. See e.g. Caney 2005a, 2009b; Gosseries 2004; Shue 1993, 1999b; Page 2012. There has been increasing recognition that it is morally unsatisfactory to focus only on the distribution of burdens between states, or between individuals taken broadly as representatives of either the rich West or the developing world. See e.g. Harris 2010.

49. See e.g. Bell Unpublished.

50. That is, the trend towards proposals such as Caney's hybrid model (Caney 2005a, 2010).

51. Note that I am not necessarily committed to the view that, were the two to conflict, fulfilling negative weakly collective duties would take priority for Polluters over fulfilling positive weakly collective duties.

52. On the Polluter Pays Principle, see e.g. Caney 2005a, 2010; Neumayer 2000; Shue 1999b.

53. See e.g. Caney 2005a: 771–2. This might be rejected on the grounds that duty-bearers should not be expected to pick up the slack for non-compliers. (Murphy 1993, 2000.) I will counter this in Chapter Six. (In this context, see also Roser and Hohl 2011.) For now, note simply that this is not a case (of the type Murphy has in mind) of one individual duty-bearer facing apparently limitless cases of harm. Rather, our focus is on a number of individuals (making up a potential collectivity) who could between them put an end to the harm at relatively small cost to each of them.

54. This is a familiar point from the debate on the allocation of burdens between states. See especially Shue 1992: 397.

55. To reiterate, this argument is limited to The Young more narrowly construed, as those currently in a position to prevent the harm to themselves. Given the need for mitigation (not just adaptation) to prevent the serious suffering of future generations, the reasoning does not transfer to them.

56. Gosseries 2004. See also e.g. Caney 2005a: 756–8; Page 2012; Shue 1999b: 533–7.

NOTES ON CHAPTER FOUR

1. Bentham 1789: 311.

2. Palmer 2011: 291.
3. For an earlier discussion of the place of non-human animals, species, and eco-systems in a capabilities model of justice, see Cripps 2010.
4. See e.g. Palmer 2010: 11–18.
5. Nussbaum identifies a list of central capabilities for non-human animals, but has been criticized for taking the human capabilities as her starting point. See e.g. Nussbaum 2006: 392–401; Schlosberg 2007: 153–7.
6. See Schlosberg 2007: 144–7.
7. Bernstein et al. 2007: 48.
8. Stern 2006: vi. See also e.g. Thomas et al. 2004.
9. See e.g. Derocher et al. 2004. The Worldwide Fund for Nature (2012b) warns of food shortages for a number of animals, including Asian elephants and mountain gorillas, as impacts of climate change.
10. See e.g. Singer 1976.
11. Example borrowed from Graham 2002: 71–2; Searle 1995: 38. See also Sheehy 2006: 129–30.
12. The three conditions, taken to be generally plausible, were borrowed from Graham 2002: 68–9.
13. Townley 2010: 515.
14. See e.g. Michael Pollan's account of the small-scale, high-welfare Polyface Farm. (2006: 185–238.) This is not necessarily the case for all organic farms, however, as Pollan's coverage of 'industrial' organic illustrates. (2006: 130–84.)
15. That is not to suggest that the factory farmer and bully do not have moral duties (which they are violating) to their victims. Quite the reverse, as later sections make clear.
16. This was discussed in Chapter Two. See also Cripps 2011b: 16.
17. See Stern 2006: xii.
18. Palmer 2011: 288–9.
19. Leopold 1966: 203–10.
20. On extending the capabilities approach, see especially Nussbaum 2006: 325–7, 346–407.
21. McMahan 2008: 81.
22. Singer 1976.
23. Diamond 1978.
24. See e.g. Engster 2006; Francis and Norman 1978; Gunnarsson 2008.
25. Townley 2010.
26. McMahan 2008: 81.
27. This point is made regularly in the literature. See e.g. Nussbaum 2006: 402; Singer 1976: 222–4.
28. See e.g. Nuffield Council on Bioethics 2005.
29. On the difficulty of providing any such account, see Carter 2011: 351–4.
30. Based on Singer 1972: 231.
31. Nussbaum 2006: 379–80. For an alternative defence of policing nature, see Cowen 2003.
32. See Donaldson and Kymlicka 2011; Palmer 2010. For brief comments on Palmer's relational model, see Cripps 2012.

33. A variant on the first would be to take the no-harm principle as having priority and argue that interfering to prevent harm to the prey would require actively harming the predator. However, there are two difficulties with this: it is not clear that it fits with our responses to (even innocent) threats in the human case, and it is by no means universally agreed that death in itself is a central deprivation for a being who lacks a consciously espoused plan of life. See e.g. Nussbaum 2006: 384–8; T. Regan 2004: 99–103; Singer 1979: 198–201.

34. This is broadly in line with Nussbaum 2006: 379–80.

35. To bridge the gap, one might argue that running the risk of being eaten is in the interest of each and every gazelle. I have discussed difficulties with this elsewhere. (Cripps 2010: 16–17.)

36. See Endnote 33. For some animals, the effect of the extermination of others in the community might be considered a central loss: a point Nussbaum herself stresses in relation to elephants. (2011: 229, 33–4.) However, this would not necessarily rule out all such policies.

37. A familiar point from ecological ethics. See e.g. Leopold 1966: 219–20; Taylor 1981: 207–9.

38. Holland 2008, 2012; Norton 1986; Page 2007. See also Tim Hayward's notion of enlightened self-interest. (1998: 61–117.)

39. Nussbaum 2000b: 80. See also e.g. the critique of Norton's convergence theory in Nolt 2011b: 707–8. (Norton 2005: 508–10.)

40. The former expands on Palmer's *laissez-faire intuition.* (2010: 63–95.) The latter has similarities to the rights-based approach of Donaldson and Kymlicka (2011: esp. 156–209).

41. Gardiner 2011b: 41.

42. Schlosberg 2007: 129–59, 2012, Unpublished. I focus on his work because he attempts specifically to expand the capabilities approach to include species and systems. However, he acknowledges a debt to earlier theorists, especially Rodman 1977, 1983.

43. Schlosberg 2007: 148.

44. Schlosberg 2007: 149.

45. Schlosberg 2007: 151–2.

46. Schlosberg Unpublished.

47. In particular, this is a central tenet of Leopold's approach (1966: 219–20).

48. Schlosberg 2007: 154; personal correspondence 17 May 2012. See also Adrian Armstrong 2012 for a list of proposed capabilities (or, in his vocabulary, *consideranda*) for ecosystems (2012: 117–20). However, Armstrong also proposes consideranda for Gaia, or the earth as a whole, as part of his account of environmental justice. This goes well beyond anything considered here.

49. This is in parallel with Baxter 2005: 127–31.

50. See e.g. Cahan 1988; Taylor 1981.

51. For Schlosberg, this is less of a problem, since he aims to extend capabilities justice also to human communities. (E.g. Schlosberg and Carruthers 2010.)

52. E.g. Anderson 2004; Baxter 2005: 86–7; Cripps 2010: 6–9; Nussbaum 2006: 393–405; Schinkel 2008.

53. Schlosberg Unpublished. He moves from the Humean/Rawlsian circumstances of justice, within which, at least in theory, the entitlements of all can be met,

to an idea of justice as more of a balancing act: a case of incremental improvements, driven by public reason and democratic engagement, rather than aspiring to achieve some ideal world model. This is closer to Sen (2009) than to Nussbaum's capabilities model.

54. Baxter 2005: 127–31. Taylor 1981 appeals to just such interests to argue that such living organisms, while not rights-holders, are nonetheless of ethical significance. See also Rolston III 1994. As he puts it, 'though things do not matter *to* plants, things matter *for* them' (1994: 18).

55. Baxter 2005: 127.

56. Rolston III 1994: 15. See also e.g. Caldicott 1986; Singer 1979: 203–4. Of course, there are various understandings of 'intrinsic value', on some of which the relevant environmental ethic would come close to the kind of flourishing-based claim to consideration, discussed above. See e.g. O'Neill 1992.

57. Note, however, that a parallel challenge would arise to that acknowledged for the expanded interests-based model. We would need an account of what exactly this value consisted in (of what was to be preserved) that was sensitive to the evolving nature of ecosystems, including the potential for non-destructive human interaction. Otherwise, there might again be a practical case for focusing on populations.

58. Palmer 2011: 291.

59. See Palmer 2011: 288–90.

60. Compare for example Shiffrin's or Harman's approaches with that of Parfit himself, or Hare's proposal. (See C. Hare 2007; Harman 2004; Parfit 1984: 381–417; Shiffrin 1999.)

61. Suppose an individual, Jane, has a one-off chance to give a pill to her cat, Kitty. If Kitty is not given the pill this week, she will conceive three kittens, Kit, Cathy, and Cassie. Kit will be healthy, but Cathy and Cassie will be significantly disabled (though have lives worth living). If Kitty is given the pill, she will conceive a few weeks later instead, and will again have three kittens, Mog, Meg, and Mogens. Mog and Meg will be healthy, but Mogens will be disabled (though with a life worth living). It is not intuitively clear that Jane acts wrongly in giving the pill. Appealing to the no-harm principle to condemn her decision as impermissible requires focusing narrowly on her *actively having* taken a decision which deprived some future individual cat, Mogens, of some of his fundamental interests, without allowing as mitigation the fact that the only alternative future was one in which two cats (who also don't exist at the point of decision) were born to comparable deprivation.

62. Palmer 2011: 290.

63. Palmer 2011: 285–6.

64. Singer 1979: 196.

65. See e.g. Bernstein et al. 2007: 45, 53–4; Committee on Abrupt Climate Change et al. 2002: esp. 107–17; Hansen 2008.

66. Nolt 2011b: 709.

67. Palmer 2011: 279.

68. Barnosky et al. 2011. Also cited in Nolt 2011b: 702.

69. Bernstein et al. 2007: 48. See also: Worldwide Fund for Nature 2012a.

70. See Kirchner and Weil 2000; Nolt 2011b: 709.

71. Some mitigation and adaptation could be complementary: the IPCC report highlights that collapse of ecosystems in turn makes climate change worse. (Bernstein et al. 2007: 48.)
72. See e.g. Hettinger 2012; Light 2012.
73. Nussbaum 2006: 371.
74. This former option would not rule out all duties to aid the non-human victims of climate change: following section (i), relational models could account for specific duties to aid domestic or even liminal animals. (See e.g. Donaldson and Kymlicka 2011: 73–155, 210–51.)
75. Lomborg 2001: 300–24. See also e.g. Nordhaus 1997.
76. See e.g. Caney 2008, 2009c; Stern 2008: 12–15.
77. Schlosberg Unpublished.
78. Carter 2011.
79. This should be obvious, but I will hammer it home with a small-scale analogy. Suppose I had two daughters and a son with such wildly conflicting needs that I could not possibly do everything for them all, or even for both of my daughters. I would be justified neither in doing nothing at all for any of them, nor focusing only on giving my son everything from dental care to music lessons—because his interests can at least then fully be secured—and leaving my daughters without even basic food or clothing.
80. Gardiner 2011b: 41.
81. Carter 2011.

NOTES ON CHAPTER FIVE

1. Sinnott-Armstrong 2005: 304.
2. Garvey 2010: 99.
3. This example (discussed as *Beach rescue* in Chapter Three) is borrowed from May 1992: 111–12.
4. On the distribution of burdens, see e.g. Caney 2005a, 2009b; Gosseries 2004; Shue 1993, 1999b; Page 2012. It is also worth distinguishing my forward-looking focus on individual duties from another potential discussion: the backward-looking debate over assigning fault or liability—or even shares of punishment—to individuals. (See e.g. May 1992; Vanderheiden 2008: 165–8.)
5. These are classified by objective, rather than by the details of the actions involved, as these may overlap. It is precisely because of this—because of a distinction between mimicking *duties* and mimicking *actions*, which latter may be defended as means of fulfilling promotional or direct duties—that Chapter Six can reopen the question to make a derivative case for some individual emissions cuts.
6. An alternative terminology, suggested to me by Tim Hayward and Henry Shue respectively, would be *anticipatory duties* and *transitional duties*.
7. Maltais Forthcoming.
8. Murphy 1993, 2000.
9. Murphy 1993, 2000: 8. However, in his discussion of individual duties of justice, Murphy puts more emphasis on direct duties than I do in Chapter Six. He argues that rich individuals can often do more good acting directly than by promoting

institutional action, and so have a primary duty to do so. (1998: 279–82.) For a counter-argument, see Young 2011: 68–70.

10. Lichtenberg 2010.
11. Sinnott-Armstrong 2005.
12. Nolt 2011a: 9.
13. Nolt 2011a. John Broome also treats our individual actions as harmful in the climate change case. (2008: 69.) Avram Hiller (2011) argues that even driving a gas-guzzling car for an afternoon can be castigated as equivalent to ruining someone's afternoon.
14. See e.g. Lichtenberg 2010: 564–7.
15. See also Vanderheiden 2008: 163–4.
16. Or rather, as Kagan puts it, of being one of a set including exactly *x*. (Kagan 2011: 125.)
17. Kagan 2011: 141.
18. Kagan 2011: 110–11, 21–8.
19. Contra, for example, Lomborg 2001: 300–24.
20. Parfit 1984: 74.
21. Kagan 2011: 128.
22. See also Garvey 2011: 161–4 for concerns about transferring threshold-based arguments from the vegetarianism to the climate change case.
23. Maltais Forthcoming.
24. The appeal to overdetermination is distinct from that in cases where the individual's act in isolation would have caused harm, but was not, as it happened, necessary to the harm. For example, Daniel Farber's case of several polluters releasing dangerous chemicals into a lake, each of whose contribution would have been sufficient to destroy all the fish. Farber argues that, in assigning liability for climate change to individual *states*, overdetermination is not a sufficient excuse. (2008: 389–92.) However, the cases are significantly different because major polluting states, unlike individuals, can plausibly be expected to increase overall emissions sufficiently to be *sure* of triggering perceptible additional harm. To return to Kagan's example, the US is like someone buying (at least) 25 chickens.
25. May 1992: 37–42.
26. Maltais Forthcoming.
27. May 1992. Jamieson himself does not present this as a rule-consequentialist argument but as a way out of a motivation problem facing the individual utilitarian. However, *if* the idea is to appeal ultimately to consequences, the argument effectively relies on the assumption that rule-consequentialism is an appropriate response to climate change. If, on the other hand, the argument makes a more direct appeal to considerations of moral character, then it falls under the discussion of section (v).
28. Jamieson 1992, 2007a: 480–1, 2007b.
29. On the rational altruist's dilemma, see e.g. Arntzenius and McCarthy 1997; Kutz 2002; Otsuka 1991; Parfit 1984: 75–86.
30. See D. Regan 1980: x.
31. E.g. R. B. Brandt 1988; Foot 1985; Hooker 1990; Smart 1956.
32. Miller 2009.
33. Hooker 1990: 74. (Italics in original.)

34. R. B. Brandt 1988: 358–9; Hooker 1990.
35. R. B. Brandt 1988: 358–9. The same example is used in Hooker 1990: 73.
36. Thanks to Tim Mulgan for the example.
37. See also Lichtenberg 2010.
38. Garvey 2011: 171.
39. Garvey 2010: 99.
40. Sinnott-Armstrong 2005: 304.
41. Maltais Forthcoming; personal correspondence 1 June 2012.
42. Maltais Forthcoming.
43. See e.g. Caney 2009b, 2010; Shue 1999b.
44. Personal correspondence, 1 June 2012.
45. Personal correspondence, 1 June 2012. (Italics in original.)
46. Maltais himself recognizes this. (Personal correspondence, 1 June 2012.) His point is the more limited one that the higher an individual's emissions now, the less likely she is to be able to cancel the debt later.
47. Maltais Forthcoming.
48. Garvey 2010, 2011; Glover 1975: 184, quoting Aleksandr Solzhenitsyn's Nobel lecture. (Solzhenitsyn 1970.)
49. Jamieson 2007a: 480.
50. Aristotle 350 BC: 1729–42. See also Foot 2001.
51. Hourdequin 2010: 449.
52. Williams 1981: 45. Indeed, Williams himself points out that it is not clear why integrity in itself should be a virtue (1981: 49).
53. E.g. Johnson 2003: 278–81.
54. Lichtenberg makes the parallel point that concern for integrity 'need not exclude responsibilities to make the world better'. (Lichtenberg 2010: 570.)
55. Building on work in progress by Kerri Woods, an alternative case might be made for the weakly collective duty to act on climate change, by appeal to a 'collective' virtue of stewardship. Woods suggests assessing institutional frameworks on the criterion 'what would the virtuous environmental steward do?' (Woods Unpublished.) However, this still leaves a dilemma for the individual who is not living within a virtuous institutional framework.
56. See e.g. Foot 1985.
57. See e.g. Hursthouse 2007; Taylor 1986: 169–218; Trachtenberg 2010.
58. Hursthouse 2007: 170. She draws on Taylor 1986: 169–219.
59. The former is Hursthouse's example (2007: 168).
60. Hursthouse 2007: 170.
61. Trachtenberg 2010: 340.
62. '[A]ct only in accordance with that maxim through which you can at the same time will that it become a universal law.' (Kant 1785: 31. Italics in original.)
63. Korsgaard 1986: 338.
64. Garvey 2008: 149.
65. Sinnott-Armstrong 2005. See also Jamieson 2007b.
66. Kant 1785: 32. (Paraphrased from original.)
67. Korsgaard 1996: 93–101.
68. Some, including R. M. Hare (1993) and David Cummiskey (2003), have read Kant as a consequentialist. However, on such readings, the success or

failure of Kantian attempts to defend mimicking duties will follow that of rule-consequentialist efforts to do so. Indeed, Cummiskey himself suggests that on this reasoning it would be permissible, because universalizable, to break a promise if that would lead to more promise-keeping overall. (Cummiskey 2003: 59.) The analogy with emissions is, I hope, obvious.

69. Thanks to Catriona McKinnon for clarity on this point.
70. Rawls 1989: 82.
71. Korsgaard 1986: 345.
72. Jamieson 2007b: 161.
73. Jamieson 2007b: 161, quoting Korsgaard 1996: 275. (Italics in original.) It is worth also noting that, whatever Kant's own view, there are Kantian approaches which allow for deviation in some non-ideal situations. (See Korsgaard 1986; Schapiro 2006.) Rawls, who builds on a later version of the categorical imperative as a way of determining the appropriate principles for the basic structure of a just institution, defends individual duties to promote such institutions. (1971: 99.)

NOTES ON CHAPTER SIX

1. Franklin et al. 1776.
2. Interview while awaiting sentencing for disrupting a gas and oil industry auction. (Ask Umbra 2011.)
3. Johnson 2003 makes a parallel case for promotional duties in the context of the tragedy of the commons. As such, his argument is relevant to The Young. However, this chapter aims to consider the problem more generally. See e.g. Gardiner 2011b: 103–84 on the limits of the classic game theory case as an analogy for the collective action problem posed by climate change.
4. Sinnott-Armstrong 2005.
5. Sinnott-Armstrong 2005: 304.
6. Gardiner (2011a: 54) makes this point.
7. See e.g. Caney (2005b: 148–88) for a discussion of possible modifications to state sovereignty, in the global justice context. Going beyond such changes, to borrow a point from Gardiner, we should not automatically assume that the state system is an inevitable or a necessary part of a future in which we fulfil our weakly collective duties. (2011b: 125.)
8. Unlike Maltais (Forthcoming), I do not claim that voting green is sufficient to fulfil promotional duties. Voting for the Green Party candidate may actually be comparatively costly because it means giving up voting on other issues considered important (Maltais acknowledges this), while being comparatively unlikely, given how others can be expected to vote, to make any difference. Contributions to campaigns to influence those already in power can be lower cost and arguably more effective.
9. Jamieson 2011: 36.
10. Goodin 1985: 139. See also Shue 1980: 51–60.
11. The Forth Road Bridge, which joins Edinburgh to Fife, was notorious until recently for allegedly needing painting again at one end as soon as the other end had been painted.

12. See also Lichtenberg 2010: 576–7.
13. Of course, this is not always the case. It might be more arduous to promote a collective solution and persuade or legitimately coerce others into doing their share than simply to solve the problem yourself. Then, whatever the unfairness of their not participating, taking the collective route looks like cutting off your nose to spite your face. To use an example no doubt depressingly familiar to many readers, consider efforts to nag one's partner into doing a fair share of the housework.
14. Gardiner 2011b: 95–6; Victor 2006.
15. Jamieson 2011: 36.
16. See e.g. Caney 2005a: 771–2; Roser and Hohl 2011.
17. Gardiner 2011b: 84, citing Marland et al. 2008.
18. Gardiner 2011b: 95–6. Positing an emissions ceiling of a 20 per cent cut on 1990 levels, Gardiner points out that it would only take the Chinese or Indians emitting at current US rates to render such a cut impossible 'even if the rest of the world cut its emissions down to nothing'. (Italics in original.)
19. Maltais, who doubts that we have promotional duties beyond voting, nonetheless acknowledges this distinction. He argues that, while individuals can expect in practice to make no difference to overall harm by cutting emissions, 'the average individual can only be expected to make a very small difference to how others act with any of the promotional strategies they adopt'. (Maltais Forthcoming.) However, in leaving open to each individual the small chance of making a significant difference, this paves the way for the kind of 'moral mathematics' consequentialism inappropriate in Chapter Five.
20. Thanks to Kerri Woods for pressing this point.
21. Barbaro et al. 2012.
22. Hourdequin 2010: 450–1.
23. See e.g. BBC 2003.
24. The same point is made by Johnson 2003: 285. See also Hourdequin 2010: 451.
25. Of course, as an individual, the appropriate response could be to set up such a boycott, which could include refraining from buying the company's products in anticipation. However, this would again be as a means of fulfilling promotional duties.
26. Jamieson 2011: 36.
27. Norgaard stresses that local 'political renewal' must be understood as part of this global context, not as an end in itself. (Norgaard 2011: 228.)
28. Jamieson 2007b: 166.
29. In line with Singer's less stringent version of the principle. (Singer 1972: 231.)
30. See e.g. Lichtenberg 2010.
31. Murphy 1993, 2000.
32. Murphy 1993: 278. See also Unger 1996: 39.
33. Murphy 1993: 282.
34. Anja Karnein makes an intriguing alternative case against the compliance condition: that slack-taking should be regarded as 'fulfilling the duty one would have had had nobody else been around' (Karnein Unpublished). However, in the current context—of individual duties explained as derivative of a weakly collective duty—this response is unavailable. Richard Arneson also rejects the

condition, appealing to its implausible verdicts in many cases. (Arneson 2004: 33–58.)

35. Murphy 2000: 92.

36. Murphy 2000: 92.

37. Singer 1972. Indeed, to reiterate, in some ways Murphy is more demanding than I am: requiring high levels of sacrifice in emergency cases, or situations where the set of duty-bearers is comparatively small. (Murphy 2000: 97–101.)

38. It would, however, affect the question of whether (as in section (ii)) subsets that could achieve a collective end directly have a duty to do so. Roser and Hohl 2011, making their case for states to take up the burdens of non-compliers, also reject the compliance condition.

39. Chapter Three made the point, with Gardiner against Jamieson, that unless one is committed to an internalist view of moral reasoning, it need not follow from the fact that we are not motivated to do something that we do not have a duty to do it, or even that we do not properly understand that we should do so. (Gardiner 2011a: 41–2; Jamieson 2010: 435–8.)

40. Unger 1996: 24–54.

41. Unger 1996: 101.

42. See e.g. Doran and Zimmerman 2009: 22.

43. Stoll-Kleemann et al. 2001: 107. The study involved fourteen integrated-assessment focus groups, of mostly six to eight people, over 1997–9.

44. Norgaard 2011: 207.

45. Norgaard 2011: 221, building on S. Cohen 2001: esp. 293.

46. Stoll-Kleemann et al. 2001: 107.

47. May 1992: 114–16, 21.

48. Gardiner 2011b: 433.

49. Thanks to Dale Jamieson and Kerri Woods for clarifying discussion on this point.

50. I have said nothing here about the legitimacy of coercion in the climate change case, although I have made a prima facie case elsewhere for the permissibility of coercion of Polluters, by some legitimate authority, on the basis of a collectivized version of Mill's harm principle. (Cripps 2011a: 182–9; Mill 1859: 14.)

51. For example, Jamieson is pessimistic about the chances of an institutional response. (Jamieson 2008, 2011: 35–7.) For a legal analysis of the progress (or lack thereof) on securing an effective international deal, see Lavanya Rajamani's series of articles in *International and Comparative Law Quarterly*. (Most recently, Rajamani 2011, 2012.) For an account of the persistent features of the situation that have made it so very difficult to secure an ethically appropriate response, see Gardiner's account of climate change as a 'perfect moral storm'. (Gardiner 2011b.) For sociological work on communications strategies to motivate citizen action, see e.g. Moser and Dilling 2004; Moser and Walser 2008. See also Norgaard 2011: 222–9.

NOTES ON CHAPTER SEVEN

1. Hugo 1862: 159.

2. Gardiner 2010: 301.

3. I apply the notion of marring choices at a different level to Gardiner himself. He argues primarily that we wrong future generations by leaving them with marring choices (in particular, whether to undertake geoengineering). However, he suggests also that developed countries inflict marring choices on those in the developed world, and that politicians can be marred by their failure to act on climate change. Finally, he says there is a sense in which we are marred ourselves, as a generation, and highlights the possibility that imposing a marring choice is itself marring. (Gardiner 2010, 2011b: 339–96.)

4. Although it owes a great deal to Nagel 1991, my argument—as will become clear—diverges considerably from his.

5. Nagel 1991: 1–10.

6. See e.g. Nussbaum 1990, 2000b.

7. We are born into many of these relations, but they still need some nurturing (however minimal) to acquire this significance.

8. Gardiner, in referring to 'moral baggage' in cases such as *Sophie's Choice*, must have this in mind. (See e.g. Gardiner 2011b: 386.)

9. See e.g. Goodin 1985: 92–9.

10. Williams 1981: 18; Goodin 1985: 92–9.

11. Stocker 1976: 456.

12. Lichtenberg makes a related point about the costs of reducing suffering in general. She points out that both research costs and the so-called mindfulness costs of breaking convenient habits can be reduced by collective action. (2010: 576.)

13. Murphy 1993, 2000.

14. Singer 1972: 231.

15. May 1992: 120.

16. Appiah 1986–7: 187–8.

17. May 1992: 153.

18. See e.g. Dodd and Laville 2012; Dodd 2012.

19. E.g. Gardiner 2011a; Kutz 2000: 171–91.

20. May 1992: 158, building on Jean Paul Sartre's notion of taking responsibility for who one is. (Sartre 1956.)

21. Glover 1975: 184; Solzhenitsyn 1970.

22. May 1992: 120.

23. The individual has, of course, the option of publicly disavowing her connection with the other holidaymakers. However, to do so without having attempted to promote collective action would look unconvincing at best, hypocritical at worst.

24. May 1992: 158.

25. Appiah 1986–7: 193.

26. See Lichtenberg 2010. That is not to deny that, because the grounding of the duty is negative in the weakly collective harm case, the individual's correlative moral duties might have a greater pull on her. (This was left open in Chapter Six.) However, because the harm is collective, the pull on her of not being part of it cannot count as independent of that of helping to prevent it, because they have the same source: the weakly collective responsibility of the potential collectivity. By contrast, an individual may have reasons not directly to cause

serious suffering which are incommensurate with her reasons to prevent serious suffering (or for that matter to fulfil duties derived from collective harms).

27. Iris Marion Young offers a related argument, in the context of actual collectivities. (2011: 75–93.)
28. I realize this term is more apt than grammatically accurate, but it can be considered an abbreviation of the rather less snappy term: 'choices between fundamental and irreconcilable alternatives'.
29. Gardiner 2010, 2011b: 385–90; Styron 1979: 542–3.
30. Sartre 1956: 355.
31. Sen 1999: 8.
32. Marcus 1980; Nagel 1979: 53–74.
33. Williams 1973. See also Gardiner 2011b: 393.
34. Simpson 1997: 100–6.
35. This is based on William Godwin's example of the choice between saving his mother and saving Archbishop Fénelon. Although Godwin himself, as a stalwart utilitarian, would plump for the latter, such examples are generally used to demonstrate the overdemandingness of utilitarianism. (Godwin 1793: 82–3.)
36. Pullman 2000: 509–48.
37. Singer 1972: 231.
38. Dickens 1853.
39. Phillips 2011; Ribeiro da Silva 2011. More than 1,150 rural activists are reported to have been killed in land and logging conflicts in the last twenty years, and more than 125 know their lives to be in danger. (Catholic Land Pastoral data, cited in Carrington 2011.)
40. Goldenberg 2011.
41. For a parallel point, see e.g. Hursthouse (2007: 133–41), as discussed in Chapter Five.
42. To reiterate, I do not deny that many so-called 'green' lifestyle changes, far from imposing such terrible choices, are in fact positive for the individual. The point is merely that, for some, emissions cuts would come at a fundamental personal or interpersonal cost.
43. Again, this argument is much inspired by Nagel (1991: 53–62), although without his commitment to the view that the personal standpoint requires equality, nor his restriction of the argument to a case for state-level political institutions. It can also be seen as filling out a proposal by Simon Hailwood (2011: 219), who acknowledges a Nagel-style case for political action on climate change to reconcile the personal and the impersonal perspective.
44. Gardiner 2010: 301.
45. Wolff and de-Shalit 2007: 72.
46. Gardiner 2010: 301.
47. Williams 1981: 28. See also Appiah 1986–7: 188.
48. Bagnoli 2000.
49. It also narrows down the idea of fundamental regret—marring regret—from Bagnoli's notion, which, while not including such trivial cases, does include regret in choices between two means of satisfying the same central capability. (Bagnoli 2000: 170.)

50. Still further along the spectrum, there might be a lesser kind of regret in cases where a person's body has been used by someone else to cause harm.

51. This, recalling Chapter Six, is a distinct wrong from that which he would have committed if the cost to her had been less (say, if saving the second child would only make her late for a business meeting). Then, he would have increased the cost to her of fulfilling her moral duties.

52. I am grateful to Ben Colburn for an illuminating discussion on this point.

53. Williams 1981: 28.

54. This also, importantly, allows me to reject any comparison with the more unpleasant deviations of communitarianism that require individuals to comply with some comprehensive moral view (often a religious view) allegedly for the sake of themselves and of the rest of their society.

55. See e.g. S. Cohen 2001: esp. 293; Norgaard 2011: 211–22; Stoll-Kleemann, et al. 2001; Unger 1996: 24–54.

56. Hailwood calls for 'a politics able to address such demands in a satisfactory way collectively…making it possible for us to face our responsibility and recognize, rather than disown, the world we are making, without going mad or it seeming like personal suicide'. (2011: 219.)

57. Norgaard 2011.

58. Norgaard 2011; Stoll-Kleemann et al. 2001.

59. See e.g. Lichtenberg 2010; Scheffler 2001. Gardiner suggests that to some extent this institutionalization of our moral duties has been the victim of its own success, further explaining our detachment from the moral perspective in the climate context: individuals are so used to thinking of the state as meeting the moral claims of the needy and leaving us free to live our own lives that the revelation that it no longer fully does so is 'deeply jarring'. (Gardiner 2011a: 54–5.)

60. See Norgaard 2011: 221–9.

61. Where they prove unlearnable, the collective-level alternative is to ban the relevant individual actions, for example by organizing society so that it is illegal to commit suicide and donate organs to specified loved ones.

62. Bagnoli 2000. This kind of 'valuing' of the option not taken falls outside the *fundamental* agent-regret highlighted in section (v) because it does not require an agent to give up on a central capability category, but to decide between two options within one of them (practical reason).

63. Wolf 1982.

64. Duffy 1999: 21–2.

65. Wolf 1982: 419.

66. According to Stocker, act-utilitarianism is as schizophrenic as egoism: in pursuing only aggregate welfare, we neglect the very personal projects and relations that would best increase it. (1976: 458–60.)

67. Gardiner 2012: 241.

NOTES ON CONCLUSION

1. See e.g. Gardiner 2011b; Jamieson 2008: 35–7, 2011; Rajamani 2011, 2012; Moser and Dilling 2004; Moser and Walser 2008; Norgaard 2011: 222–9.

2. See e.g. Caney 2005a, 2009b; Gosseries 2004; Page 2012; Shue 1993, 1999b. Most recently (while this project has been in press), Risse (2012) has published a discussion of the fair distribution of adaptation and mitigation burdens which starts from the notion (also defended) of common ownership of the earth. From this starting point, he also develops a very different account from that explored in Chapter Two of individuals as co-members of what might broadly be termed a global-level group: of human rights as membership rights in a global, but still state-dominated, *order*.

3. See e.g. Vanderheiden 2008: 169.

4. Goodin 1985: 134–41; May 1992: 111; Shue 1980: 35–64.

5. See e.g. Moellendorf 2002; Pogge 2002; Young 2011.

Bibliography

Academia Brasiliera de Ciências Brazil, et al. (2005), 'Joint Science Academies' Statement: Global Response to Climate Change'. <http://royalsociety.org/policy/publications/2005/global-response-climate-change/>, accessed 30 June 2012.

African Academy of Sciences, et al. (2007), 'Joint Statement by the Network of African Science Academies to the G8 on Sustainability, Energy Efficiency and Climate Change' (Nairobi: NASAC). <http://www.interacademies.net/File.aspx?id=4825>.

American Association for the Advancement of Science, American Chemical Society, American Geophysical Union, American Institute of Biological Sciences, American Meteorological Society, American Society of Agronomy, American Society of Plant Biologists, American Statistical Association, Association of Ecosystem Research Centers, Botanical Society of America, Crop Science Society of America, Ecological Society of America, Natural Science Collections Alliance, Organization of Biological Field Stations, Society for Industrial and Applied Mathematics, Society of Systematic Biologists, Soil Science Society of America, University Corporation for Atmospheric Research (2009), 'Letter to the US Senate' (date of letter: 9 December).

American Association of Petroleum Geologists (2007), 'Climate Change'. <http://dpa.aapg.org/gac/statements/climatechange.cfm>, accessed 11 July 2012.

American Geophysical Union (2003), 'AGU Position Statement: Human Impacts on Climate'.

American Meteorological Society (2007), 'Climate Change: An Information Statement of the American Meteorological Society', *Bulletin of the American Meteorological Society*, 1 February. <http://www.ametsoc.org/policy/2007climatechange.html>, accessed 30 May 2012.

Anderson, Elizabeth (2004), 'Animal Rights and the Values of Nonhuman Life', in Cass R. Sunstein and Martha Nussbaum (eds), *Animal Rights: Current Debates and New Directions* (New York: Oxford University Press), 277–9.

Appiah, Anthony (1986–7), 'Racism and Moral Pollution', *Philosophical Forum, 18* (2–3), 185–202.

Aristotle (350 BC), 'Nicomachean Ethics', in Jonathan Barnes (ed.), *The Complete Works of Aristotle* (Vol. II; Princeton: Princeton University Press).

Armstrong, Adrian (2012), *Ethics and Justice for the Environment* (London and New York: Routledge).

Arneson, Richard (2004), 'Moral Limits on the Demands of Beneficence', in Deen K. Chatterjee (ed.), *The Ethics of Assistance: Morality and the Distant Needy* (Cambridge: Cambridge University Press), 33–58.

Arnold, Denis G. (2011), 'Introduction: Climate Change and Ethics', in Denis G. Arnold (ed.), *The Ethics of Global Climate Change* (Cambridge: Cambridge University Press).

Arntzenius, Frank and McCarthy, David (1997), 'Self Torture and Group Beneficence', *Erkenntnis, 47*, 129–44.

Ashford, Elizabeth (2006), 'The Inadequacy of Our Traditional Conception of the Duties Imposed by Human Rights', *Canadian Journal of Law and Jurisprudence*, *19* (2), 217–35.

Ask Umbra (2011), 'Climate Activist Tim DeChristopher Talks about His Guilty Verdict', *Grist*, 11 March. < http://grist.org/climate-change/2011-03-10-tim-dech ristopher-talks-about-his-guilty-verdict/>.

Australian Academy of Sciences, et al. (2001), 'Science of Climate Change'. < http:// royalsociety.org/policy/publications/2001/science-climate-change/>, accessed 30 May 2012.

Bagnoli, Carla (2000), 'Value in the Guise of Regret', *Philosophical Explorations*, *3* (2), 169–87.

Barbaro, Michael, Cooper, Helene, and Parker, Ashley (2012), 'Romney Camp Stirred Storm Over Gay Aide', *New York Times*, 2 May. <http://www.nytimes.com/2012/05/03/ us/politics/richard-grenell-resigns-from-mitt-romneys-foreign-policy-team. html>, accessed 14 June 2012.

Barnosky, Anthony D., et al. (2011), 'Has the Earth's Sixth Mass Extinction Already Arrived?' *Nature, 471*, 51–7.

Baxter, Brian (2005), *A Theory of Ecological Justice* (Oxford: Routledge).

BBC (2003), 'Abbott Criticised Over School Choice', *BBC News*. <http://news.bbc. co.uk/1/hi/education/3218593.stm>, accessed 20 July 2012.

Bell, Derek (Unpublished), 'How Should We Think About Climate Justice?'

Bentham, Jeremy (1789), *An Introduction to the Principles of Morals and Legislation* (1876 edn; Oxford: Clarendon Press).

Berkeley Earth Surface Temperature (2012), '250 Years of Global Warming: Berkeley Earth Releases New Analysis' (Berkeley: Berkeley Earth Surface Temperature). <http://berkeleyearth.org/results-summary/>, accessed 31 July 2012.

Bernstein, Lenny, et al. (2007), 'Climate Change 2007: Synthesis Report', (Valencia: Intergovernmental Panel on Climate Change). <http://www.ipcc.ch/pdf/ assessment-report/ar4/syr/ar4_syr.pdf>.

Brandt, Richard B. (1979), *A Theory of the Good and the Right* (Oxford: Oxford University Press).

Brandt, Richard B. (1988), 'Fairness to Indirect Optimific Theories in Ethics', *Ethics, 98* (2), 341–60.

Brighouse, Harry (2010), 'Thomson's Violinist: What Is the Point of Thought Experiments in Moral Philosophy?' *Crooked Timber*, 23 January. <http://crook-edtimber.org/2010/01/23/thomsons-violinist-what-is-the-point-of-thought-experi-ments-in-moral-philosophy/>, accessed 8 June 2012.

Broome, John (2008), 'The Ethics of Climate Change', *Scientific American, 69–73*.

Cahan, Harley (1988), 'Against the Moral Considerability of Ecosystems', *Environmental Ethics, 10*, 196–216.

Caldicott, J. Baird (1986), 'On the Intrinsic Value of Non-Human Species', in Bryan Norton (ed.), *The Preservation of Species: the Value of Biological Diversity* (Princeton: Princeton University Press), 138–72.

Caney, Simon (2005a), 'Cosmopolitan Justice, Responsibility, and Global Climate Change', *Leiden Journal of International Law, 18*, 747–75.

Caney, Simon (2005b), *Justice Beyond Borders: A Global Political Theory* (Oxford: Oxford University Press).

Caney, Simon (2006), 'Cosmopolitan Justice, Rights and Global Climate Change', *Canadian Journal of Law and Jurisprudence, 19* (2), 255–78.

Caney, Simon (2008), 'Human Rights, Climate Change, and Discounting', *Environmental Politics, 17* (4), 536–55.

Caney, Simon (2009a), 'Climate Change, Human Rights, and Moral Thresholds', in Stephen Humphreys (ed.), *Human Rights and Climate Change* (Cambridge: Cambridge University Press), 69–90.

Caney, Simon (2009b), 'Justice and the Distribution of Greenhouse Gas Emissions', *Journal of Global Ethics, 5* (2), 125–46.

Caney, Simon (2009c), 'Climate Change and the Future: Discounting for Time, Wealth, and Risk', *Journal of Social Philosophy, 40* (2), 163–86.

Caney, Simon (2010), 'Climate Change and the Duties of the Advantaged', *Critical Review of International Social and Political Philosophy, 13* (1), 203–28.

Carrington, Damien (2011), 'Peasant Activist Shot Dead in Brazil's Amazon Region', *The Guardian*, 15 June 2011. <http://www.guardian.co.uk/world/2011/jun/15/peasant-activist-killed-brazil>, accessed 18 February 2012.

Carter, Alan (2001), 'Can We Harm Future People?' *Environmental Values, 10*, 429–54.

Carter, Alan (2011), 'Towards a Multidimensional, Environmentalist Ethics', *Environmental Values, 20* (3), 347–74.

Caws, Peter (2005), 'The Distributive Structure of the Social Group', *Journal of Social Philosophy, 36* (2), 218–32.

Cocker, Jarvis, et al. (1995), 'Common People' (Polygram).

Cohen, G. A. (1989), 'On the Currency of Egalitarian Justice', *Ethics, 99* (4), 906–44.

Cohen, Stanley (2001), *States of Denial: Knowing About Atrocities and Suffering* (Cambridge: Polity Press).

Committee on Abrupt Climate Change, et al. (2002), 'Abrupt Climate Change: Inevitable Surprises' (Washington, DC: National Academy Press). <http://www.nap.edu/openbook.php?record_id=10136&page=R1>.

Cowen, Tyler (2003), 'Policing Nature', *Environmental Ethics, 25*, 169–82.

Cripps, Elizabeth (2010), 'Saving the Polar Bear, Saving the World: Can the Capabilities Approach do Justice to Humans, Animals and Ecosystems?' *Res Publica, 16* (1), 1–22.

Cripps, Elizabeth (2011a), 'Climate Change, Collective Harm and Legitimate Coercion', *Critical Review of International Social and Political Philosophy, 14* (2), 171–93.

Cripps, Elizabeth (2011b), 'Collectivities Without Intention', *Journal of Social Philosophy, 42* (1), 1–20.

Cripps, Elizabeth (2012), 'Review of Clare Palmer: Animal Ethics in Context', *Environmental Values, 21* (2), 238–40.

Cummiskey, David (2003), *Kantian Consequentialism* (Oxford and New York: Oxford University Press).

Derocher, Andrew E., Lunn, Nicholas J., and Stirling, Ian (2004), 'Polar Bears in a Warming Climate', *Integrative and Comparative Biology, 44*, 163–76.

Diamond, Cora (1978), 'Eating Meat and Eating People', *Philosophy, 53* (206), 465–79.

Dickens, Charles (1837), 'The Adventures of Oliver Twist' (1994 edn; London: Everyman).

Dickens, Charles (1853), 'Bleak House' (1993 edn; Ware, Herts.: Wordsworth).

Dodd, Vikram (2012), 'Stephen Lawrence: Theresa May Orders Review into Police Corruption Claims', *The Guardian*, 1 June. <http://www.guardian.co.uk/uk/2012/jun/01/stephen-lawrence-theresa-may-review-police-corruption>, accessed 21 July 2012.

Dodd, Vikram and Laville, Sandra (2012), 'Stephen Lawrence Verdict: Dobson and Norris Guilty of Racist Murder', *The Guardian*, 3 January. <http://www.guardian.co.uk/uk/2012/jan/03/stephen-lawrence-verdict-guilty-murder>, accessed 21 July 2012.

Donaldson, Sue and Kymlicka, Will (2011), *Zoopolis: A Political Theory of Animal Rights* (Oxford: Oxford University Press).

Doran, Peter T. and Zimmerman, Maggie Kendall (2009), 'Examining the Scientific Consensus on Climate Change', *Eos, Transactions American Geophysical Union*, *90* (3), 22–3.

Dostoyevsky, Fyodor (1866), 'Crime and Punishment', (1980 edn; Oxford: Oxford University Press).

Duffy, Carol Ann (1999), *The World's Wife* (London: Picador).

Dworkin, Ronald (1981a), 'Equality of What? Part 1: Equality of Welfare', *Philosophy and Public Affairs, 10* (3), 185–246.

Dworkin, Ronald (1981b), 'Equality of What? Part 2: Equality of Resources', *Philosophy and Public Affairs, 10* (3), 283–345.

Elster, Jon (1983), *Sour Grapes: Studies in the Subversion of Rationality* (Cambridge: Cambridge University Press).

Engster, Daniel (2006), 'Care Ethics and Animal Welfare', *Journal of Social Philosophy*, *37* (4), 521–36.

European Academy of Sciences and Arts (2007), 'Let's Be Honest' (Salzburg: European Academy of Sciences and Arts). <http://www.euro-acad.eu/memorandas?page=2>.

European Geosciences Union, 'Position Statement on Climate Change and Recent Letters from the Chairman of the U.S. House of Representatives Committee on Energy and Commerce'. <http://www.egu.eu/statements/position-statement-of-th e-divisions-of-atmospheric-and-climate-sciences-7-july-2005.html>, accessed 23 July 2012.

Farber, Daniel (2008), 'The Case for Climate Compensation: Justice for Climate Change Victims in a Complex World', *Utah Law Review, 377* (2), 377–413.

Feinberg, Joel (1970), *Doing and Deserving: Essays in the Theory of Responsibility* (Princeton: Princeton University Press).

Feinberg, Joel (1987), *The Moral Limits of the Criminal Law Volume I: Harm to Others* (Oxford: Oxford University Press).

Finkelstein, Claire (2003), 'Is Risk a Harm?' *University of Pennsylvania Law Review*, *151* (3), 963–1001.

Foot, Philippa (1978), *Virtues and Vices and Other Essays in Moral Philosophy* (Oxford: Blackwell).

Foot, Philippa (1985), 'Utilitarianism and the Virtues', *Mind, 94* (384), 196–209.

Foot, Philippa (2001), *Natural Goodness* (Oxford: Clarendon).

Francis, Leslie Pickering and Norman, Richard (1978), 'Some Animals Are More Equal Than Others', *Philosophy, 53*, 507–27.

Franklin, Benjamin, et al. (1776), 'The Unanimous Declaration of the Thirteen United States of America' (Philadelphia). <http://www.archives.gov/exhibits/charters/declaration_transcript.html>, accessed 14 June 2012.

Gansberg, Martin (1964), 'Thirty-Eight Who Saw Murder Didn't Call the Police', *New York Times*, March 27.

Gardiner, Stephen M. (2004), 'Ethics and Global Climate Change', *Ethics, 114* (3), 555–600.

Gardiner, Stephen M. (2006), 'A Perfect Moral Storm: Climate Change, Intergenerational Ethics and the Problem of Moral Corruption', *Environmental Values, 15* (3), 397–413.

Gardiner, Stephen M. (2009), 'Saved by Disaster? Abrupt Climate Change, Political Inertia, and the Possibility of an Intergenerational Arms Race', *Journal of Social Philosophy, 40* (2), 140–62.

Gardiner, Stephen M. (2010), 'Is "Arming the Future" with Geoengineering Really the Lesser Evil?' in Stephen M. Gardiner, et al. (eds), *Climate Ethics: Essential Readings* (Oxford and New York: Oxford University Press), 284–312.

Gardiner, Stephen M. (2011a), 'Is No-One Responsible for Global Environmental Tragedy? Climate Change as a Challenge to Our Ethical Concepts', in Denis G. Arnold (ed.), *The Ethics of Global Climate Change* (Cambridge: Cambridge University Press), 38–59.

Gardiner, Stephen M. (2011b), *A Perfect Moral Storm: The Ethical Tragedy of Climate Change* (Oxford and New York: Oxford University Press).

Gardiner, Stephen M. (2012), 'Are We the Scum of the Earth? Climate Change, Geoengineering and Humanity's Challenge', in Allen Thompson and Jeremy Bendik-Keymer (eds), *Ethical Adaptation to Climate Change: The Human Virtues of the Future* (Cambridge, MA: MIT Press), 241–59.

Garvey, James (2008), *The Ethics of Climate Change: Right and Wrong in a Warming World* (London: Continuum).

Garvey, James (2010), 'Climate Change and Moral Outrage', *Human Ecology Review, 17* (2), 96–101.

Garvey, James (2011), 'Climate Change and Causal Inefficacy: Why Go Green When It Makes No Difference?' in A. O'Hear (ed.), *Philosophy and the Environment* (Cambridge: Cambridge University Press), 157–74.

Gilbert, Margaret (1989), *On Social Facts* (London: Routledge).

Gilbert, Margaret (2006), *A Theory of Political Obligation* (Oxford and New York: Oxford University Press).

Global Footprint Network (2012), 'Carbon Footprint', <http://www.footprintnet/work.org/en/index.php/GFN/page/carbon_footprint/>, accessed 26 July 2012.

Glover, Jonathan (1975), 'It Makes No Difference Whether or Not I Do It', *Proceedings of the Aristotelian Society*, Supplement *49*, 171–209.

Godwin, William (1793), *An Enquiry Concerning Political Justice*, (Vol. I; Oxford and New York: Woodstock Books (1992)).

Goldenberg, Suzanne (2011), 'US Eco-Activist Jailed for Two Years', *The Guardian*, 27 July. <http://www.guardian.co.uk/world/2011/jul/27/tim-dechristopher-jailed-two-years>, accessed 18 February 2012.

Goodin, Robert E. (1985), *Protecting the Vulnerable: A Reanalysis of Our Social Responsibilities* (Chicago and London: University of Chicago Press).

Gosseries, Axel (2004), 'Historical Emissions and Free-Riding', *Ethical Perspectives*, *11* (1), 36–60.

Gould, Carol C. (1988), *Rethinking Democracy: Freedom and Social Cooperation in Politics, Economy, and Society* (Cambridge: Cambridge University Press).

Graham, Keith (2002), *Practical Reasoning in a Social World* (Cambridge: Cambridge University Press).

Gunnarsson, Logi (2008), 'The Great Apes and the Severely Disabled: Moral Status and Thick Evaluative Concepts', *Ethical Theory and Moral Practice, 11*, 305–26.

Hailwood, Simon (2011), 'Disowning the Weather', *Critical Review of International Social and Political Philosophy, 14* (2), 215–34.

Hampton, Jean (1986), *Hobbes and the Social Contract Tradition* (Cambridge: Cambridge University Press).

Hansen, J. (2008), 'Tipping Point: Perspective of a Climatologist', in E. Fearn (ed.), *State of the Wild 2008–2009: A Global Portrait of Wildlife, Wildlands, and Oceans* (Washington: Island Press), 6–15.

Hare, Caspar (2007), 'Voices from Another World: Must We Respect the Interests of People Who Do Not, and Will Never, Exist?' *Ethics, 117* (3), 498–523.

Hare, R. M. (1993), 'Could Kant Have Been a Utilitarian?' in R. M. Dancy (ed.), *Kant and Critique: New Essays in Honor of W. H. Werkmeister* (Dordecht, Boston, and London: Kluwer Academic Publishers), 91–113.

Harman, Elizabeth (2004), 'Can We Harm and Benefit in Creating?' *Philosophical Perspectives, 18*, 89–113.

Harman, Elizabeth (2009), 'Harming as Causing Harm', in M. A. Roberts and D. T. Wasserman (eds), *Harming Future Persons: Ethics, Genetics and the Nonidentity Problem* (Dordrecht: Springer), 137–54.

Harris, Paul (2010), *World Ethics and Climate Change: From International to Global Justice* (Edinburgh: Edinburgh University Press).

Hayward, Tim (1998), *Political Theory and Ecological Values* (Cambridge: Polity Press).

Held, Virginia (1970), 'Can a Random Collection of Individuals be Morally Responsible?' *Journal of Philosophy, 67* (14), 471–81.

Hettinger, Ned (2012), 'Nature Restoration as a Paradigm for the Human Relationship with Nature', in Allen Thompson and Jeremy Bendik-Keymer (eds), *Ethical Adaptation to Climate Change: Human Virtues of the Future* (Cambridge, Mass. and London: The MIT Press), 27–46.

Hiller, Avram (2011), 'Climate Change and Individual Responsibility', *The Monist, 94* (3), 349–68.

Hobbes, Thomas (1651), 'Leviathan', (1996 edn; Cambridge: Cambridge University Press).

Holland, Breena (2008), 'Justice and the Environment in Nussbaum's Capabilities Approach: Why Sustainable Ecological Capacity is a Meta-Capability', *Political Research Quarterly, 61* (2), 319–32.

Holland, Breena (2012), 'Environment as a Meta-capability: Why a Dignified Human Life Requires a Stable Climate System', in Allen Thompson and Jeremy Bendik-Keymer (eds), *Ethical Adaptation to Climate Change: Human Virtues of the Future* (Cambridge, Mass. and London: MIT Press), 145–64.

Hooker, Brad (1990), 'Rule-Consequentialism', *Mind, 99* (393), 67–77.

Hourdequin, Marion (2010), 'Climate, Collective Action, and Individual Ethical Obligations', *Environmental Values, 19*, 443–64.

Hugo, Victor (1862), 'Les Misérables', (Vol. I; Ware, Herts.: Wordsworth Classics).

Hursthouse, Rosalind (2007), 'Environmental Virtue Ethics', in Rebecca L. Walker and Philip J. Ivanhoe (eds), *Working Virtue: Virtue Ethics and Contemporary Moral Problems* (Oxford: Oxford University Press), 155–209.

InterAcademy Council (2007), 'Lighting the Way: Towards a Sustainable Energy Future' (Amsterdam: IAC). <http://www.interacademycouncil.net/24026/25142.aspx>.

International Council of Academies of Engineering and Technological Sciences (2007), 'Environment and Sustainable Growth: A Statement by CAETS, International Council of Academies of Engineering and Technological Sciences, Inc' (Tokyo: CAETS).

IPCC (2007), 'Summary for Policymakers', in B. Metz, et al. (eds), *Climate Change 2007: Mitigation. Contribution of Working Group III to the Fourth Assessment Report of the Intergovernmental Panel on Climate Change* (Cambridge and New York: Cambridge University Press), 1–23.

Jamieson, Dale (1992), 'Ethics, Public Policy, and Global Warming', *Science, Technology and Human Values, 17* (2), 139–53.

Jamieson, Dale (2007a), 'The Moral and Political Challenges of Climate Change', in Susanne C. Moser and Lisa Dilling (eds), *Creating a Climate for Change: Communicating Climate Change and Facilitating Social Change* (Cambridge: Cambridge University Press), 475–82.

Jamieson, Dale (2007b), 'When Utilitarians Should Be Virtue Theorists', *Utilitas, 19* (2), 160–83.

Jamieson, Dale (2008), 'The Post-Kyoto Climate: A Gloomy Forecast', *Georgetown Journal of International Environmental Law, 20*, 537–51.

Jamieson, Dale (2010), 'Climate Change, Responsibility, and Justice', *Science and Engineering Ethics, 16*, 431–45.

Jamieson, Dale (2011), 'Energy, Ethics, and the Transformation of Nature', in Denis G. Arnold (ed.), *The Ethics of Global Climate Change* (Cambridge: Cambridge University Press), 16–37.

Johnson, Baylor L. (2003), 'Ethical Obligations in a Tragedy of the Commons', *Environmental Values, 12* (3), 271–87.

Kagan, Shelly (2011), 'Do I Make a Difference?' *Philosophy and Public Affairs, 39* (2), 105–41.

Kamm, F. M. (2004), 'The New Problem of Distance in Morality', in Deen K. Chatterjee (ed.), *The Ethics of Assistance: Morality and the Distant Needy* (Cambridge: Cambridge University Press), 59–74.

Kant, Immanuel (1785), *Groundwork of the Metaphysics of Morals* (1998 edn; Cambridge: Cambridge University Press).

Karl, Thomas R., Melillo, Jerry M., and Paterson, Thomas C. (eds) (2009), *Global Climate Change Impacts in the United States* (New York: Cambridge University Press).

Karlsson, Rasmus (2006), 'Reducing Asymmetries in Intergenerational Justice: Descent from Modernity or Space Industrialization?' *Organization & Environment, 19* (2), 233–50.

Karnein, Anja (Unpublished), 'Putting Fairness in Its Place: Why There is a Duty to Take Up the Slack'.

Kernohan, Andrew (1998), *Liberalism, Equality, and Cultural Oppression* (New York: Cambridge University Press).

Kirchner, James W. and Weil, Anne (2000), 'Delayed Biological Recovery from Extinctions Throughout the Fossil Record', *Nature, 404*, 177–80.

Korsgaard, Christine (1986), 'The Right to Lie: Kant on Dealing with Evil', *Philosophy and Public Affairs, 15* (4), 235–349.

Korsgaard, Christine (1996), *Creating the Kingdom of Ends* (New York: Cambridge University Press).

Kutz, Christopher (2000), *Complicity: Ethics and Law for a Collective Age* (Cambridge and New York: Cambridge University Press).

Kutz, Christopher (2002), 'The Collective Work of Citizenship', *Legal Theory, 8*, 471–94.

Leopold, Aldo (1966), *A Sand County Almanac: With Other Essays on Conservation from Round River* (New York: Oxford University Press).

Lichtenberg, Judith (2004), 'Absence and the Unfond Heart: Why People Are Less Giving Than They Might Be', in Deen K. Chatterjee (ed.), *The Ethics of Assistance: Morality and the Distant Needy* (Cambridge: Cambridge University Press), 75–97.

Lichtenberg, Judith (2010), 'Negative Duties, Positive Duties, and the "New Harms"', *Ethics, 120* (3), 557–78.

Light, Andrew (2012), 'The Death of Restoration?' in Allen Thompson and Jeremy Bendik-Keymer (eds), *Ethical Adaptation to Climate Change: Human Virtues of the Future* (Cambridge, Mass. and London: The MIT Press), 105–21.

Lomborg, Bjørn (2001), *The Skeptical Environmentalist: Measuring the Real State of the World* (Cambridge: Cambridge University Press).

Macdonald, Graham and Pettit, Philip (1981), *Semantics and Social Science* (London: Routledge & Kegan Paul).

Maltais, Aaron (Forthcoming), 'Radically Non-Ideal Climate Politics and the Obligation to at Least Vote Green', *Environmental Values*.

Marcus, Ruth Barcan (1980), 'Moral Dilemmas and Consistency', *The Journal of Philosophy, 77* (3), 121–36.

Marland, G., Boden, T., and Andreas, R. J. (2008), 'Global CO2 Emissions from Fossil-fuel Burning, Cement Manufacture, and Gas Flaring: 1751–2005'. <http://cdiac.ornl.gov/trends/emis/em_cont.html>.

May, Larry (1987), *The Morality of Groups: Collective Responsibility, Group-Based Harm, and Corporate Rights* (Notre Dame, Ind. University of Notre Dame Press).

May, Larry (1992), *Sharing Responsibility* (Chicago and London: University of Chicago Press).

McDermott, Daniel (2008), 'Analytical Political Philosophy', in David Leopold and Marc Stears (eds), *Political Theory: Methods and Approaches* (Oxford: Oxford University Press), 11–28.

McKinnon, Catriona (2009), 'Runaway Climate Change: A Justice-Based Case for Precautions', *Journal of Social Philosophy, 40* (2), 187–203.

McMahan, Jeff (2008), 'Challenges to Human Equality', *Journal of Ethics, 12*, 81–104.

Mill, John Stuart (1859), 'On Liberty', in John Gray (ed.), *John Stuart Mill: On Liberty and Other Essays* (1991 edn; Oxford: Oxford University Press).

Mill, John Stuart (1869), 'The Subjection of Women', in John Gray (ed.), *John Stuart Mill: On Liberty and Other Essays* (1991 edn; Oxford: Oxford University Press).

Miller, Richard B. (2004), 'Moral Closeness and World Community', in Deen K. Chatterjee (ed.), *The Ethics of Assistance: Morality and the Distant Needy* (Cambridge: Cambridge University Press), 101–22.

Miller, Richard B. (2009), 'Actual Rule Utilitarianism', *The Journal of Philosophy, 106* (1), 5–28.

Moellendorf, Darrel (2002), *Cosmopolitan Justice* (Boulder, Colo.; Oxford: Westview Press).

Moellendorf, Darrel (2011), 'A Normative Account of Dangerous Climate Change', *Climatic Change, 108* (1–2), 391–410.

Moser, Susanne C. and Dilling, Lisa (2004), 'Making Climate Hot', *Environment, 46* (10), 32–46.

Moser, Susanne C. and Walser, Maggie L. (2008), 'Communicating Climate Change Motivating Citizen Action', *Encyclopedia of Earth*. <http://www.eoearth.org/article/Communicating_climate_change_motivating_citizen_action>, accessed 23 July 2012.

Muller, Richard A. (2012), 'The Conversion of a Climate-Change Skeptic', *New York Times*, 28 July. <http://www.nytimes.com/2012/07/30/opinion/the-conversion-of-a-climate-change-skeptic.html?_r=3&pagewanted=all>, accessed 31 July 2012.

Murphy, Liam B. (1993), 'The Demands of Beneficence', *Philosophy and Public Affairs, 22* (4), 267–92.

Murphy, Liam B. (1998), 'Institutions and the Demands of Justice', *Philosophy and Public Affairs, 27* (4), 251–91.

Murphy, Liam B. (2000), *Moral Demands in Nonideal Theory* (New York: Oxford University Press).

Nagel, Thomas (1979), *Mortal Questions* (Cambridge: Cambridge University Press).

Nagel, Thomas (1991), *Equality and Partiality* (New York and Oxford: Oxford University Press).

Nagel, Thomas (2005), 'The Problem of Global Justice', *Philosophy and Public Affairs, 33* (2), 113–47.

Neumayer, Eric (2000), 'In Defence of Historical Accountability for Greenhouse Gas Emissions', *Ecological Economics, 33*, 185–92.

Nolt, John (2011a), 'How Harmful Are the Average American's Greenhouse Gas Emissions?' *Ethics, Policy and Environment, 14* (1), 3–10.

Nolt, John (2011b), 'Nonanthropocentric Climate Ethics', *WIREs Climate Change, 2*, 701–11.

Nolt, John (2011c), 'Greenhouse Gas Emission and the Domination of Posterity', in Denis G. Arnold (ed.), *The Ethics of Global Climate Change* (Cambridge: Cambridge University Press), 60–76.

Nordhaus, William (1997), 'Discounting in Economics and Climate Change', *Climatic Change, 37*, 315–28.

Norgaard, Kari Marie (2011), *Living in Denial: Climate Change, Emotions, and Everyday Life* (Cambridge, Mass.: MIT Press).

Norton, Bryan G. (1986), 'On the Inherent Danger of Undervaluing Species', in Bryan G. Norton (ed.), *The Preservation of Species: The Value of Biological Diversity* (Princeton: Princeton University Press), 110–37.

Norton, Bryan G. (2005), *Sustainability: A Philosophy of Adaptive Ecosystem Management* (Chicago: Chicago University Press).

Nozick, Robert (1974), *Anarchy, State and Utopia* (Oxford: Blackwell).

Nuffield Council on Bioethics (2005), 'The Ethics of Research Involving Animals', (London: Nuffield Council on Bioethics).

Nussbaum, Martha (1990), 'Aristotelian Social Democracy', in R. Bruce Douglass, Gerald M. Mara, and Henry S. Richardson (eds), *Liberalism and the Good* (New York: Routledge), 203–52.

Nussbaum, Martha (1992), 'Human Functioning and Social Justice: In Defense of Aristotelian Essentialism', *Political Theory, 20* (2), 202–46.

Nussbaum, Martha (1998), 'The Good as Discipline, the Good as Freedom', in David A. Crocker and Toby Linden (eds), *Ethics of Consumption: The Good Life, Ethics and Global Stewardship* (Lanham, Md. and Oxford: Rowman & Littlefield), 312–41.

Nussbaum, Martha (2000a), 'Aristotle, Politics, and Human Capabilities: A Response to Antony, Arneson, Charlesworth, and Mulgan', *Ethics, 111* (1), 102–40.

Nussbaum, Martha (2000b), *Women and Human Development: The Capabilities Approach* (Cambridge: Cambridge University Press).

Nussbaum, Martha (2006), *Frontiers of Justice: Disability, Nationality, Species Membership* (Cambridge, Mass. and London: Harvard University Press).

Nussbaum, Martha (2011), 'The Capabilities Approach and Animal Entitlements', in Tom L. Beauchamp and R. G. Frey (eds), *The Oxford Handbook of Animal Ethics* (New York: Oxford University Press), 228–51.

Obama, Barack (2011), 'Remarks by the President to Parliament in London, United Kingdom' (London). <http://www.whitehouse.gov/the-press-office/2011/05/25/re marks-president-parliament-london-united-kingdom>, accessed 7 June 2012.

Omenn, Gilbert S., et al. (2006), 'AAAS Board Statement on Climate Change', (American Association for the Advancement of Science).

O'Neill, John (1992), 'The Varieties of Intrinsic Value', *The Monist, 75* (2), 119–37.

Oreskes, Naomi (2004), 'Beyond the Ivory Tower: The Scientific Consensus on Climate Change', *Science, 306* (5702), 1686.

Oreskes, Naomi and Conway, Erik M. (2010), *Merchants of Doubt: How a Handful of Scientists Obscured the Truth on Issues from Tobacco Smoke to Global Warming* (New York: Bloomsbury).

Orwell, George (1933), *Down and Out in Paris and London* (1949 edn; London: Secker & Warburg).

Otsuka, Michael (1991), 'The Paradox of Group Beneficence', *Philosophy and Public Affairs, 20*, 132–49.

Page, Edward (2006), *Climate Change, Justice and Future Generations* (Cheltenham and Northampton, MA: Edward Elgar).

Page, Edward (2007), 'Intergenerational Justice of What: Welfare, Resources or Capabilities?' *Environmental Politics, 16* (3), 455–71.

Page, Edward (2012), 'Give It Up for Climate Change: A Defence of the Beneficiary Pays Principle', *International Theory, 4* (2), 300–30.

Palmer, Clare (2010), *Animal Ethics in Context* (New York: Columbia University Press).

Palmer, Clare (2011), 'Does Nature Matter? The Place of the Nonhuman in the Ethics of Climate Change', in Denis G. Arnold (ed.), *The Ethics of Global Climate Change* (Cambridge: Cambridge University Press), 272–91.

Parfit, Derek (1984), *Reasons and Persons* (1987 Corrected reprint edn; Oxford: Clarendon Press).

Parfit, Derek (1986), 'Comments', *Ethics*, 96 (4), 832–72.

Pearce, Fred (2007), *With Speed and Violence* (Boston: Beacon Press).

Perry, Stephen (2007), 'Risk, Harm, Interests, and Rights', in Tim Lewens (ed.), *Risk: Philosophical Perspectives* (London and New York: Routledge), 190–209.

Petersen, John (2008), 'A Green Curriculum Involves Everyone on Campus', *The Chronicle of Higher Education*.

Peterson, Thomas C., Stott, Peter A., and Herring, Stephanie (2012), 'Explaining Extreme Events of 2011 from a Climate Perspective', *American Meteorological Society*, 93 (7), 1041–67. <http://chronicle/article/A-Green-Curriculum-Involves/7662/>.

Phillips, Tom (2011), 'Amazon Rainforest Activist Shot Dead', *The Guardian*, 24 May. <http://www.guardian.co.uk/world/2011/may/24/amazon-rainforest-activist-killed>, accessed 10 February 2012.

Pogge, Thomas (2002), *World Poverty and Human Rights: Cosmopolitan Responsibilities and Reforms* (Cambridge: Polity).

Pollan, Michael (2006), *The Omnivore's Dilemma* (London: Bloomsbury).

Priestley, J. B. (1950), 'An Inspector Calls', *The Plays of J B Priestley* (Vol. III; London: William Heinemann).

Pullman, Philip (2000), *The Amber Spyglass* (London: Scholastic).

Rajamani, Lavanya (2011), 'The Cancun Climate Agreements: Reading the Text, Subtext and Tea Leaves', *International and Comparative Law Quarterly*, 60, 499–519.

Rajamani, Lavanya (2012), 'The Durban Platform for Enhanced Action and the Future of the Climate Regime', *International and Comparative Law Quarterly*, 61, 501–18.

Rawls, John (1971), *A Theory of Justice* (Revised 1999 edn; Oxford: Oxford University Press).

Rawls, John (1989), 'Themes in Kant's Moral Philosophy', in E. Forster (ed.), *Kant's Transcendental Deductions: The Three Critiques and the Opus postumum* (Stanford, Calif.: Stanford University Press), 81–113.

Raz, Joseph (1986), *The Morality of Freedom* (Oxford: Clarendon Press).

Regan, Donald (1980), *Utilitarianism and Co-operation* (Oxford: Oxford University Press).

Regan, Tom (2004), *The Case for Animal Rights* (2nd edn; Berkeley, Calif. and London: University of California Press).

Ribeiro da Silva, José Cláudio (2011), 'Speech to TedX Amazonia'. <http://en.tedxamazonia.com.br/tedtalk/ze-claudio>, accessed 21 July 2012.

Risse, Mathias (2012), *On Global Justice* (Princeton and Oxford: Princeton University Press).

Rodman, John (1977), 'The Liberation of Nature', *Inquiry*, 20 (1), 83–145.

Rodman, John (1983), 'Four Forms of Ecological Consciousness Reconsidered', in Donald Scherer and Thomas Attig (eds), *Ethics and the Environment* (Englewood Cliffs, NJ.: Prentice Hall), 82–92.

Rolston III, Holmes (1994), 'Value in Nature and the Nature of Value', in Robin Attfield and Andrew Belsey (eds), *Philosophy and Natural Environment* (Cambridge: Cambridge University Press), 13–30.

Roser, Dominic and Hohl, Sabine (2011), 'Stepping in for the Polluters? Climate Justice under Partial Compliance', *Analyse and Kritik, 33* (2), 477–500.

Ross, W. D. (1930), *The Right and the Good* (2002 edn; Oxford: Oxford University Press).

Sartre, Jean-Paul (1956), 'Existentialism is a Humanism', in Walter Kaufman (ed.) (1989 edn), *Existentialism from Dostoyevsky to Sartre* (Seattle: Meridian Publishing Company), 345–69.

Schapiro, Tamara (2006), 'Kantian Rigorism and Mitigating Circumstances', *Ethics, 117* (1), 32–57.

Scheffler, Samuel (1995), 'Individual Responsibility in a Global Age', *Social Philosophy and Policy, 12*, 219–36.

Scheffler, Samuel (2001), *Boundaries and Allegiances: Problems of Justice and Responsibility in Liberal Thought* (Oxford: Oxford University Press).

Schelling, Thomas C. (1997), 'The Cost of Combating Global Warming: Facing the Tradeoffs', *Foreign Affairs, 76* (6), 8–14.

Schinkel, Anders (2008), 'Martha Nussbaum on Animal Rights', *Ethics and the Environment, 13*, 41–69.

Schlosberg, David (2007), *Defining Environmental Justice: Theories, Movements and Nature* (New York: Oxford University Press).

Schlosberg, David (2012), 'Justice, Ecological Integrity, and Climate Change', in Allen Thompson and Jeremy Bendik-Keymer (eds), *Ethical Adaptation to Climate Change: Human Virtues of the Future* (Cambridge, Mass.: MIT Press).

Schlosberg, David (Unpublished), 'Rethinking Ecological Justice: Capabilities and Critics'.

Schlosberg, David and Carruthers, David (2010), 'Indigenous Struggles, Environmental Justice, and Community Capabilities', *Global Environmental Politics, 10* (4), 12–35.

Searle, John (1995), *The Construction of Social Reality* (New York: The Free Press).

Sen, Amartya (1980), 'Equality of What?' in Sterling M. McMurrin (ed.), *Liberty, Equality and Law: Selected Tanner Lectures on Moral Philosophy* (Cambridge: Cambridge University Press, 1987), 195–220.

Sen, Amartya (1987), *On Ethics and Economics* (Oxford: Blackwell).

Sen, Amartya (1992), *Inequality Reexamined* (New York and Oxford: Clarendon Press).

Sen, Amartya (1993), 'Capability and Well-Being', in Martha Nussbaum and Amartya Sen (eds), *The Quality of Life* (New York: Oxford University Press), 30–53.

Sen, Amartya (1999), *Development as Freedom* (Oxford: Oxford University Press).

Sen, Amartya (2009), *The Idea of Justice* (London: Allen Lane).

Sheehy, Paul (2002), 'On Plural Subject Theory', *Journal of Social Philosophy, 33* (3), 377–94.

Sheehy, Paul (2006), *The Reality of Social Groups* (Aldershot and Burlington: Ashgate).

Shiffrin, Seana Valentine (1999), 'Wrongful Life, Procreative Responsibility, and the Significance of Harm', *Legal Theory, 5*, 117–48.

Shrader-Frechette, K. S. (2002), *Environmental Justice: Creating Equity, Reclaiming Democracy* (Environmental ethics and science policy series; New York: Oxford University Press).

Shue, Henry (1980), *Basic Rights: Subsistence, Affluence, and U.S. Foreign Policy* (Princeton: Princeton University Press).

Shue, Henry (1981), 'Exporting Hazards', *Ethics, 91* (4), 579–606.

Shue, Henry (1988), 'Mediating Duties', *Ethics, 98* (4), 687–704.

Shue, Henry (1992), 'The Unavoidability of Justice', in Andrew Hurrell and Benedict Kinsbury (eds), *The International Politics of the Environment* (Oxford: Oxford University Press), 373–97.

Shue, Henry (1993), 'Subsistence Emissions and Luxury Emissions', *Law and Policy, 15* (1), 39–60.

Shue, Henry (1999a), 'Bequeathing Hazards: Security Rights and Property Rights of Future Humans', in Mohammed Dore and Timothy Mount (eds), *Global Environ-mental Economics: Equity and the Limits to Markets* (Oxford: Blackwell), 38–53.

Shue, Henry (1999b), 'Global Environmental and International Equality', *International Affairs, 75* (3), 531–45.

Shue, Henry (2010), 'Deadly Delays, Saving Opportunities: Creating a More Dangerous World?' in Stephen M. Gardiner, et al. (eds), *Climate Ethics: Essential Readings* (New York: Oxford University Press), 146–62.

Simpson, Joe (1997), *Touching the Void* (London: Vintage).

Singer, Peter (1972), 'Famine, Affluence, and Morality', *Philosophy and Public Affairs, 72* (1), 229–43.

Singer, Peter (1976), 'All Animals Are Equal', in Peter Singer (ed.), *Animal Ethics* (Oxford: Oxford University Press), 213–28.

Singer, Peter (1979), 'Not for Humans Only: The Place of Nonhumans in Environmental Issues', in Kenneth Goodpaster (ed.), *Ethics and Problems of the 21st Century* (Notre Dame, Ind.: University of Notre Dame Press), 191–205.

Singer, Peter (2002), *One World: The Ethics of Globalization* (New Haven and London: Yale University Press).

Singer, Peter (2004), 'Outsiders: Our Obligations to the Distant Needy', in Deen K. Chatterjee (ed.), *The Ethics of Assistance: Morality and the Distant Needy* (Cambridge: Cambridge University Press), 11–32.

Sinnott-Armstrong, Walter (2005), 'It's Not My Fault: Global Warming and Individual Moral Obligations', in Walter Sinnott-Armstrong and Richard Howarth (eds), *Perspectives on Climate Change: Science, Economics, Politics, Ethics* (Oxford: Elsevier), 285–307.

Smart, J. J. C. (1956), 'Extreme and Restricted Utilitarianism', *The Philosophical Quarterly, 6* (25), 344–54.

Solzhenitsyn, Aleksandr (1970), 'Nobel Lecture: One Word of Truth Outweighs the Whole World'. <http://www.nobelprize.org/nobel_prizes/literature/laureates/1970/solzhenitsyn-lecture.html>.

Stern, Nicholas (2006), 'Stern Review on the Economics of Climate Change. Executive Summary' (London: HM Treasury). <http://webarchive.nationalarchives.gov. uk/+/http://www.hm-treasury.gov.uk/d/Executive_Summary.pdf>, accessed 23 June 2011.

Stern, Nicholas (2008), 'The Economics of Climate Change', *American Economic Review, 98* (2), 1–37.

Stewart, Frances (1996), 'Basic Needs, Capabilities, and Human Development', in Avner Offer (ed.), *In Pursuit of the Quality of Life* (New York: Oxford University Press), 46–65.

Stocker, Michael (1976), 'The Schizophrenia of Modern Ethical Theories', *The Journal of Philosophy, 73* (14), 453–66.

Stoll-Kleemann, S., O'Riordan, Tim, and Jaeger, Carlo C. (2001), 'The Psychology of Denial Concerning Climate Mitigation Measures: Evidence from Swiss focus Groups', *Global Environmental Change, 11*, 107–17.

Streeten, Paul, et al. (1981), *First Things First: Meeting Basic Human Needs in the Developing Countries* (New York: Oxford University Press).

Styron, William (1979), *Sophie's Choice* (1980 edn; London: Corgi).

Taylor, Paul W. (1981), 'The Ethics of Respect for Nature', *Environmental Ethics, 3*, 197–218.

Taylor, Paul W. (1986), *Respect for Nature: A Theory of Environmental Ethics* (Princeton: Princeton University Press).

The Guardian, 'The Ultimate Climate Change FAQ'. <http://www.guardian.co.uk/ environment/series/the-ultimate-climate-change-faq>, accessed 26 July 2012.

The Truman Show (1998), Weir, Peter (dir.).

Thomas, Chris D., et al. (2004), 'Extinction Risk from Climate Change', *Nature, 427*, 145–8.

Thomson, Judith Jarvis (1990), *The Realm of Rights* (Cambridge, Mass. and London: Harvard University Press).

Townley, Cynthia (2010), 'Animals and Humans: Grounds for Separation?' *Journal of Social Philosophy, 41* (2), 512–26.

Trachtenberg, Zev (2010), 'Complex Green Citizenship and the Necessity of Judgement', *Environmental Politics, 19* (3), 339–55.

Tuomela, Raimo (2002), *The Philosophy of Social Practices: A Collective Acceptance View* (Cambridge: Cambridge University Press).

Unger, Peter (1996), *Living High and Letting Die* (New York: Oxford University Press).

Vanderheiden, Steve (2008), *Atmospheric Justice: Political Theory of Climate Change* (New York: Oxford University Press).

Verbruggen, Aviel (2007), 'Annex 1: Glossary', in B. Metz, et al. (eds), *Climate Change 2007: Mitigation. Contribution of Working Group III to the Fourth Assessment Report of the Intergovernmental Panel on Climate Change* (Cambridge and New York: Cambridge University Press), 809–22.

Victor, David G. (2006), 'Toward Effective International Cooperation on Climate Change: Numbers, Interests and Institutions', *Global Environmental Politics, 6* (3), 90–103.

Vine, Barbara (2002), *The Blood Doctor* (London: Penguin).

Waugh, Evelyn (1934), *A Handful of Dust* (London: Chapman and Hall).

Weinberg, Rivka (2008), 'Identifying and Dissolving the Non-Identity Problem', *Philosophical Studies, 137* (1), 3–18.

Wenar, Leif (2003), 'What We Owe to Distant Others', *Politics, Philosophy and Economics, 2* (3), 283–304.

Wiggins, David (1987), *Needs, Values, Truth* (Oxford: Oxford University Press).

Wikipedia (2012), 'Scientific Opinion on Climate Change', <http://en.wikipedia.org/wiki/Scientific_opinion_on_climate_change>, accessed 10 July.

Williams, Bernard (1973), 'A Critique of Utilitarianism', in J. C. C. Smart and Bernard Williams (eds), *Utilitarianism: For and Against* (Cambridge: Cambridge University Press), 77–151.

Williams, Bernard (1981), *Moral Luck: Philosophical Papers* (Cambridge: Cambridge University Press).

Wolf, Susan (1982), 'Moral Saints', *The Journal of Philosophy, 79* (8), 419–39.

Wolff, Jonathan and de-Shalit, Avner (2007), *Disadvantage* (Oxford: Oxford University Press).

Woods, Kerri (Unpublished), 'Rights, Responsibility and the Virtues of Stewardship in Climate Change Ethics'.

Woodward, James (1986), 'The Non-Identity Problem', *Ethics, 96* (4), 804–31.

Woodward, James (1987), 'Reply to Parfit', *Ethics, 97* (4), 800–16.

Woollard, Fiona (2012), 'Have We Solved the Non-Identity Problem?' *Ethical Theory and Moral Practice, 15* (5), 677–90.

Worldwide Fund for Nature (2012a), 'Species Threatened by Climate Change'. <http://wwf.panda.org/about_our_earth/aboutcc/problems/impacts/species/>, accessed 26 July 2012.

Worldwide Fund for Nature (2012b), 'Climate Change and Animals'. <http://www.wwf.org.uk/what_we_do/tackling_climate_change/impacts_of_climate_change/climate_change_and_animals.cfm>, accessed 10 July 2012.

Young, Iris Marion (2011), *Responsibility for Justice* (New York: Oxford University Press).

Index